Junior High Edition

FAITH & WORD EDITION
BLEST ARE WE

The Story of Our Church

Series Authors
Rev. Richard N. Fragomeni, Ph.D.
Maureen Gallagher, Ph.D.
Jeannine Goggin, M.P.S.
Michael P. Horan, Ph.D.

Scripture Co-editor and Consultant
Maria Pascuzzi, S.S.L., S.T.D.

Multicultural Consultant
Angela Erevia, M.C.D.P., M.R.E.

The Subcommittee on the Catechism, United States Conference
of Catholic Bishops, has found this catechetical text, copyright 2010,
to be in conformity with the Catechism of the Catholic Church.

ROMAN
MISSAL
THIRD EDITION

Cincinnati, Ohio

Contributing Writers
Kim Duty, Carole MacClennan

Contributing Authors
Feasts and Seasons: Rita Ferrone M.Div.; Janie Gustafson, Ph.D.
History and Mystery: Janie Gustafson, Ph.D.
Get Connected: Greg "Dobie" Moser
Our Catholic Teachings, We Care: Richard Reichert, M.A.
Unit Organizers: Joyce A. Crider
Unit Reviews: Joyce A. Crider, Robert Heman

Advisory Board
Patricia M. Feeley, S.S.J., M.A.; Edmund F. Gordon; Rose Ann Hickey, M.S.;
Rev. Daniel Kelly; Dorothy Sanning; Kevin Staszkow; Barry Thornton;
Cris V. Villapando, D.Min.

Music Advisor
Kathryn M. Lewis

On the Cover: The name Jesus in Greek ('Ιησὺ) has been shortened to the first three Greek letters in capitals (ΙΗΣ) and written as IHS to form a decorative symbol for Jesus Christ. In our cover design, it signifies that our Church is the Mystical Body of Christ.

Acknowledgments

Excerpts from the *New American Bible* with Revised New Testament and Psalms Copyright © 1991, 1986, 1970 Confraternity of Christian Doctrine, Inc., Washington, DC. Used with permission. All rights reserved. No portion of the *New American Bible* may be reprinted without permission in writing from the copyright holder.

All adaptations of Scripture are based on the *New American Bible* with Revised New Testament and Psalms Copyright © 1991, 1986, 1970 Confraternity of Christian Doctrine, Inc., Washington, DC.

Excerpts from the English translation of *Rite of Baptism for Children* © 1969, International Committee on English in the Liturgy, Inc. (ICEL); excerpts from the English translation of *Rite of Holy Week* © 1972, ICEL; excerpts from the English translation of *The Roman Missal* © 2010, ICEL; excerpts from the English translation of *The Liturgy of the Hours* © 1974, ICEL; excerpts from the English translation of *Rite of Penance* © 1974, ICEL; excerpts from the English translation of *Ordinations of Deacons, Priests, and Bishops* © 1975, ICEL; excerpts from the English translation of *Rite of Christian Initiation for Adults* © 1985, ICEL; excerpts from *Catholic Household Blessings and Prayers (revised)* ©2007, United States Conference of Catholic Bishops, Washington, D.C. All rights reserved.

Excerpts from the English translation of the *Catechism of the Catholic Church* © 1994, 1997, United States Conference of Catholic Bishops. Libreria Editrice Vaticana. Used with permission. All rights reserved.

Music selections copyrighted and/or administered by GIA publications are used with permission of GIA Publications, Inc., 7404 S. Mason Avenue, Chicago, IL 60638-9927. Music selections copyrighted and/or administered by World Library Publications are used with permission of World Library Publications, 3825 N. Willow Road, Schiller Park, IL 60176-0703. Please refer to songs for specific copyright dates and information.

Nihil Obstat
Rev. Msgr. Robert Coerver
Censor Librorum

Imprimatur
✠ Most Reverend Kevin J. Farrell, D.D.
Bishop of Dallas

January 16, 2009

The *nihil obstat* and *imprimatur* are official declarations that the material reviewed is free of doctrinal and moral error. No implication is contained therein that those who have granted the *nihil obstat* and *imprimatur* agree with the contents, opinions, or statements expressed.

Send all inquiries to:
RCL Benziger Publishing LLC
8805 Governor's Hill Dr, Suite 400
Cincinnati, Ohio 45249

Toll Free   877-275-4725
Fax   800-688-8356

Visit us at RCLBenziger.com
        BlestAreWe.com

Blest Are We® is a trademark of RCL Benziger, or its affiliates.

S6208   ISBN 978-0-7829-1287-6 (*The Story of Our Church* Student Book)
S6218   ISBN 978-0-7829-1289-0 (*The Story of Our Church* Teacher Guide)
S6228   ISBN 978-0-7829-1291-3 (*The Story of Our Church* Catechist Guide)

8th Printing. January 2016.

CONTENTS

WHAT CATHOLICS BELIEVE

HOW CATHOLICS WORSHIP

HOW CATHOLICS LIVE

HOW CATHOLICS PRAY

UNIT 5 · Returning to the Roots of Christianity 259

♪ *Unit Song* • "Send Down the Fire" 260

FEASTS AND SEASONS 317

OUR CATHOLIC HERITAGE 395

BLEST ARE WE

Words and Music by David Haas
Spanish translation by Ronald F. Krisman

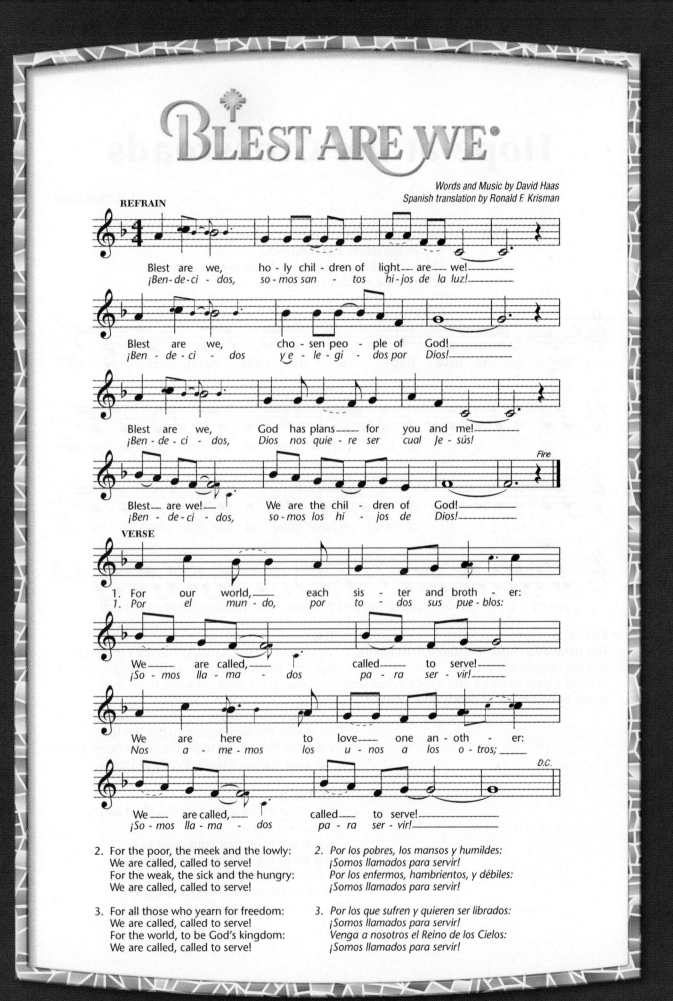

REFRAIN

Blest are we, ho-ly chil-dren of light are we!
¡Ben-de-ci - dos, so-mos san - tos hi-jos de la luz!

Blest are we, cho-sen peo - ple of God!
¡Ben-de-ci - dos y e - le-gi - dos por Dios!

Blest are we, God has plans for you and me!
¡Ben-de-ci - dos, Dios nos quie-re ser cual Je - sús!

Fine

Blest are we! We are the chil - dren of God!
¡Ben-de-ci - dos, so-mos los hi - jos de Dios!

VERSE

1. For our world, each sis - ter and broth - er:
1. Por el mun - do, por to - dos sus pue-blos:

We are called, called to serve!
¡So - mos lla-ma - dos pa - ra ser-vir!

We are here to love one an-oth - er:
Nos a - me-mos los u-nos a los o-tros;

D.C.

We are called, called to serve!
¡So - mos lla-ma - dos pa - ra ser - vir!

2. For the poor, the meek and the lowly:
   We are called, called to serve!
   For the weak, the sick and the hungry:
   We are called, called to serve!

2. Por los pobres, los mansos y humildes:
   ¡Somos llamados para servir!
   Por los enfermos, hambrientos, y débiles:
   ¡Somos llamados para servir!

3. For all those who yearn for freedom:
   We are called, called to serve!
   For the world, to be God's kingdom:
   We are called, called to serve!

3. Por los que sufren y quieren ser librados:
   ¡Somos llamados para servir!
   Venga a nosotros el Reino de los Cielos:
   ¡Somos llamados para servir!

Hope at the Crossroads

Michael Mahler

VERSE 1   We come together now from different walks of life
to join our hands and celebrate.
Our Lord will come again, and take away our strife.
We must be watchful as we wait.

We've got to have hope at the cross - roads. *Es - pe - ran - za en la vi - da.* Got to have hope at the cross - roads. *Es - pe - ran - za en la vi - da.* Need to have hope at the cross - roads. *Es - pe - ran - za en la vi - da.* Got to be strong and pre-pare for the com-ing of the Lord!

VERSE 2
This generation holds the future in its hands,
and the responsibility
to build a path to peace and justice in our land
where hope can set all people free. *(Refrain)*

RAP
This world keeps changing and life's unsteady,
but God keeps calling, so we are ready
to stand up for what we know to be true:
that Jesus is alive in me and you.
Like Mary our mother, we've got to say yes,
no matter the burden, no matter the test.
We must face all our trials, but we're never alone.
Our God is always there, steady as stone.

VERSE 3
Now that the love of Christ has filled and
    made us whole,
we've got to let that light shine out
and bring the message to the ones who
    cannot hope,
so all can dance and sing and shout!

LET US PRAY

The Sign of the Cross

In the name of the Father,
and of the Son,
and of the Holy Spirit.

Amen.

Signum Crucis SIHG-noom KROO-chees

Line 1. In nómine Patris
ihn NOH-mee-nay PAH-trees,

2. et Fílii,
et FEE-lee-ee

3. et Spíritus Sancti.
et SPEE-ree-toos SAHNK-tee.

Amen.
AH-men.

The Lord's Prayer

Our Father, who art in heaven,
hallowed be thy name;
thy kingdom come,
thy will be done
on earth as it is in heaven.
Give us this day our daily bread,
and forgive us our trespasses,
as we forgive those who trespass
    against us;
and lead us not into temptation,
but deliver us from evil.

Amen.

Oratio Dominica

Pater noster qui es in caelis:
PAH-tair NOHS-tair kwee es ihn CHAY-lees:
sanctificétur nomen tuum;
sahnk-tee-fee-CHAY-tor NOH-men TOO-oom;
advéniat regnum tuum;
ahd-VEH-nee-aht REG-noom TOO-oom;
fiat volúntas tua, sicut in caelo, et in terra.
FEE-aht voh-LOON-tahs TOO-ah, SEE-koot ihn
CHAY-loh, et ihn TAIR-ah.
Panem nostrum cotidiánum da nobis hódie;
PAH-nem NOH-stroom koh-tee-dee-AH-noom dah
NOH-bees OH-dee-ay;
et dimítte nobis débita nostra,
et dih-MEET-tay NOH-bees DEH-bee-tah NOH-strah,
sicut et nos dimíttimus debitóribus nostris;
SEE-koot et nohs dih-MIHT-ee-moos
day-bee-TOR-ee-boos NOH-strees;
et ne nos indúcas in tentatiónem;
et nay nohs ihn-DOO-kahs ihn ten-taht-see-OH-nem;
sed líbera nos a malo.
sed LEE-bair-ah nohs ah MAH-loh.

Amen.
AH-men

* The lines in the Latin prayers are numbered to match the lines in the English prayers.

Glory Be

Glory be to the Father
and to the Son
and to the Holy Spirit,
as it was in the beginning
is now, and ever shall be
world without end.

Amen.

The Hail Mary

Hail, Mary, full of grace,
the Lord is with thee.
Blessed art thou among women
and blessed is the fruit of thy
   womb, Jesus.
Holy Mary, Mother of God,
pray for us sinners,
now and at the hour of our death.

Amen.

Glória Patri

GLOR-ee-ah PAH-tree

Lines 1.–2. Glória Patri et Fílio
GLOR-ee-ah PAH-tree et FEE-lee-oh

3. et Spirítui Sancto.
et spee-REE-too-ee SAHNK-toh.

4. Sicut erat in princípio,
SEE-koot AIR-aht ihn prihn-CHEE-pee-oh,

5. et nunc et semper
et noonk et SEM-pair

6. et in saécula saeculórum.
et ihn SAY-koo-lah say-koo-LOR-oom.

Amen.
AH-men.

Ave, María AH-vay, mah-REE-ah

1. Ave, María, grátia plena,
AH-vay, mah-REE-ah, GRAHT-see-ah PLAY-nah,

2. Dóminus tecum.
DOH-mee-noos TAY-koom.

3. Benedícta tu in muliéribus,
bay-nay-DEEK-tah too ihn moo-lee-AIR-ee-boos,

4-5. et benedíctus fructus ventris tui, Iesus.
et bay-nay-DEEK-toos FROOK-toos VEN-trees TOO-ee, YAY-zoos.

6. Sancta María, Mater Dei,
SAHNK-tah mah-REE-ah, MAH-tair DAY-ee,

7. ora pro nobis peccatóribus,
OR-ah proh NOH-bees pek-uh-TOR-ee-boos,

8. nunc et in hora mortis nostrae.
noonk et ihn OR-ah MOR-tees NOHS-tray.

Amen.
AH-men.

The Apostles' Creed

I believe in God,
the Father almighty,
Creator of heaven and earth,
and in Jesus Christ, his only Son, our Lord,
who was conceived by the Holy Spirit,
born of the Virgin Mary,
suffered under Pontius Pilate,
was crucified, died and was buried;
he descended into hell;
on the third day he rose again from the dead;
he ascended into heaven,
and is seated at the right hand of God
   the Father almighty;
from there he will come to judge
   the living and the dead.

I believe in the Holy Spirit,
the holy catholic Church,
the communion of saints,
the forgiveness of sins,
the resurrection of the body,
and life everlasting.

Amen.

Hail, Holy Queen

Hail, holy Queen, Mother of Mercy:
Hail, our life, our sweetness, and our hope.
To you do we cry,
poor banished children of Eve.
To you do we send up our sighs,
mourning and weeping
   in this vale of tears.
Turn, then, most gracious advocate,
your eyes of mercy toward us;
and after this our exile show to us
   the blessed fruit of your womb, Jesus.
O clement, O loving, O sweet Virgin Mary.

Amen.

Grace Before Meals

Bless us, O Lord, and these thy gifts,
which we are about to receive
from thy bounty,
through Christ our Lord.

Amen.

The Rosary

The Rosary is a prayer that honors Mary, the Mother of Jesus, and helps us meditate on the life of Christ. We pray the Rosary using a set of beads. A group of ten beads is called a decade. Before each decade, we recall one of the mysteries, or important times in the lives of Mary and Jesus. There are twenty mysteries, shown at right. The prayers for the beads are shown below.

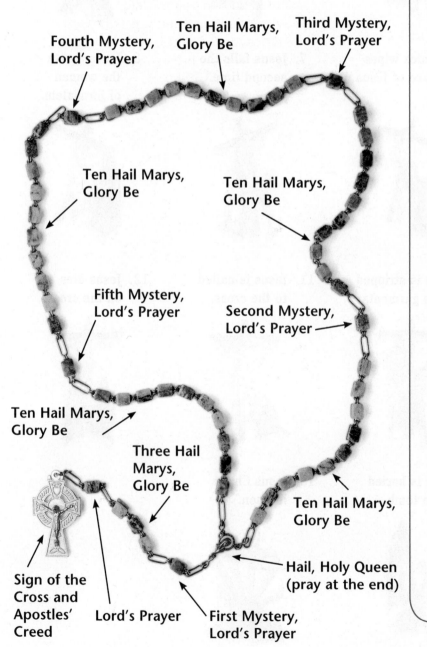

Fourth Mystery, Lord's Prayer

Ten Hail Marys, Glory Be

Third Mystery, Lord's Prayer

Ten Hail Marys, Glory Be

Ten Hail Marys, Glory Be

Fifth Mystery, Lord's Prayer

Second Mystery, Lord's Prayer

Ten Hail Marys, Glory Be

Three Hail Marys, Glory Be

Ten Hail Marys, Glory Be

Sign of the Cross and Apostles' Creed

Lord's Prayer

First Mystery, Lord's Prayer

Hail, Holy Queen (pray at the end)

The Mysteries of the Rosary

The Joyful Mysteries

1. The Annunciation
2. The Visitation
3. The Nativity
4. The Presentation in the Temple
5. The Finding of the Child Jesus After Three Days in the Temple

The Luminous Mysteries

1. The Baptism at the Jordan
2. The Miracle at Cana
3. The Proclamation of the Kingdom and the Call to Conversion
4. The Transfiguration
5. The Institution of the Eucharist

The Sorrowful Mysteries

1. The Agony in the Garden
2. The Scourging at the Pillar
3. The Crowning with Thorns
4. The Carrying of the Cross
5. The Crucifixion and Death

The Glorious Mysteries

1. The Resurrection
2. The Ascension
3. The Descent of the Holy Spirit at Pentecost
4. The Assumption of Mary
5. The Crowning of the Blessed Virgin as Queen of Heaven and Earth

The Stations of the Cross

1. Jesus is condemned to death.

2. Jesus accepts the cross.

3. Jesus falls the first time.

4. Jesus meets his mother.

5. Simon helps Jesus carry the cross.

6. Veronica wipes the face of Jesus.

7. Jesus falls the second time.

8. Jesus meets the women of Jerusalem.

9. Jesus falls the third time.

10. Jesus is stripped of his garments.

11. Jesus is nailed to the cross.

12. Jesus dies on the cross.

13. Jesus is taken down from the cross.

14. Jesus is buried in the tomb.

15. Jesus Christ is risen.

HISTORY AND MYSTERY

A LOOK INSIDE THE CATHOLIC CHURCH

When you think about your family, you probably think about your parents, brothers and sisters, grandparents, and aunts and uncles. But do you ever include your Church family? As a Catholic, you belong to a family that is more than one billion members strong! It's true. The Catholic Church is a diverse Church whose family members come from all walks of life and are found in every inhabited corner of the globe. This is a far cry from the humble beginnings of the Church 2,000 years ago, when Jesus Christ's small family of disciples struggled to keep the faith alive. They worked hard to continue Jesus' mission on Earth as they faced persecution from their enemies and disagreements among themselves. The Apostles, under the leadership of Saint Peter, the first pope, and Saint Paul, the Apostle to the Gentiles, or non-Jews, stayed faithful to the mission that Jesus Christ had entrusted to them: "Go, therefore, and make disciples of all nations, baptizing them in the name of the Father, and of the Son, and of the holy Spirit, teaching them to observe all that I have commanded you" (Matthew 28:19–20).

You might wonder how such a large family is able to stay together. Well, it certainly is not easy. Jesus Christ promised the Apostles that God the Father would send the Holy Spirit to help guide them to do God's will. The Holy Spirit guides the Church today. The Church also has traditions that have been passed down to us from the Apostles and the early Church. The Church also has four distinct *Marks*, or characteristics. It is *one, holy, catholic,* and *apostolic*. This means that it is unified in Christ, in communion with God, open to all, and faithful to the teachings of the Apostles.

Just as every organization has a unique purpose, so the Church has a specific job, or mission. The Church preaches the Gospel, the Good News of Jesus, and helps people grow in holiness. Throughout the world, Catholics share the same beliefs, celebrate the same Seven Sacraments, and try to live the Gospel in their daily life. This year you will better understand your Catholic identity within the Church family as you learn more about the history of the Catholic Church.

Catholic faithful gather in Saint Peter's Square for a papal audience.

What Is Your Church History IQ?

How much do you know about the Catholic Church? Take this fun quiz to find out!

1. To whom did Jesus say, "You are the rock on which I will build my church" (based on Matthew 16:18)?

   (a) Saint James
   (b) Saint John
   (c) Saint Peter
   (d) Saint Paul

2. The early Church was led by

   (a) the Apostles.
   (b) religious brothers and sisters.
   (c) Blessed Pope John Paul II.
   (d) Emperor Augustus.

3. The role of the pope is to

   (a) rule the world.
   (b) lead the universal Catholic Church.
   (c) wage war against non-Catholics.
   (d) write books and become famous.

4. During the Middle Ages, monasteries became important centers of

   (a) farming and agriculture.
   (b) biology and horticulture.
   (c) learning and education.
   (d) tourism.

5. Beginning in the 1500s, priests accompanied the Spanish Conquistadors to

   (a) the New World.
   (b) the Old World.
   (c) celebrate the Mass.
   (d) the British Isles.

6. Which Church leader defended the Church against heresy in the fourth century?

   (a) Arius
   (b) Augustine
   (c) Gregory the Great
   (d) Thomas Aquinas

7. The Church ordered military crusades to try to

   (a) spread the Gospel to every nation.
   (b) convert the Jews.
   (c) free the Holy Land from Muslim control.
   (d) defeat the Vikings.

8. Who painted the ceiling of the Sistine Chapel in Rome?

   (a) Leonardo da Vinci
   (b) Fra Angelico
   (c) Michelangelo
   (d) Rembrandt

9. Saint Catherine of Siena is known for having

   (a) donated a lot of money to the Church.
   (b) helped paint the ceiling of the Sistine Chapel.
   (c) given counsel to popes.
   (d) seen the Blessed Virgin Mary at Fatima.

10. Saint Benedict is known as the father of

    (a) Eastern prayer.
    (b) Vatican City.
    (c) the Rosary.
    (d) Western monasticism.

11. What was the most recent Church Council?

    (a) Jerusalem II
    (b) Vatican I
    (c) Vatican II
    (d) Trent

Check your score on page 26!

THE HISTORY OF THE CHURCH

1. APOSTOLIC AGE AND EARLY CHURCH (A.D. 30–400)

Pentecost is the day the Holy Spirit descended upon the disciples. After Jesus Christ's Ascension into Heaven, the disciples continued to preach the Good News. Wherever they went, they founded Christian communities. The early Christians worshiped together and helped bring Jesus Christ's message of hope, love, and Salvation to others. Between A.D. 50 and 60, Saint Paul wrote letters (part of the New Testament) to the early Christians. The Gospels were written between A.D. 65 and 100, and the New Testament was completed by A.D. 120. The early Church often had to worship in secret places for fear that they might be arrested or even put to death by their Roman rulers. Persecution of Christians continued until A.D. 313, when Emperor Constantine legalized Christianity in the Roman Empire. In A.D. 325, the Council of Nicaea developed the Nicene Creed, a statement of the Church's beliefs.

2. EARLY MIDDLE AGES (A.D. 400–1000)

Saint Jerome translated the Old and New Testaments from Hebrew and Greek into Latin. Saint Augustine of Hippo and other Church leaders worked hard to keep the Church faithful to the teachings of Jesus Christ as handed on to the Church by the Apostles. Saint Benedict and Saint Scholastica helped bring monasticism, a religious way of life, to the Western Church. Around A.D. 530 Saint Benedict wrote his monastic rule. In A.D. 590 Gregory the Great became the first monk to become pope. He helped reform the Church and

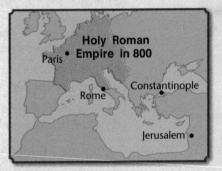

Holy Roman Empire in 800

Paris • • Rome • Constantinople • Jerusalem •

A TIME LINE OF CHURCH EVENTS

IN THE CHURCH

	APOSTOLIC AGE & EARLY CHURCH A.D. 30–400	EARLY MIDDLE AGES A.D. 400–1000	LATE MIDDLE AGES A.D. 1000–1500

30 Ascension of Jesus Christ; Pentecost

50–60 Conversion of Saint Paul

51 Council of Jerusalem

65–120 New Testament is written.

313 Constantine legalizes Christianity.

325 Council of Nicaea

400 Saint Jerome translates Bible.

500 Saint Benedict helps build first monasteries.

590 Gregory the Great becomes pope.

800 Pope Leo III crowns Charlemagne emperor of Holy Roman Empire.

1054 Schism between Christians in East and West

1095 First Crusade

1231 Church establishes Inquisition.

IN THE WORLD

117–313 Persecution of Christians

410 Rome is sacked.

622 Muhammad founds Islam.

900 Mayan Empire collapses.

1220 Genghis Khan unites Mongol Empire.

1347–52 Bubonic plague ravages Europe.

sent missioners to France, Spain, England, and Africa. In A.D. 800, Pope Leo III crowned Charlemagne emperor of the Holy Roman Empire.

3. LATE MIDDLE AGES (A.D. 1000—1500)

In the Schism of 1054, most of the Church in the East in the Byzantine Empire split from the Roman Catholic Church. In 1095, Pope Urban II authorized the First Crusade to save the holy places of Palestine from Islamic rulers. In 1204, during the Fourth Crusade, Christians destroyed much of Constantinople, a city revered by Eastern Christians. The Church established the Inquisition in the thirteenth century to root out heresies.

4. REFORMATION AND COUNTER-REFORMATION (A.D. 1500—1869)

The Protestant Reformation began in 1517 when Martin Luther posted ninety-five theses on the doors of the castle church in Wittenberg, Germany. In 1533, the pope excommunicated King Henry VIII, who established the Church of England. The Counter-Reformation (within the Church) followed. The Council of Trent met between

1545 and 1563 and clarified Church teachings, such as the Real Presence of Jesus in the Eucharist and the necessity of both faith and good works for Salvation. During the eighteenth century, many missionaries came to the New World. John Carroll became the first Catholic bishop in the United States of America.

5. MODERN AND POSTMODERN ERA (A.D. 1869—THE PRESENT)

In 1869, the First Vatican Council defined papal infallibility and confronted modern trends of secular thought. In 1917, the Church issued the Code of Canon Law. The Second Vatican Council, which met from 1962 to 1965, emphasized relations with other faiths and brought about a major change in the rites of the Liturgy. The Church issued the Revised Code of Canon Law in 1983 and approved the new *Catechism of the Catholic Church* in 1992. In 2001, Pope John Paul II was the first pope in more than 1,000 years to make an official visit to Greece, to bring peace between the Roman Catholic Church and Eastern Orthodox churches. In 2013, Francis became pope.

1545–63
Council of Trent

1517
Martin Luther posts ninety-five theses at Wittenburg, Germany.

1769
Blessed Junipero Serra begins nine missions in California.

1809
Saint Elizabeth Ann Seton founds first U.S. religious community for women.

1917
Code of Canon Law

1869 Vatican I

1962–65
Vatican II

1992
Approval of new *Catechism of the Catholic Church*

2013
Francis became pope

REFORMATION & COUNTER-REFORMATION A.D. 1500–1869

1492
Christopher Columbus arrives in the New World.

1564
Galileo is born.

1591
Shakespeare writes *Romeo and Juliet*.

1789
French Revolution

1776
American Revolution

MODERN & POSTMODERN ERA A.D. 1869—THE PRESENT

1879
Thomas Edison invents lightbulb.

1939–45
World War II

1969
First man lands on moon.

1990
Tim Berners-Lee invents World Wide Web.

1914–18 World War I

THE CHURCH THEN . . .

Jesus chose Saint Peter the Apostle to be the foundation of his Church. The rest of the Apostles had the mission to spread the Good News throughout the world and to baptize people.

The first followers of Jesus considered themselves to be Jews and worshiped in a synagogue on the Jewish Sabbath, which begins at sundown on Friday and ends at sundown on Saturday evening. They gathered for Eucharist in one another's homes.

The Church taught that the only way people could have their sins forgiven was through the Sacrament of Baptism. Eventually, through the Sacrament of Penance, the Church provided forgiveness and reconciliation to people who committed sins after Baptism. People celebrated the Sacrament of Penance only once, usually just before death.

In the church buildings of the Western Church, people were separated from the altar by means of a communion rail.

Throughout the Middle Ages, there were no pews in churches. People stood throughout the liturgy—men on one side of the church and women on the other. Catholics placed great emphasis on seeing the Eucharistic host during its elevation after the consecration, but many did not receive Holy Communion. They felt they were too unworthy.

For more than 1,300 years, the priest said Mass with his back turned to the people. He said the prayers of the liturgy in Latin, a language that many people could not understand.

. . . AND NOW

The pope is the successor of Saint Peter the Apostle as the visible head of the Church on Earth. The other bishops are the successors of the other Apostles. Together, the pope and bishops form the *Magisterium*, or teaching office of the Church. They spread the Gospel of Jesus and baptize people in God's name.

Jesus Christ is the Messiah who will come again in glory at the end of time. Catholics believe that God's Word is contained in both the Old Testament (the Scriptures of ancient Israel) and in the New Testament. Groups of Catholics gather for Eucharist in parish churches on Saturday night or Sunday.

Catholics frequently celebrate God's forgiveness in the Sacrament of Penance and Reconciliation. There are two ways that Catholics usually celebrate this Sacrament: (1) privately while concealed from the priest by a screen; privately but in face-to-face conversation with the priest; (2) and communally in a service with individual confession and absolution.

Church buildings are no longer required to have communion rails and altar screens.

In many churches today, pews surround the altar. During Mass, people stand, sit, and kneel at appropriate times. Catholics who are in a state of grace (without mortal sins to confess in the Sacrament of Penance and Reconciliation) may receive Holy Communion.

The entire assembly of Catholics take part in the celebration of Mass. Since the Second Vatican Council (1962–65), the Eucharist and the other Sacraments have been celebrated in the *vernacular*, the language of each community. This helps Catholics everywhere actively participate in the liturgy. The priest, who faces the people, is in constant dialogue with the assembly.

PEOPLE IN CHURCH HISTORY

The following people are among some of the more well-known Catholics in history who have served and helped the Church grow.

Saints Peter and Paul, Apostles

Jesus instructed Peter to lead his followers. Paul became a follower of Christ after seeing a vision of the Risen Christ. He founded many Christian communities and wrote some of the New Testament Epistles (letters). Both Peter and Paul arranged the Church's first gathering: the Council of Jerusalem. As a result, Gentiles were allowed to belong to the Church without first becoming Jews. Peter and Paul died as martyrs.

Saint Augustine of Hippo

Augustine repented, was baptized, was ordained a priest and bishop. He became a strong opponent of *heresies,* or teachings that go against Catholic beliefs. He wrote many homilies and books that continue to influence Christians today.

Saint Gregory the Great

As pope, Gregory brought discipline and organization to the Church. Gregorian chant and the Gregorian calendar are both named after him.

Saint Benedict of Nursia

Benedict founded the first monastery in the Western Church. He wrote a *rule*, or set of guidelines, for his monks that was based on the motto "Pray and work." In the Church today, many religious sisters and brothers continue to follow the Rule of Saint Benedict.

Saint Francis of Assisi

Francis set out to reform the Church by founding the Orders of Friars Minor, a community devoted to poverty and simplicity—the heart of the Gospel message.

Saint Thomas Aquinas

This thirteenth-century Dominican priest and Doctor of the Church is known as one of the greatest teachers in the history of the Church. The *Summa Theologiae,* his encyclopedia of religious topics, is taught in colleges and seminaries today.

Saint Teresa of Jesus (Saint Teresa of Ávila)

This sixteenth-century Carmelite nun wrote extensively about spirituality. She reformed Carmelite convents so that they were real houses of prayer. Today we honor her as a Doctor of the Church.

Pope Saint John XXIII

Born "Angelo Roncalli" to peasant parents, this man rose to become one of the Church's most beloved popes. He recognized that the Church had to be renewed so that it could better serve and minister in a modern world. In 1962, Pope John XXIII set about to set this work in motion by convening the Second Vatican Council.

THE CHURCH COMMUNITY

Every person in the church throughout the world is important. Here is a summary of how the Church is structured.

The Pope and the Bishops. The pope, the Bishop of Rome, is the head of the universal Church. He exercises his authority as the successor of Saint Peter, the first pope. Bishops are ordained in the Sacrament of Holy Orders and are named by the pope to lead geographical areas of the Church called dioceses. They have authority over every aspect of their dioceses. Together, the pope and bishops serve the Church and teach about matters of faith and morals.

Priests and Deacons. Priests and deacons are also ordained in the Sacrament of Holy Orders to serve the Church. Priests are coworkers with their bishop. They preside at Mass and many of the Sacraments. In a diocese, a priest who has authority over his particular parish is called a pastor. Deacons help bishops and priests. They generally fulfill their service to the bishop of their diocese through the work they perform in parishes, under the authority of a pastor. Some priests and deacons are members of religious orders approved by the Church.

Religious Sisters and Brothers. Religious sisters and brothers are members of religious orders. They take vows or promises of poverty, chastity, and obedience. They lead consecrated lives, either alone or in groups. Some are contemplative—engaged mainly in prayer. Others are active religious, serving the Church through their work in education, social work, health care, and other works.

The Laity. The laity make up about 99.5 percent of all the members of the Church. These disciples of Christ live the Gospel in their daily lives, specifically through their families and their work. Here are some ministries of laypeople in the Church:

- **Parish administrators** help run and maintain the parish.
- **Parish council members** advise the pastor and help carry out important decisions in the parish.
- **Catechists** teach religious education and help people prepare for the Sacraments.
- **Liturgists** plan parish celebrations of prayer and the Sacraments.
- **Altar servers** assist the priest during Mass and the Sacraments.
- **Lectors** proclaim the Scripture readings at Mass and the Sacraments.
- **Extraordinary ministers of Holy Communion** distribute communion at Mass and bring the Eucharist to those who are sick at home or in nursing homes.
- **Music ministers** arrange music for Mass and other celebrations.
- **Ministers of hospitality** welcome people to church and help them find seats.
- **Fundraiser volunteers** help with specific projects, such as bazaars, carnivals, raffles, bingo, dinners, and so on, to raise money for charitable causes.

The Laity

Religious Sisters & Brothers

Priests & Deacons

Pope & Bishops

A CLOSER LOOK AT THE FAITH OF OUR CHURCH

Growing in faith means developing a personal relationship with God the Father, Son, and Holy Spirit. Growing in faith involves *learning* about faith and *practicing*, or living, the faith of the Church.

Learning About Faith

People wishing to join the Catholic Church enter a process called the Rite of Christian Initiation of Adults (RCIA). This is a process that includes religious instruction, reflection on God's Word, and prayer and service.

People who are already baptized are called *candidates*. Those who have never been baptized are called *catechumens*. Candidates and catechumens listen closely to the Sunday homilies, participate in parish activities and faith-sharing groups, and observe Church teachings and practices. Many Catholics are enrolled in religious education programs or Catholic schools to learn more about their Catholic faith.

Practicing Faith

Growing in faith involves *practicing* faith. We practice our faith whenever we participate in the Mass and the Sacraments, pray, make good moral decisions, imitate Jesus, and open ourselves to the grace of the Holy Spirit. Growing in faith is a lifelong journey for which we need God's love and grace. Our faith-filled involvement in the Church and the world can help others grow in faith, too.

IT'S YOUR TURN

1. The work of an organization is explained in a mission statement. Write a mission statement for the Church.

   _____

   _____

2. Write a mission statement for yourself as a Catholic.

   _____

   _____

   _____

   _____

Answers to "What Is Your Church History IQ?" (page 19)

1) c,   2) a,   3) b,   4) c,   5) a,   6) b,   7) c,   8) c,   9) c,   10) d,   11) c

Scoring:

Give yourself one point for each correct answer.

8–11 points: You are a Catholic champion!

5–7 points: You get a B in Church history!

3–4 points: Brush up on Catholic history just a bit.

1–2 points: Don't worry. You will improve your Church history IQ this year!

The Marks of the Church from the Beginning

The first disciples built their church communities around the celebration of the Lord's Supper and the Gospel message. Their belief in the Kingdom of God and the ongoing presence of Christ sustained them through many times of trial and persecution.

[Jesus' followers] devoted themselves to the teaching of the apostles and to the communal life, to the breaking of the bread and to the prayers.

Acts 2:42

This fresco from the catacomb of Saint Priscilla in Rome shows the early disciples celebrating the presence of Christ in the Eucharist. Today, we profess our faith in Christ in the Eucharist.

27

We Are Called

Based on Micah 6:8

David Haas

1. Come! Live in the light! _____
2. Come! O - pen your heart! _____
3. Sing! Sing a new song! _____

Shine with the joy and the love of the Lord! We are
Show your mer - cy to all those in fear! We are
Sing of that great day when all will be one! God will

called _____ to be light for the king - dom, to
called _____ to be hope for the hope - less so all
reign, _____ and we'll walk with each oth - er as

live in the free - dom _ of the cit - y _____ of God!
ha - tred and blind - ness _____ will be _____ no more!
sis - ters and broth - ers _____ u - nit - ed _____ in love!

We are called to act _ with jus - tice, _____ we are called _ to

love ten - der - ly, _____ we are called _ to serve one _ an - oth - er; _____

_____ to walk hum - bly with God! _____

Get CONNECTED

with family and friends

Apostolic: Founded on the Apostles

The Apostles devoted their lives to following Jesus and passing on his teachings to others. Jesus commissioned Peter to be the leader of the Apostles and the first leader of the Church. In every age the Church shares in the mission of the Apostles to proclaim to the world the Good News of Jesus Christ.

Activity

Have you ever had some exciting news that you couldn't wait to tell someone about? The Apostles did. After Jesus ascended to his Father in Heaven, the Apostles, filled with the Holy Spirit, set out to tell the whole world about Jesus. We too are called by God to share the Good News of Jesus with others.

Do one of the following.

1. Have a family discussion in which family members share how they are challenged to live out their Catholic faith in their daily lives. Be sure to offer each other support and encouragement.

2. Pass on your Catholic faith to a younger sibling or cousin by teaching them the Rosary (see page 160), the Stations of the Cross, a novena, or another prayer.

Trivia

- Church History
- Social Studies
- Arts & Culture
- People & Places

The Azores, a group of nine subtropical Portuguese islands in the Atlantic, are a place where the Catholic faith imbues countless aspects of the landscape and of everyday life. Azoreans have a special devotion to the Holy Spirit. Dozens of *imperios* (small chapels dedicated to the Holy Spirit) dot the islands and welcome visitors for prayer.

Quotable Scripture

"You are Peter, and upon this rock I will build my church, and the gates of the netherworld shall not prevail against it."
—Matthew 16:18

Get CONNECTED
with family and friends

✝ Scripture Background

In the Early Church

The Christian Community in Jerusalem In the Acts of the Apostles, Luke describes the growth of the early Church. Acts contains three passages (2:42–47, 4:32–37, and 5:12–16) that describe the early Church in Jerusalem. The Church at this early stage was comprised largely of Jews who kept their traditions and did not see themselves as following a new religion. For them, Jesus was the long-awaited Messiah of Israel. To teach that Jesus was the Messiah, Peter referred to the Old Testament. The early Church preached that everyone received the call to repentance and Baptism. This call required accepting the teachings of the Apostles, daily prayer in the synagogue, a Eucharist-centered life, and the sharing of one's possessions to meet the needs of the entire community.

WEEKLY PLANNER

On Sunday

Pay special attention to the prayers that are spoken at Mass by the priest. These prayers remind us again and again of who we are and what we believe.

On the Web

blestarewe.com

Visit our Web site for the saint of the day and the reflection question of the week.

Saint of the Week

Saint Peter the Apostle

Saint Peter appears in the Gospels more than any other disciple and was at Jesus' side at many key events in Jesus' ministry. Jesus appointed Peter the "rock" on which he would build his Church. Saint Peter was martyred in A.D. 64.

Patron Saint of: the universal Church

Feast Day: June 29

A Prayer for the Week

Lord, help us learn what our Catholic faith teaches, and help us live it faithfully. Guide us to be good Catholics in all that we do and in all that we say. Amen.

1   Apostolic: Founded on the Apostles

[Jesus' followers] devoted themselves to the teaching of the apostles and to the communal life, to the breaking of the bread, and to the prayers.

Acts of the Apostles 2:42

Share

Catholics belong to a local faith community called a parish. Each parish member has certain responsibilities to fulfill.

Think about the groups you belong to: family, parish, school, clubs, teams, neighborhood, and so on. Each of these groups forms a community with a particular purpose and goals. For a community to thrive, each member must understand and work responsibly toward the goals of the group and use their time wisely to support the other members. When each member tries to fulfill their responsibilities, the group can be successful.

Activity

Choose a group to which you belong or one to which you would like to belong. Imagine that you have been chosen to recruit new members. Design a poster that would attract new members to your group. Include the following: the name of the group, its goals, the duties of members, the benefits of membership, and the most important thing you want others to remember about your group.

GROUP NAME

GOALS

DUTIES

BENEFITS

REMEMBER

Why is the Church apostolic?

✝ Scripture Peter and the Early Church

The Catholic Church is **apostolic**. This means that the Catholic Church is founded by Jesus Christ on the Apostles.

The first followers of Jesus were primarily Jews. Before they came to understand that Jesus was indeed the Savior of all people, of both Jews and non-Jews alike, these first followers of Jesus truly believed that only Jews were included in the divine plan of Salvation.

The Acts of the Apostles, however, describes that Peter and others came to understand that God invites and calls all people to Salvation in Christ. In the Acts of the Apostles, Luke describes both the vision of Peter and the vision and conversion of Cornelius, a centurion in the Roman army, and his household to Christ.

[An angel of the Lord God appeared to Cornelius, saying,] " 'Cornelius, your prayer has been heard and your almsgiving remembered before God. Send therefore to Joppa and summon Simon, who is called Peter. He is a guest in the house of Simon, a tanner, by the sea.' So I sent for you immediately, and you were kind enough to come. Now therefore we are all here in the presence of God to listen to all that you have been commanded by the Lord."

Then Peter proceeded to speak and said, "In truth, I see that God shows no partiality. Rather, in every nation whoever fears him and acts uprightly is acceptable to him. You know the word [that] he sent to the Israelites as he proclaimed peace through Jesus Christ, who is Lord of all, what has happened all over Judea, beginning in Galilee after the baptism that John preached, how God anointed Jesus of Nazareth with the holy Spirit and power. He went about doing good and healing all those oppressed by the devil, for God was with him. We are witnesses of all that he did both in the country of the Jews and [in] Jerusalem. They put him to death by hanging him on a tree. This man God raised [on] the third day and granted that he be visible, not to all the people, but to us, the witnesses chosen by God in advance, who ate and drank with him after he rose from the dead. He commissioned us to preach to the people and testify that he is the one appointed by God as judge of the living and the dead. To him all the prophets bear witness, that everyone who believes in him will receive forgiveness of sins through his name."

While Peter was still speaking these things, the holy Spirit fell upon all who were listening to the word. The circumcised believers who had accompanied Peter were astounded that the gift of the holy Spirit should have been poured out on the Gentiles also, for they could hear them speaking in tongues and glorifying God. Then Peter responded, "Can anyone withhold the water for baptizing these people, who have received the holy Spirit even as we have?" He ordered them to be baptized in the name of Jesus Christ. Then they invited him to stay for a few days.

Acts of the Apostles 10:31–49

Many wonders and signs were done through the Apostles. The number of followers of Jesus increased as the disciples of Jesus stayed true to the teachings of Jesus that were passed on to them by the Apostles.

The Holy Spirit Guides Peter

A man named Cornelius sent a message to Peter. Cornelius had heard that Peter was teaching people about Jesus, and Cornelius had a great desire to learn about the Lord. He invited Peter to come to his house to teach him and his family and servants. Peter was troubled by this invitation. Cornelius was not Jewish, and it was against Jewish law for a Jew to enter the home of a Gentile.

Peter was not certain about what he should do, but the Holy Spirit prompted him to go to Cornelius. Then Peter realized that Jesus wanted him to teach not only Jews, but all people. In Cornelius' house, Peter taught that Jesus was anointed by God with the Holy Spirit. He taught about Jesus' ministry of doing good and about his Death and Resurrection. Peter told that Jesus appeared to the Apostles after his death and how they ate and drank with him. He taught the people that all who believe in Jesus could receive forgiveness of their sins through his name. Peter could teach all these things because Jesus had given him the authority to do so.

The authority of Peter and the other Apostles to teach the Word of God has been passed on to the pope and bishops. The pope and bishops serve the Church by instructing the Church and leading her members to holiness. The pope and the bishops form the **Magisterium**, the teaching office of the Church. As the pope and bishops teach, they are guided by the Holy Spirit. The Holy Spirit ensures the Church's fidelity to the teaching of Jesus and the Apostles in matters of faith and morals. When the pope or the bishops together with the pope officially proclaim a teaching on morality or faith, such a teaching is infallible. We, the faithful, trust the teaching of the Church and follow it. We live in unity as the People of God, the Body of Christ, and the Temple of the Holy Spirit. This unity reflects the **Trinitarian** nature of the Church.

A Church Community Is Born

Peter and the other Apostles taught that Jesus Christ had died to redeem sins so that all who believe in him might be saved. Jews and Gentiles responded to the Apostles' teachings by repenting for their sins, being baptized, and living together united in love. They cared for each other's needs, prayed together during the day, and in the evening gathered in someone's home to share a meal. They remembered Jesus' life by sharing stories of his life and his teachings. The reading of the Scriptures of ancient Israel was also an important part of their worship life, just as the reading of God's Word is essential to our life today. The disciples remembered Jesus' Death and Resurrection and celebrated his presence with them in the Breaking of Bread, the Eucharist.

Activity

List three things the early Church did that showed they understood the message of Jesus and his Apostles.

_____

_____

_____

As Christians today, how do we show that we understand and practice this message?

_____

_____

Faith Words

apostolic The Catholic Church is apostolic because Jesus founded the Church on the Apostles, and the Church is faithful to the teachings of Jesus Christ passed on to her by the Apostles.

Magisterium The Magisterium is the teaching office of the Church, guided by the Holy Spirit, to authentically and accurately interpret the Word of God—Scripture and Tradition.

Trinitarian *Trinitarian* means "reflecting the unity of the Blessed Trinity."

How does the Church grow?

33

Hear & Believe

✝ Scripture   Peter Is Chosen

The early Church looked to Peter as a leader. Peter spoke with special authority because Jesus had chosen him to lead the Church. We read in the following Scripture passages how Jesus singled out Peter to hold a position of great trust.

The Apostles traveled with Jesus as he preached and taught. One day Jesus asked his disciples who people thought he was. The Apostles replied that people thought he might be John the Baptist or another prophet.

Then Jesus asked them directly, "Who do you say that I am?" Simon spoke up and said, "You are the Messiah, the Son of the living God."

Jesus said to him, "Simon, you are blessed. Only my Father in Heaven could have revealed this to you. From now on, your name will be Peter, which means 'rock,' I will build my church on you and I will give you the keys to the Kingdom of Heaven. Whatever you bind or loose on Earth will be bound or loosed in Heaven."

At the Last Supper on the night before he died, Jesus singled out Peter and said to him, "I have prayed that your own faith will be strong. You must strengthen your brothers."

Based on Matthew 16:13–19, Luke 22:31–32

Jesus prayed for Peter's faith to be strong because he understood the challenges and hardships that Peter would face. Peter did become a strong and effective leader, a man of great faith and vision. Peter guided the early Church wisely and well.

A CLOSER LOOK

The Altar Table

In the Old Testament the first altars were piles of stones. Animals were placed on the stones and sacrificed. The first Christian altars, however, were the tables at which people ate their meals. In the first 200 years of the Church, Christians gathered in private homes. People would gather around an ordinary wooden table, where they would eat supper, pray, read the Scriptures of ancient Israel, listen to the teachings of the Apostles, and share in the Breaking of Bread as Jesus had commanded them to do.

Our Church Teaches

Jesus sent his Apostles and other disciples out into the world to teach the Good News. He chose Peter to lead the disciples and proclaim to the world that all Salvation comes from Christ through the Church.

The People of God recognize that Peter was the first pope. The pope is the leader of the universal Catholic Church and is responsible for the care of souls throughout the Church. There is an unbroken line of succession from Peter, who received his authority from the Son of God, to the pope today. The bishops, the successors of the other Apostles, are the chief teachers of the Church, in union with the pope.

The Holy Spirit guides the Church to be faithful to the teachings of Jesus. Through her life, teaching, and worship, the Church passes on to every generation all that she is and all that she believes.

We Believe

The Church, led by the pope and the bishops, continues the mission of the Apostles.

Activities

1. Like Peter, every pope has faced challenges while leading the Church. Think about the challenges that our present pope faces. Then complete the activity below.

List three challenges that the pope faces today.

_____

_____

_____

_____

_____

_____

_____

_____

_____

List some ways in which the pope shows leadership in these areas.

_____

_____

_____

_____

_____

_____

_____

_____

_____

2. Because we belong to the Catholic Church, we are called to support the Church. What are some ways that young people can support the Church?

_____

_____

_____

Who carries on Peter's work today?

Respond

Peter's Message Continues

Much has changed in the world since Jesus said to Peter, "Upon this rock I will build my church" (Matthew 16:18). Catholics now live on every inhabited continent, and worldwide membership totals more than one billion people. The pope today teaches the Good News of Jesus using modern technologies, such as the Internet, TV, and audio and video recordings. The pope also travels throughout the world by plane, train, ship, helicopter, automobile, or "popemobile."

The message carried by the pope is the same message carried by Saint Peter. It is the Good News that God the Father so loved the world that he sent us his only Son, Jesus Christ, our Lord. Jesus was anointed with the Holy Spirit. Jesus was put to death, but rose from the dead on the third day. Appearing to the Apostles, the Risen Jesus commissioned them to preach and teach the Gospel and the forgiveness of sins and to baptize people. This work has been passed on to the Church from the Apostles. The Church continues this mission today and will proclaim the Gospel to all people to the end of time.

Activities

1. What makes it easy for the Church to continue spreading the Gospel in the twenty-first century? What makes it difficult?

_____

_____

_____

_____

2. What message from the Gospels would you like to pass on to the believers of tomorrow?

_____

_____

_____

_____

_____

Why do you feel this message is important?

_____

_____

_____

_____

How can you help spread this message?

_____

_____

_____

_____

3. The early Christians shared their possessions with one another. They spent time together praying, reading the Scriptures, listening to the teachings of the Apostles, and sharing in the Eucharist. Each image on this page represents an activity of the early Church. On the lines below each image, describe how your family or parish community participates in the activity.

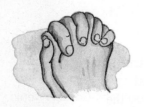

_____

_____

_____

_____

_____

_____

_____

_____

_____

_____

4. Sometimes people might question your Catholic beliefs. Peter had the same problem. His critics believed his teachings were something he had made up. How do you think Peter answered them? (*Hint:* Read 2 Peter 1:12–21.)

_____

_____

_____

_____

How did the early Church pray?

✝ Prayer Celebration

The Apostles' Creed

Catholics pray the Apostles' Creed because it is the true summary of the Apostles' faith. It is an ancient creed that has been taught for almost 2,000 years. When we pray the Apostles' Creed, we are united with God the Father, the Son, and the Holy Spirit, as well as the whole Church.

Let us stand and unite our voices with those of the Apostles and Catholics around the world as we proclaim our faith.

I believe in God, the Father almighty,

Creator of heaven and earth,

and in Jesus Christ, his only Son, our Lord,

who was conceived by the Holy Spirit,

born of the Virgin Mary, suffered under Pontius Pilate,

was crucified, died and was buried;

he descended into hell;

on the third day he rose again from the dead;

he ascended into heaven,

and is seated at the right hand of God the Father almighty;

from there he will come to judge the living and the dead.

I believe in the Holy Spirit,

the holy catholic Church,

the communion of saints,

the forgiveness of sins,

the resurrection of the body,

and life everlasting. Amen.

1 Chapter Review

A **Complete** the sentences with words from the box.

succession
Holy Spirit
Jews
Gentiles
prayer
Peter
Salvation
Apostles'

1. Jesus' early followers believed that people who were not

   _____ could not take part in God's _____.

2. A prayer of beliefs that the Church has said from earliest times of the

   Church is the _____ Creed.

3. The early Christians devoted themselves to communal life, the

   teaching of the Apostles, the breaking of bread, and

   _____.

4. The _____ guided Peter to reach out to the _____.

5. There is an unbroken line of _____ from _____ to the

   present pope.

B **Circle** the letter of the best answer.

1. The _____, or teaching authority of the Church, is made up of the bishops in communion with the pope, the bishop of Rome.
   a. synod
   b. Magisterium
   c. Gospel
   d. diocese

2. The Church is _____ because it is founded by Jesus Christ on the Apostles.
   a. catholic
   b. Trinitarian
   c. holy
   d. apostolic

3. The Church is _____ because it reflects the unity of the Trinity. The Church is the People of God, the Body of Christ, and the Temple of the Holy Spirit.
   a. the Light of the world
   b. Trinitarian
   c. apostolic
   d. universal

4. When the Magisterium officially proclaims a teaching on morals or faith, such a teaching is _____.
   a. apostolic
   b. understandable
   c. temporary
   d. infallible

C **Match** Column A with Column B by writing the correct number in the space provided.

A

1. Cornelius

2. Jesus

3. Peter

4. the pope

5. The Holy Spirit

B

___ prayed for Peter's faith to be strong

___ received the keys of the kingdom from Jesus

___ has guided the Church throughout the centuries to be faithful to the teachings of Jesus

___ invited Peter to come to his house and teach him and his family and servants about Jesus

___ teaches the same message carried by Peter

D **Complete** these statements from the Apostles' Creed.

I believe in God, the _____ almighty, . . .

and in Jesus Christ, his _____, our _____, . . .

I believe in the Holy _____,

the holy catholic _____,

the communion of _____,

the _____ of sins,

the _____ of the body,

and life _____.

E **List** some ways in which you might share the Good News of Jesus with others as Peter did with Cornelius.

_____

_____

_____

_____

_____

_____

Get CONNECTED

with family and friends

Holy: Jesus Christ in the Sacraments

The Seven Sacraments are encounters with the living Christ. They are vital ways in which we experience God's profound love at important times in our lives. The Sacraments help us connect God with the ordinary and extraordinary events in our lives. They are God's gifts of love, and we always celebrate them within the Church. Sacraments celebrate our life in Christ and are actions that are to be lived. They bring God's love and grace into every aspect of our lives.

Activity

Each of us has moments to remember—some big and some small. Some of these moments involve God, such as receiving a Sacrament for the first time. What Sacraments have you received? Do you remember how you prepared to receive each Sacrament? Do you remember who helped you? Do you remember how you felt on the day you received each Sacrament?

Do one of the following.

1. Dig up photos or videos of big moments in your life in which God played a part. Talk to your parents about the way that God was present on those special occasions.

2. Make a list of some special moments in your life. Recall with your family how you celebrated these moments.

Trivia

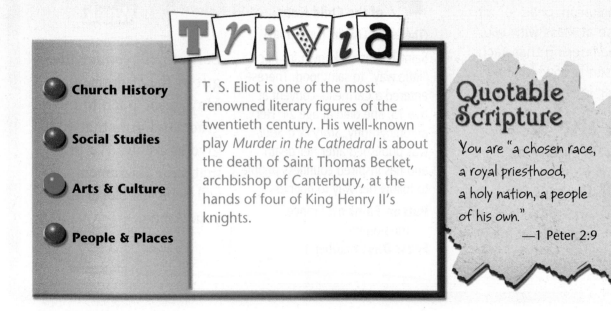

- ● **Church History**
- ● **Social Studies**
- ● **Arts & Culture**
- ● **People & Places**

T. S. Eliot is one of the most renowned literary figures of the twentieth century. His well-known play *Murder in the Cathedral* is about the death of Saint Thomas Becket, archbishop of Canterbury, at the hands of four of King Henry II's knights.

Quotable Scripture

You are "a chosen race, a royal priesthood, a holy nation, a people of his own."

—1 Peter 2:9

Get CONNECTED

with family and friends

✝ Scripture Background

In the Early Church

The Origin of the Sunday Mass In the earliest Eucharistic celebrations, prayers were spoken by priests who presided over these gatherings. These celebrations, as they do today, commemorated the Last Supper, where Jesus instituted the Eucharist and the priesthood. These shared meals adapted several Jewish customs and prayers. Usually held early in the morning and eventually on Sunday, these celebrations also commemorated the Resurrection. During the second century, Saint Justin wrote about Christian practices in *The First Apology,* in which he described a Eucharistic celebration. The celebration included Scripture readings, a sermon, common prayers, an offertory, a sign of peace, a Eucharistic prayer, and the distribution of Holy Communion.

Read Acts 2:43–47 to learn more about how the early Christians gathered to celebrate the Eucharist.

WEEKLY PLANNER

On Sunday

After you receive Holy Communion, pray for all those at Mass with you, remembering that each person is your brother or sister in Christ.

On the Web

blestarewe.com

New! Visit our Web site for the saint of the day and the reflection question of the week.

Saint of the Week

Saint Thérèse of the Child Jesus

(Thérèse of Lisieux) (1873–1897)

Saint Thérèse is known for her "little way" to sainthood. Thérèse entered a Carmelite convent at age 15. She died at age 24. Her autobiography, *Story of a Soul,* was published after her death and has inspired countless people to follow her way to holiness.

Patron Saint of: France, missionaries

Feast Day: October 1

Lord, thank you for the gift of the Sacraments. May we be open to the grace and gifts that you give so freely. We pray that your Sacraments will bring us closer to you. Amen.

2   Holy: Jesus Christ in the Sacraments

And it happened that, while he was with them at table, he took bread, said the blessing, broke it, and gave it to them. With that their eyes were opened and they recognized him.

Luke 24:30–31

Share

Jason was on the basketball court trying to get in the game, and it seemed like an eternity before anyone picked him to play. His mom's words kept ringing in his head: *No one ever said this was going to be easy.* He thought about how much he disliked his new home. It was a shock—moving into a Latino neighborhood.

Jason thought, *I bet they'll pick me last 'cause I'm new and I look different.*

The next day, Sunday, Jason did everything he could to convince his mom he was too sick to go to Mass. He had been thinking about what happened the day before and how the kids had acted like he was from another world.

"I knew this was going to happen," Jason whispered to his mom when they were at the church.

"What do you mean?" his mom asked.

"It's strange here. Our church was never like this," Jason said. "Why do they have to use Spanish for so many prayers?"

Then, at the Sign of Peace, Jason recognized the kid standing behind him.

Alex reached out and shook Jason's hand and smiled, saying, "Hey, what's up, Jason? That was a good game you played yesterday."

Jason smiled back and said, "Thanks, Alex."

Activity

Before the Second Vatican Council—a worldwide gathering of bishops that began in 1962 and ended in 1965—the Catholic Church celebrated Mass in only one language, Latin. Since Vatican II, however, Catholics all over the world have been celebrating Mass in their native languages.

Imagine what it would be like if you attended Mass at which the prayers were said in an unfamiliar language to you. What parts of the Mass do you think you would understand, no matter what language was spoken?

_____

_____

_____

_____

_____

Where do we encounter Jesus?

43

Worship   Breaking Bread Together

This Scripture story in Luke's Gospel about the Risen Jesus' appearance to two of his disciples on the road to Emmaus is often read during the Easter Season.

On the third day after Jesus had been put to death on a cross, Cleopas and his companion traveled from Jerusalem to the village of Emmaus. As they walked, Cleopas and his companion talked about the events that led to the Crucifixion of Jesus. Jesus' Death had left them feeling defeated, crushed, and abandoned.

Cleopas asked his companion, "Do you think we misunderstood Jesus?" At that moment, the Risen Jesus appeared beside them. But the two disciples did not recognize him.

"What are you discussing as you walk along?" Jesus asked them.

Cleopas and his friend stopped, looking downcast. "Are you the only visitor to Jerusalem who does not know of the things that have taken place there in these last few days?" asked Cleopas.

Jesus replied, "What things?"

"The things that happened to Jesus, the Nazarene, who was a mighty prophet. He spoke and did great things," they explained. "But he was handed over to the Romans to be crucified. We had been hoping that he would be the one who would save our people."

Jesus asked them, "Do you think that it was not necessary that the Messiah should suffer these things and enter into his glory?" Then beginning with Moses and all the Prophets, he explained what the Scriptures said about the Messiah.

The things that Jesus said to the two disciples made sense. The more Cleopas and his companion listened to Jesus' words, the more they wanted to hear. As the three of them approached Emmaus, Jesus gave the impression that he was going to walk on farther. But by now, Cleopas and his companion were not yet ready to say goodbye to the stranger.

"Stay with us a little while longer," they said. While he was with them at the table, Jesus took bread, said the blessing, broke the bread, and gave it to them. With that, their eyes were opened and they recognized that the traveler was Jesus. But then, just as quickly as he had appeared to them on the road from Jerusalem, Jesus vanished from their sight.

The two set out at once, returned to Jerusalem to the other disciples, and explained what had taken place.

Based on Luke 24:13–35

The Gospel story describes that it was in the "breaking of bread" that Cleopas and his companion understood that they had been talking with Jesus all along. Jesus is really present in the **Eucharist** and made known to us.

Jesus Is with Us

God the Father sent his only Son, Jesus, to be our Savior. Through our faith and Baptism in Christ, we share in the love that God the Father has for us. Even though members of the Church may have different cultural backgrounds or speak different languages, all come together as one family, the one People of God.

The experience of the two disciples on the road to Emmaus is a model of our experience as members of the Church. When we gather together for the Eucharist, Jesus Christ is with us, for he promised, "For where two or three are gathered together in my name, there am I in the midst of them" (Matthew 18:20).

Christ is always present in the sacramental life of the Church. When the Gospel is proclaimed at Mass, Jesus Christ speaks to us through the Holy Scriptures. Christ is present in a unique way in the Eucharist. Through the power of the Holy Spirit and the words and actions of the priest the bread and wine become the Body and Blood of Christ. Jesus is really and truly present in the Eucharist.

The Eucharist is "the source and summit of the Christian life." It is one of the Seven **Sacraments**,

one of the actions of the Church by which Jesus Christ, through the Holy Spirit, continues his saving work among us today. The Seven Sacraments are sacred signs and causes of grace instituted by Christ himself.

Activities

When do you most strongly encounter Jesus' presence with you?

_____

_____

Some Catholic young people today think that they do not get anything out of taking part in the celebration of Mass. What could you say to them about how receiving the Eucharist regularly can help them develop their relationship with Jesus?

_____

_____

_____

Faith Words

Eucharist In the Sacrament of the Eucharist, bread and wine become the Body and Blood of Jesus Christ. The Eucharist is the central Sacrament of the Church, the source and summit of the Christian life.

Sacrament A Sacrament is a sacred sign and cause of grace instituted by Christ, entrusted to the Church, makes us sharers in Divine life, and continues God's saving action among us. The Seven Sacraments are the main liturgical actions of the Church.

How do we become holy?

Hear & Believe

A Message from Peter

During the Easter Season, the Scripture readings at Mass, such as the Emmaus story, tell how the early Church experienced the presence of the Risen Lord. These readings also help us understand how knowledge of Jesus spread throughout the world.

The New Testament Epistles, or letters, that are read from the Scriptures during this season tell us even more about the lives and times of the early Church. These letters, which were written by Paul and other Apostles, helped the early Church understand Jesus and how to live his message. In those days, when travel was difficult and dangerous, letters were an important way to communicate.

Many communities of new believers lived within the Roman Empire, where they suffered and were rejected for their faith in Christ. To encourage one of these communities, Peter wrote:

Believe in Jesus, the cornerstone of our faith, . . . You are a chosen race, a royal priesthood, and a holy nation. You are God's own people. You have been brought out of darkness into a wonderful light. Praise God for all that he has done for you.

Based on 1 Peter 2:4–10

A CLOSER LOOK

The Word Holy

Holy is the English translation of the Hebrew word *Qadosh,* which means "separated from all that is not sacred; set apart for God." The Greek word *hagios* also means "consecrated to God." Therefore, *hagioi* are the holy ones, or saints, who separate themselves from sin and live in fellowship with God. Old English gives us *hailo* or *hal,* which means "whole" or "free from injury." We know that Jesus Christ frees us from sin, allowing us to be both whole and holy.

Our Church Teaches

Catholics worldwide celebrate the Seven Sacraments with expressions of their unique cultural traditions. These celebrations unite the Church on Earth and the Church in Heaven in our worship of God.

The Church, the People of God, is on a journey toward holiness. The Sacrament of Baptism is the first step on that journey. We cannot have to do anything to deserve Baptism because it is a grace and gift from God. Like Baptism, Confirmation is a

We Believe

Jesus Christ is made known to us through the Sacraments working to transform us into a holy people.

Sacrament of Christian Initiation that places a special spiritual mark on the soul and, therefore, can be received only once. Through Baptism and Confirmation and the Sacrament of the Eucharist, the third Sacrament of Christian Initiation, we become full members of the Church. We are strengthened to overcome temptation and sin and live as disciples of Christ. As each of us grows in holiness, so does the entire Church.

You are a chosen race, a royal priesthood, God's own people (based on 1 Peter 2:9)

Activities

1. In the Sacrament of Baptism we receive an indelible spiritual mark on our soul that can never be removed and that distinguishes us as one of God's own people. As we mature, our faith must be developed and nurtured by others and through our own choices. People cannot see our baptismal mark, but they should see from our words and actions that we are disciples of Jesus. List some everyday actions that Catholic young people can do to show that they are disciples of Christ.

2. In this space, design a poster to remind yourself and your fellow students that our words and actions should always show that we are disciples of Jesus.

How can we express appreciation for the gift of the Mass?

Respond

Saint Thérèse of the Child Jesus (Thérèse of Lisieux)

Thérèse of Lisieux was an ordinary young girl with little opportunity to do great things for God. Thérèse wanted to be a saint. She believed that her desire to be a saint came from God.

One day, as Thérèse was reading the Bible, she read, "Let the children come to me and do not prevent them; for the kingdom of God belongs to such as these" (Luke 18:16). These words were the key that Thérèse was searching for! She did not have to do great things; she could follow a "little way" to sainthood by doing ordinary things with great love for Jesus. This ordinary girl became one of the most beloved saints of all time.

Her story begins in 1873, in Alençon, France. The ninth child born into the Martin family, she was called "Little Queen" by her father. Thérèse lived life with gusto. She had an incredible desire to do God's will and was determined to serve him forever by becoming a nun. At age fifteen, Thérèse entered a convent of Carmelite sisters.

At first, Thérèse found life in the convent difficult, but accepting her daily challenges helped her grow in love. She also experienced periods of doubt. For comfort, she turned to the Gospels and the words of the saints. Thérèse copied her favorite Scripture verses and memorized them. Her prayers grew from her intense desire to love God. She once explained, "I tell God what I want quite simply, without any splendid turns of phrase, and somehow he always manages to understand me." Thérèse teaches us that what matters in life is "not great deeds, but great love."

Thérèse promised to pray even more after death. Before she died in 1897 at age twenty-four, she said, "I will spend my heaven doing good on earth. I will let fall a shower of roses."

In 1997 Pope John Paul II named Saint Thérèse of the Child Jesus (Thérèse of Lisieux) a **Doctor of the Church.**

Activities

1. Saint Thérèse wanted to do great things, but she discovered that God wanted her to do ordinary things with great love. Like Saint Thérèse, we can achieve holiness by doing ordinary things with great love for God. In the left column, list four ordinary things that you do nearly every day. In the right column, write how you might do these things in a way that better shows your love for God.

Everyday things that I do	How I can do them better
_____	_____
_____	_____
_____	_____
_____	_____

2. Take a few moments to reflect on the following questions.
   * Do I pay attention to what God wants of me each day?
   * How do I respond to God's call to me to live a life that honors and glorifies him?
   * Do I make my relationship with God an important part of each day, through prayer, reading Scripture, and simply reflecting on his presence in my life?

On the lines below, write ways that you can make God a greater part of your life every day. Then write a prayer asking God to help you put these ideas into action.

_____

_____

_____

My Prayer

_____

_____

_____

How do we offer praise and thanksgiving during the liturgy?

✝ Prayer Celebration

Eucharistic Prayer II

The Eucharist is the central act of worship of the Church. Like the travelers on the road to Emmaus, we meet the Risen Jesus in the breaking of bread. Let us now stand and pray together.

Reader 1: You are indeed Holy, O Lord,
the fount of all holiness.

Reader 2: At the time he was betrayed
and entered willingly into his Passion,
he took bread and, giving thanks,

Reader 3: broke it, and gave it
to his disciples, saying:

All: TAKE THIS, ALL OF YOU, AND EAT OF IT,
FOR THIS IS MY BODY,
WHICH WILL BE GIVEN UP FOR YOU.

Reader 4: In a similar way, when supper was ended,
he took the chalice

Reader 5: and, once more giving thanks,
he gave it to his disciples, saying:

All: TAKE THIS, ALL OF YOU, AND DRINK FROM IT,
FOR THIS IS THE CHALICE OF MY BLOOD,
THE BLOOD OF THE NEW AND ETERNAL COVENANT,
WHICH WILL BE POURED OUT FOR YOU
    AND FOR MANY
FOR THE FORGIVENESS OF SINS.
DO THIS IN MEMORY OF ME.

Reader 6: The mystery of faith.

All: We proclaim your Death, O Lord,
and profess your Resurrection
until you come again.

Roman Missal

A **Complete** the sentences with words from the box.

1. In the Sacrament of the Eucharist, _____ become the _____ of Jesus Christ.

2. A _____ is a sacred sign and cause of grace instituted by Christ and given to the Church to continue the saving action of God through the _____.

3. The Church is the _____, and her members are on a journey to _____.

4. The Mass is celebrated in different _____ and _____ the whole Church both on Earth and in Heaven.

5. When the _____ is proclaimed at Mass, _____ speaks to us through the Holy Scriptures.

| People of God |
| holiness |
| Jesus |
| languages |
| bread and wine |
| Sacrament |
| unites |
| Gospel |
| Holy Spirit |
| Body and Blood |

B **Match** Column A with Column B by writing the correct number in the space provided.

A

1. Saint Thérèse

2. Epistle

3. Eucharist

4. Baptism

5. Eucharistic Prayer

B

___ first step on our Christian journey to holiness

___ source and summit of the Christian life

___ a New Testament letter that was written by Paul or another Apostle

___ the part of the Mass in which the priest consecrates the bread and wine

___ said that what matters in life is not great deeds but great love

C **Circle** the letter of the best answer.

1. Cleopas and his friends were on the road to _____ when they met the Risen Jesus.
   a. Damascus
   b. Emmaus
   c. Jerusalem
   d. heaven

2. They recognized Jesus when he _____.
   a. instructed them in the Scriptures
   b. told them his name
   c. broke the bread
   d. met them on the road

3. The _____ of the Church unites us more closely with Jesus and the Church, the Body of Christ.
   a. origin
   b. authority
   c. mandate
   d. sacramental life

4. The _____ is the central Sacrament of the Church and the heart of Catholic worship.
   a. Eucharist
   b. Sacred Scripture
   c. homily
   d. Last Judgment

5. The Sacraments of _____ place an indelible, or permanent, spiritual mark on the soul; therefore, they may be received only once.
   a. Baptism and Penance
   b. Baptism and Confirmation
   c. Penance and Confirmation
   d. Anointing of the Sick and Matrimony

D **Write** a prayer in the style of a Eucharistic Prayer in which you thank Jesus for his Real Presence in the Eucharist.

_____

_____

_____

_____

_____

_____

_____

Catholic: Open and Respectful of All

From the early days of the Church, Catholics have been charged with the mission of spreading the Good News of Jesus Christ to every corner of the Earth. The Church's leaders and her other members did not always agree on who should be welcomed into the Church and what the requirements should be. As Catholics, we must value and respect the many ways that God works in and through people.

Activity

The Catholic Church is made up of people from all over the world. The Catholic faith that parents responsibly share with their children is celebrated in ways that respect and reflect various cultures. When we open our minds and hearts and try to understand God's work in the world, it does not take long for us to realize that we are all valued by him.

Do one of the following.

1. Look around your house to find signs of your ethnic heritage. Ask your parents about the meaning of each item.

2. Find out the countries that your ancestors came from. Ask your parents or relatives to share stories of how faith may have helped people in your family adjust to living in this country.

- **Church History**
- **Social Studies**
- **Arts & Culture**
- **People & Places**

Damascus, the capital of Syria, is believed to be the oldest continuously occupied national capital. The Church has existed in Damascus since Apostolic times.

Quotable Scripture

And they were all filled with the holy Spirit and began to speak in different tongues, as the Spirit enabled them to proclaim. —Acts 2:4

Get CONNECTED

with family and friends

✚ Scripture Background

In the Early Church

The Status of Gentiles Jesus, a Jew, knew the tenets and practices of the Jewish faith. His earliest followers, also Jews, continued to live by and practice the faith and traditions of the Jewish religion. Eventually, the Gospel was preached to Gentiles, or non-Jews. The question of whether Gentiles needed to practice the Jewish faith or whether faith in Jesus was enough for Salvation arose. The issue was settled through prayerful discernment at the Council of Jerusalem. Struggling to relate Mosaic Law to Gentiles, and recalling the conversion of Cornelius, a Gentile, Peter supported Paul's position. But some Jews reluctant to worship with Gentiles were not pleased. Peter, led by the Holy Spirit, made it clear that all people are invited to share the Gospel and to receive Salvation in Jesus Christ.

Read Acts of the Apostles 10:44–49 to learn about the Baptism of Cornelius.

WEEKLY PLANNER

On Sunday

While you are at Mass, notice the different ethnic groups that make up your parish, and express thanks for the gifts all bring to the Church.

On the Web

blestarewe.com

Visit our Web site for the saint of the day and the reflection question of the week.

Saint of the Week

Blessed Miguel Agustín Pro (1891–1927)

Father Pro is one of the heroes of the Catholic Church in Mexico. Early in the twentieth century, the Mexican government forbade Catholics from practicing their faith. Father Pro took great risk to secretly celebrate the Sacraments with the Catholic people. Because of this, Miguel Pro was arrested by government authorities and executed.

Feast Day: November 23

A Prayer for the Week

Lord, we know that all people are made in your image. Help us treat others with kindness and respect. Help us be open to our parents as they share their faith with us. Amen.

3 Catholic: Open and Respectful of All

 We believe that we are saved through the grace of the Lord Jesus, . . . **Acts of the Apostles 15:11**

Share

"There's no way we can use that music at Mass! Kids will be clapping and stomping their feet!" Anna said.

"That's exactly the point!" Nagesti replied. "The Bible says to make a joyful noise to praise the Lord!"

Nagesti had come to St. Benedict's parish from Nigeria last year. He and Anna were on the committee to choose the music for the monthly youth group Mass.

"Listen. We want the regular kind of music here!" Anna said.

"Fine! Take me off the committee!" yelled Nagesti as he rushed out the door.

Activity

Sometimes people with good intentions disagree, just as Anna and Nagesti did. In the groups you belong to, what kinds of disagreements occur? On the lines below, write what could be done to resolve disagreements in a peaceful way.

_____

_____

_____

_____

_____

What kinds of disagreements did the early Christians have?

Hear & Believe

✝ **Scripture** The Council of Jerusalem

Saint Paul the Apostle played a very important role in proclaiming the Gospel to Gentiles, or non-Jews. You might know him as the author of many of the New Testament letters to the early Church. But did you know that Paul once persecuted Christians?

In Paul's time, there were many martyrs—people who were punished and killed for proclaiming their faith in Christ. Paul, who was Jewish, and was also named Saul, was responsible for seeking out Christians and arresting them. One day something remarkable happened to him. On his way to Damascus to arrest more Christians, Paul was blinded by a light and heard Jesus say to him, "Saul, Saul, why are you persecuting me?" (Acts of the Apostles 9:4).

After this incredible event, Paul became a disciple of Jesus and devoted his life to spreading the Gospel. The following Scripture story tells about Paul and how he helped spread Christ's saving message far beyond the Jewish community.

Some Jews who had become disciples of Jesus were teaching that Gentiles would not be saved if they did not follow the **Mosaic Law**, which Jewish people had followed since the time of Moses. The disciples Paul and Barnabas, however, disagreed. So they went to Jerusalem to ask the Apostles and **presbyters** to settle the question.

After much debate by the Apostles and presbyters, Peter said to them, "Remember that God chose me to bring the Gospel to the Gentiles. God granted them the Holy Spirit just as he did us. Why are you requiring more of Gentiles than God does?" Everyone fell silent and they listened as Paul and Barnabas described the signs and wonders God had worked among the Gentiles through them.

James the Apostle then spoke out, saying, "We must stop troubling the Gentiles who turn to God."

Based on Acts of the Apostles 15:1–20

Disagreement in the Early Church

The first disciples of Jesus were Jews. They followed the Mosaic Law, which contained rules about praying, eating, dressing, working, cleansing the body, and associating with others.

In time, the Gentiles heard about Jesus and wanted to be baptized. However, some of Jesus' followers said that the Gentiles could not be baptized unless they too followed the Mosaic Law. But Paul and Barnabas argued that because the Gentiles were never Jews, the Law of Moses would be difficult for them to understand and follow. They said that the important thing was for the Gentiles to follow Jesus' Law of Love.

At the Council of Jerusalem, Paul and Barnabas presented their case to the Apostles and presbyters. The Council looked for a solution to the problem. Some Jews believed in Jesus but continued, like the Pharisees, to follow the Mosaic Law in a strict way. They insisted that it was not right to let anyone into the Church unless that person followed the Mosaic Law. Peter sided with Paul by testifying about his encounter with Cornelius. (See Acts 10.) Remember, Peter did not know if he should enter Cornelius' house because it was against Jewish law for a Jew to go into the home of a Gentile. But through the guidance of the Holy Spirit, Peter went in. He taught Cornelius and his household and saw that God sent the Holy Spirit to Jews and Gentiles alike. This experience led Peter to realize that God loves all people equally, whether Jew or Gentile, and that he freely gives his grace to all. Therefore, Peter argued that there was no reason to force Gentiles to follow the Mosaic Law.

A Catholic Church

The whole assembly listened to the arguments. Finally, the Apostle James pointed out that even the prophets had written that God wanted the Gentiles to follow him. Inspired by God, James stated that the Gentiles did not have to follow the Mosaic Law. The others agreed. All at the Council realized that all people are called to be saved by faith in Jesus Christ. The Church would be open to all. It is **catholic**.

Activity

Discuss with the class one way your parish shows that it is "catholic."

Faith Words

Mosaic Law The Mosaic Law, or Law of Moses, sets forth rules and practices for the Jewish people that are based on the first five books of the Bible.

presbyters Presbyters were the appointed religious leaders, or elders, of the early Church. In the Church today, the term *presbyter* means "priest."

catholic The word *catholic* means "universal." With a capital C, it describes the Church founded by Jesus Christ on the Apostles.

What are the responsibilities of being a Catholic?

57

Hear & Believe

✝ Scripture Together in Jesus

Many Jewish people resented the Gentiles who were being baptized into the Christian faith. After all, the Jewish people had been faithful to God for generations. They had suffered because they persisted in their faith. It seemed unfair that the Gentiles could become Christians without becoming Jews first.

Saint Paul reminded the followers of Christ that Jesus had come for everyone. He stated this very clearly in his letter to the Galatians.

Before Jesus came, we carefully followed the rule of law. We waited for Jesus to come. But now that we know Jesus, we are not under the Law. Jesus said that through faith we are all children of God. As baptized Christians we are clothed in Christ.

We no longer consider ourselves Jews or Greek, or slaves or free people. Whether we are men or women, we are all one in Christ Jesus. If we belong to Jesus, then we are all descendants of Abraham and the promise made to him.

Based on Galatians 3:23–29

In the Acts of the Apostles, we see that gradually the early Christians began to focus less on who they were before they came to know Jesus. Instead, they concentrated on who they had become since their conversion. Gentiles and Jews acted together. What was important to both was following Jesus.

Everyone was of one heart and mind. Together they gave witness to Jesus' Resurrection. No one among them remained needy. Those who owned property would sell it and give the money to be shared by all.

Based on Acts of the Apostles 4:32–35

Our Church Teaches

God offers the gift of his grace to all people. All people receive Salvation through Jesus Christ. Because Jesus brings Salvation to all people, the Church welcomes everyone. As the People of God and the Body of Christ, we continue the work Jesus gave the Apostles.

We live the Gospel by working for the common good, or for the benefit of all people. Treating all people with respect is one way of working

We Believe

Through the grace of the Lord Jesus, Salvation is for all humankind. Catholics welcome all and work for the common good.

for the common good. Another way is supporting institutions that improve the conditions of human life. Jesus instructed God's people to follow the Great Commandment, loving God and our neighbors above all else. Through the grace of the Holy Spirit, which comes to us in the Sacraments, we are strengthened to love God and others as Jesus taught and showed us to do.

Activities

Catholics are called to work for the common good. This means ensuring that all people have what they need to live. Catholics have worked for the common good for more than 2,000 years. However, many decisions in the world are still motivated by selfishness and greed. We cannot change the world all at once, but we can begin to make changes in the way we live. The New Testament Epistles and letters are filled with guidelines of how Catholics are to live.

1. Look up one or more of the following Scripture passages. Some of the passages focus on making changes that will help other people. Others deal with changing ourselves. Pray about what you read. Write what the message of the reading means for you. Think about what you can do to live out the Scripture message.

Galatians 6:1–10   James 2:1–8   1 John 4:7–12
Colossians 3:12–17   1 Peter 4:8–10   1 John 4:19–21

Scripture passage I read: _____

Message : _____

_____

_____

What I can do to live out this message: _____

_____

_____

_____

_____

2. Gather in small groups and share what you have read and written. Discuss any insights that you have gained from this activity. Decide what you can do as a small group to put into practice what you have learned. Make a plan and a timetable for accomplishing your plan. Then take action!

How do we spread the Gospel in today's world?

✝ Prayer Celebration

A Prayer of the Faithful

The Catholic Church has grown from a small group of Jesus' followers in Apostolic times that today has spread around the globe. Today the Catholic Church includes people of all nationalities, and people pray in many different languages.

Leader: Let us pray together for the needs of the Church and for all people.

Reader 1: For the pope, bishops, clergy, and all God's people, that their words and actions may reflect God's love, bringing social and economic equality to the world.

All: Lord, hear our prayer.

Reader 2: For our families, that each family member will help work for the common good of the family and that each family will work for the common good of humankind.

All: Lord, hear our prayer.

Reader 3: For the hungry, that their bodies and souls will be fed by the care and generosity of the People of God.

All: Lord, hear our prayer.

Reader 4: For the whole world, that all God's people may live in dignity, prosperity, and peace.

All: Lord, hear our prayer.

A **Write** a brief summary of what you learned in this chapter, using words from the box.

James	Paul	Jewish
Gentiles	Peter	open
Council of Jerusalem	disagreement	Cornelius

_____

_____

_____

_____

_____

_____

_____

_____

_____

B **Write** the name of the person described by each clue.

1. I once persecuted Christians and then became one. _____

2. I published the *Syllabus of Errors,* which condemned the "errors" of the modern world, and I convened Vatican Council I. _____

3. I convened the Second Vatican Council. _____

4. I told the Galatians that all people who are baptized are "clothed in Christ."

_____

5. I told the presbyters that God told me to bring the Gospel to non-Jews, or Gentiles.

_____

Get CONNECTED

with family and friends

✝ Scripture Background

In the Early Church

Speaking in Tongues   Paul lists the spiritual gifts that distinguish the members of the Church. The last of these gifts is the gift of tongues. During the Eucharistic celebrations of the early Church, some members would speak in "tongues," making sounds that were actually inspired utterances but sounded like gibberish and distracted others. Those Christians of Corinth who had received the gift of tongues felt that they were particularly gifted. Paul reminds them that members of the Church are gifted in different ways and that each follower of Christ is meant to use his or her gifts to build up the Body of Christ.

Read about Paul's teaching on spiritual gifts in 1 Corinthians 12:1–11.

WEEKLY PLANNER

On Sunday

Before Mass, examine your conscience. Try to recall when you have been a source of division and pain for others. Ask for God's forgiveness and for the grace to change your ways.

On the Web

blestarewe.com

 Visit our Web site for the saint of the day and the reflection question of the week.

Saint of the Week

Saint Helena
(250–330)

At the age of eighty Saint Helena led a pilgrimage to Palestine to search for the true Cross. Helena had a chapel built on the spot where the cross was found, and sent pieces to Rome and to Constantinople. The Feast of the Exaltation of the Holy Cross on September 14 celebrates the event.

Patron Saint of: converts, Malta

Feast Day: August 18

A Prayer for the Week

Lord, it is painful to be divided from others. As your followers, help us be faithful to you and to set aside petty differences. May the love and unity that we share be signs of our love for all people. Amen.

4 One: Praying for Unity

I pray . . . that they may all be one, as you, Father, are in me and I in you.
John 17:20–21

Share

Have you ever noticed how your opinions sometimes differ from those of your mother, father, sisters, or brothers? You might even have days when you disagree so much with another member of your family that you wonder how you could be related. Having these disagreements is also a sign that you and your family share a strong bond of love.

Activity

Look at the people in the three pictures. How do they differ from one another? If the people appear to be disagreeing, what might have caused this? List some words and actions that might bring the people together.

_____

_____

_____

_____

What differences do you notice among Christians? What similarities do Christians share? Discuss your responses with your class.

How are the People of God different yet alike?

✝ Prayer Celebration

The Lord's Prayer

The Lord's Prayer is the prayer of all Christians. Imagine that you are in the crowd near Jesus on the day he teaches his disciples the Lord's Prayer. Read the prayer together slowly, as though you were hearing it for the first time. Pause after each line to hear the leader's commentary.

All: *Read the Lord's Prayer in Luke 11:2–4.*

Leader: Father, how happy we are to know that you love us so much that we can call you "Father."

All: Father, hallowed be your name,

Leader: May we follow your Son by loving one another and building unity among all who love you, so that you may truly recognize the beginning of your kingdom on Earth.

All: your kingdom come.

Leader: May we generously share what we have so that none of your children are hungry.

All: Give us each day our daily bread

Leader: We trust you will forgive us, Father, and we know we must forgive each person who sins against us.

All: and forgive us our sins for we ourselves forgive everyone in debt to us,

Leader: Father, keep us always faithful to you,

All: and do not subject us to the final test. We believe. Amen.

A   **Complete** the following sentences.

1. The Apostle Paul wrote, "Some people God has designated in the _____

to be, first, apostles; second, prophets; third _____, then, mighty

deeds; then _____ of healing, assistance, administration, and

varieties of tongues" (1 Corinthians 12:28)

2. At _____ the Apostles began to speak in _____

they had not spoken before.

3. The four essential qualities of the Church are called _____ of the Church.

4. The _____ is the living Body of Christ, the People of God.

B   **Circle** the letter of the best answer.

1. God calls all Christians to_____.
   a. live in union with one another
   b. pray and work for unity
   c. follow Jesus
   d. all of the above

2. Saint Paul's First Letter to the Corinthians reminds us that _____.
   a. some parts of the body are more important than others
   b. we are all members of the one Body of Christ, the Church
   c. the weaker parts of the body are not really necessary
   d. we must not be too concerned about the sufferings of others

3. Through the centuries, members of the Church have _____.
   a. remained completely unified
   b. taught that prophecy is the greatest talent
   c. been part of the official religion of the world
   d. had disagreements that have sometimes led to divisions

4. _____ showed devotion to God by building new churches and beautifying existing ones.
   a. Saint Paul
   b. Saint Thérèse
   c. Saint Helena
   d. Saint Peter

Faith in Action

Religion Teachers and Catechists Religion teachers and catechists instruct their students in the teachings of the *Catechism of the Catholic Church.* This helps young people grow in their faith and become fully participating members of the Catholic Church. Religion teachers and catechists play a special role in preparing students to receive the Sacraments, especially Penance and Reconciliation, Eucharist, and Confirmation. They prepare students to receive these Sacraments and teach them to be faithful to their Catholic faith.

In Everyday Life

Activity List three ways in which your religion teacher or catechist has taught you to live as a good Catholic.

1. _____

_____

2. _____

_____

3. _____

_____

In Your Parish

Activity All Catholics can serve their parish community in a variety of ways, including as altar servers and as lectors at Mass. Name one way you can serve your parish community now and one way you can serve your parish as an adult. Briefly tell how in each of these roles you can help others grow in their faith.

Now:

_____

_____

In the future:

_____

_____

_____

Faith in Action

Auxiliary Missionaries Since the time of the Apostles, the Church has been committed to caring for the needs of others and to sharing individual gifts and possessions with those who are in need. Catholic young people contribute to this important work by volunteering to help people in their own communities who are in need or by organizing drives and fundraisers to aid the work of missionaries in faraway places. Groups of students working together to support the Church's mission of serving the poor help spread Jesus' message of love and goodness to people far and near.

In Everyday Life

Activity Service to others can sometimes mean small acts of kindness, and does not always involve a significant or long-term commitment. In the following chart, name three people for whom you can do a small act of kindness. Then tell what that act might be. An example has been done for you.

Person	My act of kindness
Dad	Help with a chore without being asked

In Your Parish

Activity Discuss with a classmate how your class can participate in an event or activity to serve those in need, either in your local community or in a faraway place. Describe at least two ideas.

_____

_____

_____

_____

A **Complete** each sentence by writing the letter of the correct answer from the box in the space provided.

a. pope and bishops	**e.** Peter	**i.** Gentiles
b. homes	**f.** Holy Spirit	**j.** Thérèse of Lisieux
c. Gospel	**g.** communal life	
d. Apostles' Creed	**h.** parish	

1. Catholics pray the _____, which is the true summary of the Apostles' faith.

2. Catholics belong to a local faith community called a _____.

3. The early Christians devoted themselves to the teaching of the Apostles and to the _____.

4. Like Paul, the early Church realized that the message of Christ was for all people, including _____.

5. During the first 200 years of Christianity, Christians gathered for worship in private _____.

6. When the _____ is proclaimed at Mass, Jesus speaks to us through the Sacred Scriptures.

7. _____ followed a "little way" to sainthood by doing ordinary things with great love for Jesus.

8. Jesus gave _____ the keys to the Kingdom of Heaven.

9. The _____ are the successors of the Apostles.

10. The _____ guides the Church to be faithful to the teachings of Jesus.

B **Complete** these petitions. After writing each petition, pray "Lord, hear our prayer."

For the bishops and priests of the Church, that they may _____

_____ .

For the government of our country, that public officials may _____

_____ .

For the poor and suffering of the world, that they may _____

_____ .

C **Match** Column A with Column B by writing the correct number in the space provided.

A

1. Theodosius
2. Helena
3. Constantine
4. Blessed Pope John XXIII
5. Peter
6. Jesus
7. Paul
8. Holy Spirit
9. Messiah
10. Emmaus

B

___ legalized Christianity in the Roman Empire

___ made Christianity the Roman Empire's official religion

___ was an emperor's mother who made a pilgrimage to Jerusalem

___ Jesus appeared to two disciples on the way to this place.

___ gave the Apostles the courage to preach

___ a title that Peter used to describe who Jesus is

___ was prompted by the Holy Spirit to go to Cornelius's house

___ heard Jesus say, "Why are you persecuting me?"

___ instructed his disciples to follow the Great Commandment

___ convened the Second Vatican Council

D **Respond** to the following.

1. Name three parts of the Mass that you could recognize easily if you were in a country where no English was spoken.

_____

_____

_____

2. What differences between you and others might you think of when you pray, "Forgive us our trespasses as we forgive those who trespass against us"?

_____

_____

_____

_____

_____

E **Match** the Faith Words in Column A with the definitions in Column B.

A   **B**

1. Magisterium   ___ reflecting the unity of the Blessed Trinity

2. Marks of the Church   ___ founded on and faithful to the teachings of Jesus Christ and the Apostles

3. catholic   ___ the teaching authority of the Church, which consists of the the bishops in communion with the pope

4. Church   ___ the Sacrament in which bread and wine become the Body and Blood of Jesus Christ

5. Trinitarian   ___ four attributes and essential characteristics of the Church and her mission

6. presbyters   ___ a word meaning "universal"; with a capital C it describes the Church founded by Jesus Christ on the Apostles.

7. Eucharist   ___ the appointed religious leaders, or elders, in the early Church

8. apostolic   ___ a term describing rules and practices that the Jewish people have followed since the time of Moses

9. Mosaic Law

                        ___ a sacred sign and cause of grace instituted by Christ and entrusted to the Church to continue the saving action of God through the Holy Spirit

10. Sacrament

                        ___ the living Body of Christ, the People of God; a word that means "convocation," or a gathering

F **Fill in** the correct word to complete each sentence.

1. Before _____ dedicated his life to Christ, he was known as Saul.

2. _____ went to the house of Cornelius to teach the Word of God.

3. James stated that the Gentiles did not have to follow the _____ Law.

4. The _____ is the Body of Christ, the People of God.

5. On _____ the Apostles began the work Jesus gave to the Church.

The Growth of Christendom

UNIT 2

Having survived persecution and internal strife, Christianity burst forth as both the dominant religion of the Mediterranean world and the organizing principle of society. Great cathedrals and basilicas embodied Christianity's spirit of faith and optimism.

And whatever you do, in word or in deed, do everything in the name of the Lord Jesus, giving thanks to God the Father through him.

Colossians 3:17

Medieval cathedrals employed hundreds of skilled artisans, similar to these master stone-carvers, working on the central doorway of St. John the Divine in New York City.

Get CONNECTED
with family and friends

✚ Scripture Background

Before the Time of Jesus

The Psalms The Old Testament Book of Psalms contains hymns of praise and thanksgiving and laments of ancient Israel—150 altogether. Written over a long period of time, the psalms present varying ways of addressing God. Some speak of the God of a single people and place, while others speak of a God of all people. The psalms describe virtually every aspect of everyday life. The Book of Psalms is truly the common book of prayer of Christians and Jews.

Choose a favorite psalm to read.

WEEKLY PLANNER

On Sunday

During the Prayer of the Faithful, pray that all Catholics will be faithful to the teachings of the Church.

On the Web

blestarewe.com

 Visit our Web site for the saint of the day and the reflection question of the week.

Saint of the Week

 Saint Sophronius (550–639)

Sophronius was a native of Damascus. He lived his last nineteen years in Jerusalem, after Persians had seized the city's holy sites in 614. Just before he died, Sophronius had to negotiate Jerusalem's surrender to the Muslim invaders.

Feast Day: March 11

 **A Prayer for the Week**

Lord, let us be people of courage and peace. Give us willing hearts to do our part to help those in need. Help us treat all people with the dignity and with the respect that you have for people. Amen.

5 Councils, Cultures, and Conflicts

I bless the LORD who counsels me. . . .
I keep the LORD always before me.

Psalm 16:7, 8

Share

In the fourth century the Church began to have more freedom, thanks to emperors Constantine and Theodosius. No longer did Church members have to fear being persecuted for what they believed. Church leaders could now openly debate theological disagreements that arose in the Church.

By this time, the Church had spread rapidly throughout the Mediterranean world and had divided into the Church in the West and the Church in the East. The Western Church was centered in Rome and included the Roman empire's territory in northern Africa. The Eastern Church was centered in Constantinople. During this time leaders in the Church began to resolve their disagreements, and the Church worked to clarify her beliefs about who Jesus Christ was.

Activity

Disagreements happen between people about all sorts of things. Sometimes the disagreements can be about something relatively unimportant, such as which movie to go see. At other times disagreements can be about something very important, such as which person is best suited to be president of the class or of the country!

Think about some disagreements you have had with other people. Then complete the following sentences.

When I have a disagreement about something not too important,
I usually handle it by

_____

_____.

When I have a disagreement about something I strongly believe in,
I usually handle it by

_____

_____.

What disagreements created problems for the early Church?

Hear & Believe

✝ Scripture Stand Firm

In the first century, after Christ's Death and Resurrection, Christians had to confront people who spread false opinions that were not true to the teachings of Christ and his Apostles. Paul wrote to the Church in Thessalonica warning about the false teaching that Christ's Second Coming and the Final Judgment were at hand. Paul wrote:

"Brothers and sisters do not be lead astray by the false teaching that the day of the Lord will come about very soon. Let no one lead you away from the truth you have received. God chose you for Salvation through your holiness by the Holy Spirit, your belief in truth, and to possess the glory of our Lord Jesus Christ. Stand firm in your faith in the traditions that you were taught either by word of mouth or by a letter of ours."

Based on 2 Thessalonians 2:1–3, 13–15

A Closer Look

Saint Augustine of Hippo

Born in A.D. 354, Saint Augustine was one of the most important theologians in the history of the Church. A great preacher and writer, he used his power of logical thinking and passionate love of God to explain and defend Church teachings. As Bishop of Hippo in northern Africa, he steered the Church through a sea of controversy. Augustine understood that when God reveals himself to his people, he remains a mystery beyond words. Augustine wrote, "If you understood him, it would not be God" and "You have made us for yourself; our heart is restless until it rests in you."

Our Church Teaches

As the early Church struggled to proclaim her beliefs, conflicts and heresies arose. Ecumenical Councils were called to teach the faith of the Church. At the First Council of Nicaea, the Church, under the guidance of the Holy Spirit, wrote the Nicene Creed. The Creed clearly states that Jesus, the Son of God, truly became man while remaining truly God. "[B]y the power of the Holy Spirit [he] was incarnate of the

We Believe

Jesus Christ is truly God and truly man. We worship one God who is Father, Son, and Holy Spirit.

Virgin Mary, and became man." Jesus is one divine Person with two natures, human and divine. There is One God in Three Divine Persons, Father, Son, and Holy Spirit.

The Church today continues to proclaim the mystery of God and his love. When conflicts and problems divide the Church, Catholics continue to work toward understanding and unity among all Christians.

Activities

1. How would you stand firm in your beliefs if they were challenged? Read the basic Catholic beliefs stated here. Below each statement, write an explanation of its meaning.

We believe in the Holy Trinity.

_____

We believe that Jesus Christ is God; he became one of us and died for us.

_____

_____

We believe that the Eucharist is Christ's Body and Blood.

_____

_____

We believe in everlasting life.

_____

_____

We believe that God is Creator of all.

_____

_____

We believe that Jesus Christ rose from the dead.

_____

_____

2. The truth that Jesus Christ is truly God and truly man is an essential teaching of our Catholic faith. Identify whether the phrases below describe Jesus' humanity or divinity by writing each on the line below the correct heading.

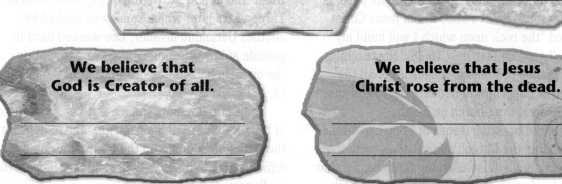

• Jesus • Gesú • Yé su • Jésus • Jesus • Gesú • Yé su • Jésus • Jesus • Gesú • Yé su • Jesus •

hears our prayers

experienced bodily pain

had parents, relatives, and friends

loves us with an everlasting, perfect love

experienced death

performs miracles and healings

was tempted by sin

saves us from sin

sends the Holy Spirit to help us

felt weak and saddened

JESUS

Truly Human

_____

_____

_____

_____

_____

Truly God

_____

_____

_____

_____

_____

• Jesus • Gesú • Yé su • Jésus • Jesus • Gesú • Yé su • Jésus • Jesus • Gesú • Yé su • Jesus •

How does a Christian stand firm in faith?

93

✝ Prayer Celebration

The Nicene-Constantinople Creed

Catholics profess their faith at Mass on Sunday. The Creed prayed at Mass is a profession of faith that was developed at the Council of Nicaea in A.D. 325 and finalized at the Council of Constantinople in A.D. 381.

Leader: Let us stand and profess our faith in God, who is Father, Son, and Holy Spirit, who loves us, created us in his image, made an everlasting Covenant with us, and promises us Salvation.

All: I believe in one God, the Father almighty,
maker of heaven and earth,
of all things visible and invisible.

I believe in one Lord Jesus Christ,
the Only Begotten Son of God,
born of the Father before all ages.
God from God, Light from Light,
true God from true God,
begotten, not made, consubstantial with the Father;
through him all things were made.
For us men and for our salvation
he came down from heaven,
(Bow your head during the following two lines.)
and by the Holy Spirit was incarnate
of the Virgin Mary, and became man.
For our sake he was crucified under Pontius Pilate,
he suffered death and was buried,
and rose again on the third day
in accordance with the Scriptures.
He ascended into heaven
and is seated at the right hand of the Father.
He will come again in glory
to judge the living and the dead
and his kingdom will have no end.

I believe in the Holy Spirit, the Lord, the giver of life,
who proceeds from the Father and the Son,
who with the Father and the Son is adored and glorified,
who has spoken through the prophets.

I believe in one, holy, catholic and apostolic Church.
I confess one Baptism for the
forgiveness of sins and I look
forward to the resurrection of the dead
and the life of the world to come. Amen.

5 Chapter Review

A **Write** a brief summary of what you learned in this chapter, using the words in the box.

_____
_____
_____
_____
_____
_____

Eastern Church
Constantine
Arius
heresy
Nicaea
Western Church
Chalcedon
Creed

B **Match** Column A with Column B by writing the correct number in the space provided.

A

1. heresy

2. Fathers of the Church

3. Ecumenical Council

B

___ a world gathering of the Pope and all the bishops

___ a teaching that is contrary to Church doctrine

___ the bishops and other writers in the first eight centuries of the Church whose teachings helped develop Christian doctrine

C **Write** the name of the person described by each clue.

1. I became the Bishop of Alexandria and fought against Arianism. _____

2. I was the Bishop of Hippo and one of the most influential theologians in the history of the Church. _____

3. I sent a letter to the Council of Chalcedon condemning the claim that Jesus Christ was not human. _____

4. I told the Thessalonians not to be deceived by false teachings about Christ's Second Coming. _____

5. When Attila the Hun was marching on Rome, I headed off his attack.

_____

D **Complete** the following lines from the Nicene Creed.

1. I believe in one God, the _____ almighty, maker of heaven

and earth, of all things visible and invisible.

2. I believe in one _____ Jesus Christ, the Only Begotten _____

of God, born of the _____ before all _____.

God from God, Light from Light, true _____ from true God,

begotten, not made, consubstantial with the _____.

3. By the _____ _____ was incarnate

of the Virgin Mary, and became _____.

4. He will come again in glory to _____ the living and the dead and

his _____ will have no end.

5. I believe in the _____ _____, the Lord, the giver of

life, who proceeds from the _____ and the Son.

E **Respond** to the following.

1. Name and describe one of the heresies that challenged the early Church. Tell why this
heresy was dangerous to the faith of the Church.

_____

_____

_____

2. Name a conflict that threatens the faith of the Church today. Explain how Catholics can
respond to this conflict.

_____

_____

_____

Get CONNECTED
with family and friends

Liturgy and Unity, Worship and Beauty

Since the earliest days of the Church, the Body of Christ has come together to worship God. These gatherings have always included specific symbols, rituals, and prayers that we know as the liturgy. Our participation in the liturgy helps us grow closer to God and to one another and to live as faithful disciples of Christ Jesus.

Activity

The ways in which we experience God include appreciating him through prayer and nature. But we encounter Christ in a unique way when we gather together as the Body of Christ to celebrate the Eucharist.

Do one of the following.

1. Have a family discussion in which family members share what participating in the Mass and receiving Christ in the Eucharist means to them.

2. Prepare a blessing that offers thanks to God for the gifts of life, family and friends, and health. Pray this blessing before your next family meal.

- Church History
- Social Studies
- Arts & Culture
- People & Places

From 1910 to 1945, the Catholic Church in Korea was under the control of the Japanese, who forced Catholics to worship in Shinto shrines. When Korea split into North and South Korea, the Catholic Church in South Korea was forced underground. But the Church survived. Today, there are about one and one half million Catholics in Korea.

Quotable Scripture

"Watch and pray that you may not undergo the test. The spirit is willing but the flesh is weak."

—Mark 14:38

Worship Early Eucharist Celebrations

On the day named after the sun, we hold a meeting in one place for all those who live in the cities or in the country nearby. The memoirs of the Apostles or the writings of the Prophets are read as long as time permits. When the reader has finished, the overseer gives a talk urging and inviting us to imitate all these good examples. Then we all stand up together and send up our prayers. . . . Bread is brought along with wine and water after we have finished our prayer. The overseer likewise sends up prayer and thanksgiving with all his might. The people give their consent by saying "Amen." Now the distribution takes place, and each one receives what has been accepted with thanksgiving. Those who are absent receive their share through the deacons.

Saint Justin Martyr

Saint Justin Martyr (A.D. 100–165) gave us the above description of a second-century celebration of the Eucharist. The first Christians gathered often to celebrate the **Paschal Mystery**—the mystery of our Salvation through Christ's Passion, Death, Resurrection, and Ascension. They did not worship in church buildings. They gathered in each other's homes, where they prayed, sang, read and discussed the Scriptures, and shared the Eucharist. It was not until later that Sunday was designated the Lord's Day. Sunday was chosen as the principal day to celebrate the Eucharist because it is the day on which the Resurrection occurred. By A.D. 150, the Church began to develop its ritual, or formal ceremony, for the celebration of the Eucharist.

The "overseers" that Saint Justin Martyr refers to later became known as priests. As the Church's **liturgy** became more structured, it also required a more formal space for prayer.

 pages 409 and 410 to learn more about the Mass.

The Church in the East

Emperor Constantine moved his capital from Rome to Byzantium, part of modern-day Turkey, and called his new capital Constantinople. This established two major centers of the Roman Empire, one in Constantinople and one in Rome. Each center was influenced by the culture around it. The Church in the East and the Church in the West soon developed different styles of celebrating the liturgy and of church architecture.

For the Church in the East, the liturgy was an expression of faith in God's beautiful kingdom at the end of time. God revealed his beauty and splendor through the senses. Therefore, the Eastern liturgy appealed to a person's senses of touch, smell, sight, hearing, and even taste. The clergy presided over the liturgy, and active participation by the worshiping assembly was not emphasized. The movements and words of the clergy were very ritualistic. First, the bishop entered in majestic robes. The priests followed, carrying the bread and wine. Incense and bells added to the mystery of the ritual. A cantor chanted the Word of God, and the people sang their responses. The consecration of the bread and wine took place behind an ornate screen, out of the people's sight.

The church buildings had a central space covered by a large dome. Often the dome would have windows around its base, allowing in light and giving the dome the appearance of floating. The dome represented Heaven. Icons decorated in gold and silver, and colorful mosaics depicting biblical scenes, adorned the walls of the church.

The Church in the West

In the Church in the West the Eucharistic liturgy celebrated Christ's Sacrifice in a dramatic way. Emphasis was placed on the altar, and worshipers moved about freely so that they could clearly see the actions of the priest.

The first church buildings were basilicas, similar to official Roman government buildings. They were long buildings that had a semicircular space at one end. The altar, which was made of stone, was placed in the semicircle. The altar acted as a symbol to help people understand that the Eucharist was a holy sacrifice. Often the relic of a martyr was buried beneath the altar. The bishop's chair was placed behind the altar and raised so that all the people could see and hear the bishop. Lecterns were placed on either side of the altar.

In time, the basilicas evolved into solid, Romanesque churches. They reflected the feeling that the Church was a powerful force in the world. The liturgy placed a greater emphasis on the clergy, and laypeople were separated from the main altar by a railing. The Romanesque churches evolved into the Gothic churches of the Middle Ages, with their high arches and spires, that celebrated God's order and perfection.

Liturgy Adapts to Culture

As the Church began to spread throughout the world, some of the prayers and rituals that make up the liturgy were adapted to the cultures of Christians living in different places. However, the essential elements of the liturgy did not change because they are part of the Church's doctrine and faith Tradition. For example, in the celebration of the Eucharist we always use bread and wine as Jesus did at the Last Supper, and the priest prays the words of consecration over the bread and wine, using the words of Jesus.

Kyrie eleison

Activity

In what ways is the celebration of Mass in your parish church the same as and different from the Eucharist in the time of Justin Martyr?

Same as: _____

_____

Different from: _____

_____

Discuss your answers with a partner.

Lord, have mercy

Faith Words

Paschal Mystery The Paschal Mystery is the saving event of the Passion, Death, Resurrection, and Ascension of Jesus Christ.

liturgy The liturgy of the Church is the official, public worship of God, especially the celebration of the Eucharist. It includes the celebration of Mass and the Sacraments. Christ is always present and leads his Church in the celebration of the liturgy.

Why is celebrating the Sacraments important for Catholics?

Hear & Believe

The Universal Catholic Church: East and West

Christ commissioned the Apostles, saying, "Go, therefore, and make disciples of all nations, baptizing them in the name of the Father, and of the Son, and of the holy Spirit" (Matthew 28:19–20). The Apostles, following the command of Jesus, traveled by land and sea throughout the lands surrounding the Mediterranean Sea. Saint Peter established the Church in Rome while the other Apostles established the Church in other parts of the Mediterranean world.

Today there are twenty-four local churches that make up the Catholic Church: the Latin Church, more commonly called the Roman Catholic Church, and twenty-three Eastern Catholic Churches. All of these churches recognize the pope as the head of the Church on Earth.

Although each Catholic Church may have its own customs, in general, there are only eight major rites, or liturgical heritages. The twenty-four Churches can be grouped into eight different rites. All of these rites are part of the "one, holy, catholic, and apostolic"

The Catholic Church
Latin Rite: Roman Catholic Church
Armenian Rite: Armenian Catholic Church
Alexandrian Rite: Coptic Catholic Church
Ge'ez Rite: Ethiopian Catholic Church
West Syrian Maronite Rite: Antiochian Syrian Maronite Catholic Church
East Syrian Rite: Chaldean Catholic Church, Syro-Malabar Catholic Church
West Syrian Rite: Syrian Catholic Church, Syro-Malankara Catholic Church
Byzantine Rite: Melkite Catholic Church, Italo-Albanian Catholic Church, Ukrainian Catholic Church, Ruthenian Catholic Church, Byzantine Catholic Church USA, Romanian Catholic Church, Greek Catholic Church in Greece, Greek Catholic Church in former Yugoslavia, Bulgarian Catholic Church, Slovak Catholic Church, Hungarian Catholic Church, Russian Catholic Church, Belarusian Catholic Church, Albanian Catholic Church, Georgian Catholic Church

Our Church Teaches

Throughout the year the Church celebrates the entire mystery of Jesus Christ in its liturgy. On special feast days, the Church also remembers and celebrates Mary the Mother of God, the Apostles, the martyrs, and all the saints. In these celebrations the Church on Earth is united with the worship of God by all who are with him in Heaven. Anyone who desires to receive the Eucharist must first be free of mortal sin and in a state of grace. If a person is not in a state of grace, he or she must receive absolution in the Sacrament of Penance and Reconciliation before receiving the Eucharist. When the faithful receive the Eucharist, they are more fully united to Christ and with the whole Church, are forgiven venial sin, and receive the grace to avoid grave sin.

We Believe

In the Eucharistic liturgy, Jesus Christ becomes present under the appearance of bread and wine.

GO TO *pages 408 and 409 to read more about the Eucharist.*

Activities

1. In Eastern Catholic Churches, children receive the Sacraments of Christian Initiation—Baptism, Eucharist, and Confirmation—at the same time, usually by the age of one. Which of these Sacraments have you received? When did you receive them?

_____

_____

_____

What might be some advantages of receiving all three Sacraments of Christian Initiation at the same time?

_____

_____

_____

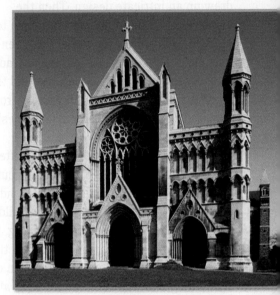

A Roman Catholic church

2. In the space below, create a poster that illustrates the Catholic Churches in the West and East, and the rites to which they belong. In your poster show that all twenty-four are part of the "one, holy, catholic, and apostolic" Church founded by Jesus Christ. Create your poster using either drawings, words, or a combination of drawings and words.

A Byzantine Catholic church

How were
the beautiful
cathedrals
of the Middle
Ages built?

Respond

Building a Cathedral

In the Middle Ages the building of a cathedral could take centuries, and many of the builders did not live to see the results of their work.

Christians worked on these majestic churches to express their faith in God. Thousands of people worked on a cathedral. A master builder drew up an intricate design. Then the master builder hired master craftsmen to oversee each part of the project. Apprentices helped the masters, learning a trade as they worked. Unskilled laborers did the digging and heavy lifting. All worked from sunrise to sunset, and sometimes they slept on the building site.

The workers dug the foundation, often to a depth of thirty feet. Stonecutters cut stone from a local quarry, shaped it, and shipped it by oxcart or barge to the building site. Once the foundation had been dug, the workers began building the walls with the cut stone. Workers developed a system of scaffolding that allowed them to work at great heights. Beautiful Gothic arches rose to heights of 150 feet. Above the vaulted ceilings, spires as high as 400 feet reached toward the heavens. The most experienced stonecutters sculpted statues of kings, bishops, saints, angels, and gargoyles.

Glassmakers created stained-glass windows depicting Bible stories.

Today, cathedrals stand as monuments in stone, inspiring us to glorify God and to imitate the faith of the builders.

Activities

1. Look at the photograph of the cathedral on this page. Carefully examine the architectural details—the tall spires, the arched windows, the stained glass, and the elaborate details in the façade. In what ways does this architecture pay homage to God?

   _____

   _____

   _____

   Imagine praying in this cathedral. How might the structure itself make you feel and inspire you?

   _____

   _____

   _____

2. Craftspeople created unique designs to decorate basilicas and cathedrals. The designs symbolized the lives of Jesus and the saints. Many people could not read, but church art helped them learn about their faith. In the space below, create your own church design.

This entrance to a cathedral in Spain shows figures of the Apostles.

3. The Church uses symbols in the liturgy to help people experience the presence of God. What are some symbols, or signs, of God's presence in your life?

How is our prayer similar to the prayer of the early Church?

107

✝ Prayer Celebration

A Eucharistic Prayer

The Eucharistic Prayers prayed by the priest at Mass today are similar to the prayers for the Mass that were written early in the third century by Hippolytus, a Church Father. In the *Church Order* of Hippolytus, we find the following prayer that a bishop would pray as he laid his hands on the bread and on the wine and water on the altar. As you quietly pray, notice the similarities with the prayers you hear at Mass.

We thank thee, God, through Thy beloved Servant Jesus Christ, Thy Son, born of the Holy Spirit and the virgin.

When he delivered himself to a voluntary Passion, to loose death, he took a loaf, gave thanks, and spake, "Take, eat, this is my body, which is given for you." Likewise, also the cup, and said, "This is my blood, which is poured out for you. As often as you do this, you make my commemoration."

Remembering therefore his death and Resurrection, we offer to Thee the loaf and the cup and give thanks to Thee. And we beseech Thee, that Thou send down Thy holy Spirit upon this offering of the Church, that we may praise and glorify Thee through Thy Servant Jesus.

Amen.

Adapted from Hippolytus, Church Order, *31, 11:21*

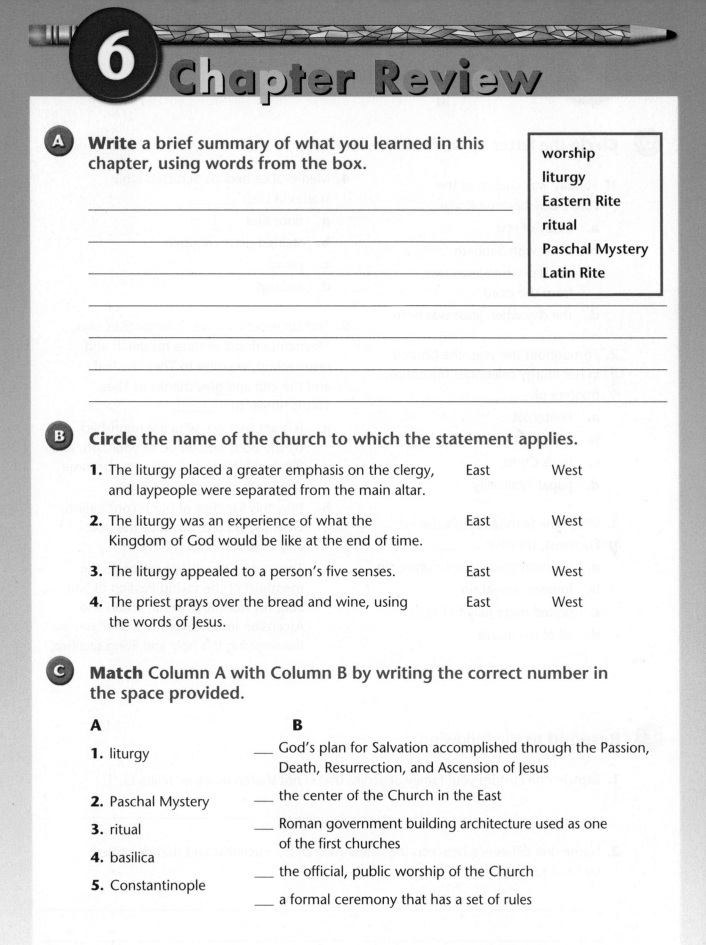

6 Chapter Review

A **Write** a brief summary of what you learned in this chapter, using words from the box.

worship
liturgy
Eastern Rite
ritual
Paschal Mystery
Latin Rite

_____

_____

_____

_____

_____

B **Circle** the name of the church to which the statement applies.

1. The liturgy placed a greater emphasis on the clergy, and laypeople were separated from the main altar.   East   West

2. The liturgy was an experience of what the Kingdom of God would be like at the end of time.   East   West

3. The liturgy appealed to a person's five senses.   East   West

4. The priest prays over the bread and wine, using the words of Jesus.   East   West

C **Match** Column A with Column B by writing the correct number in the space provided.

A

1. liturgy

2. Paschal Mystery

3. ritual

4. basilica

5. Constantinople

B

___ God's plan for Salvation accomplished through the Passion, Death, Resurrection, and Ascension of Jesus

___ the center of the Church in the East

___ Roman government building architecture used as one of the first churches

___ the official, public worship of the Church

___ a formal ceremony that has a set of rules

D **Circle** the letter of the best answer.

1. Sunday was chosen as the Lord's Day because it was _____.
   a. a day of rest
   b. the Jewish Sabbath
   c. the day when Jesus rose from the dead
   d. the day when Jesus was born

2. Throughout the year, the Church in her liturgy celebrates the entire mystery of _____.
   a. Pentecost
   b. the saints and martyrs
   c. Jesus Christ
   d. papal infallibility

3. When the faithful receive the Eucharist, they are _____.
   a. strengthened to avoid grave sin
   b. forgiven venial sin
   c. united more fully to Christ
   d. all of the above

4. Medieval cathedrals depicted Bible stories in their _____.
   a. floor tiles
   b. stained-glass windows
   c. pews
   d. ceilings

5. The Eucharistic Prayer of Hippolytus says, "Remembering therefore his death and resurrection, we offer to Thee the loaf and the cup and give thanks to Thee." This is similar to _____.
   a. [G]rant that we, who are nourished by the Body and Blood of your Son, and filled with his Holy Spirit, may become one body, one spirit in Christ.
   b. May this Sacrifice of our reconciliation, we pray, O Lord, advance the peace and salvation of all the world.
   c. Therefore, O Lord, we celebrate the memorial of the saving Passion of your Son, his wondrous Resurrection and Ascension into heaven...we offer you in thanksgiving this holy and living sacrifice.

E **Respond** to the following.

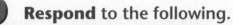

1. Explain one custom your family observes that is not shared by other relatives.

_____

2. Name one difference between the celebration of the Eucharist and that described by Saint Justin Martyr.

_____

_____

_____

Get CONNECTED

with family and friends

The Church and the Empire

God is at the center of the life of a Christian In this chapter, which covers the rise of the authority of the Church during the decline of the Roman Empire, we learn that obeying the Laws that God has written upon our hearts has priority over the laws of any human authority.

Activity

This chapter introduces us to leaders of the Church who strove to bring peace and order to the Roman Empire during a time of conflict. Before we can create an environment of peace in our communities, we must develop an inner attitude of peace. Developing this inner attitude within ourselves takes time, effort, and practice.

Do one of the following.

1. One way to create an atmosphere of peace is to have methods for dealing with conflict. One effective process for resolving conflicts is called "P.E.A.C.E." Work with family members to create a P.E.A.C.E. process certificate, such as the one you see here. Take time to review together the steps shown. Display the certificate prominently in your home.

2. Celebrate the peacemakers in your family. Develop a system in which family members earn points for actions they took to resolve conflicts at home, at school, or in the community. Choose a day of the month on which family members can submit the points they have accumulated for a reward, such as a family outing of the winner's choice.

Trivia

- **Church History**
- **Social Studies**
- **Arts & Culture**
- **People & Places**

The Hagia Sophia in Istanbul, Turkey, is perhaps the finest example of Byzantine architecture in the world. The Hagia Sophia was a Christian church until 1453, when it was captured by the Turks and transformed into a mosque. Since 1935 it has served as a museum.

Quotable Scripture

Live as children of light, for light produces every kind of goodness and righteousness and truth.

—Ephesians 5:8–9

Get CONNECTED
with family and friends

✚ Scripture Background

In the Time of Jesus

The Beatitudes   The word *beatitude* comes from the Latin word for "blessed"—the word that begins each Beatitude in Matthew 5:3–10. The Old Testament also contains many "Blessed are" statements. Although Jesus' declarations followed a traditional form, the values they expressed challenged the Old Testament tradition. According to Old Testament beliefs, blessings, or riches, are given in this lifetime to those who keep God's Law. Jesus proclaimed that the poor of the world are "blessed." Jesus further taught that the authentic reward for living a virtuous life comes after death, in God's kingdom.

Read the Beatitudes in Matthew 5:3–11.

WEEKLY PLANNER

On Sunday

Try to understand the readings at Mass from the perspective of those who are powerless and vulnerable. Pray for those who suffer most in your school, your town, and your country.

On the Web

blestarewe.com

Visit our Web site for the saint of the day and the reflection question of the week.

Saint of the Week

Saint Gregory the Great (540–604)

Gregory the Great was the son of a wealthy Roman senator. He sold his possessions and used his money to build six Benedictine monasteries in Sicily and one in Rome. As pope, he worked to bring Christianity to England. He is credited with initiating Gregorian chant, a style of liturgical music that is still popular today.

Feast Day: September 3

✚ A Prayer for the Week

Lord, help me be a peacemaker. Teach me to handle conflicts without hurting myself or others. Open my mind and heart to the suffering of those who live with conflict and war. Amen.

7 The Church and the Empire

LET US PRAY

And whatever you do, in word or in deed, do everything in the name of the Lord Jesus, giving thanks to God the Father through him.

Colossians 3:17

Share

In the 2,000-plus years since the Church was founded, Christianity has become so widespread that there are now about two billion Christians worldwide, over one billion of them Catholic. Christians make up almost one-third of the world's population.

In some countries, such as Malta and Brazil, Catholics account for a large percentage of the population. The Catholic faith has become an important part of everyday life in these countries.

The Europeans who colonized America brought many religious customs with them. Shown at right, the famous New Orleans Mardi Gras celebration—held the day before Lent begins— is an example of a social custom that has roots in Catholicism.

Activity

There are many Christian influences in the customs and celebrations of our society. Think about what some of those influences might be. Then, in the space provided, list customs or celebrations that seem to have Christian roots and ones that do not.

Christian	Not Christian
_____	_____
_____	_____
_____	_____
_____	_____

How did the Church establish Christianity in the Roman Empire?

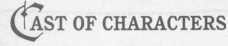

Witness Augustine and the Kingdom

CAST OF CHARACTERS

AUGUSTINE OF CANTERBURY a Roman monk
QUEEN BERTA Queen of Kent, a Christian
KING ETHELBERT Berta's pagan husband

Act I Scene I

A.D. 597 *Near the Kent castle in England. Enter Augustine. He has just arrived on a mission to convert pagans in the kingdom.*

Queen: Welcome, Reverend Father.

King: We have been anticipating your arrival.

Augustine: It's been a long, hard journey. I myself was not sure that I would ever arrive here in Roman Britain.

King: And yet, you are here.

Augustine: Yes! Praise God! The pope gave me a letter appointing me abbot of my fellow monks.

King: At least you come with priests—not an army.

Augustine: True faith cannot be forced, your Grace.

Queen: Quite so, but do you realize the difficult task you have here? People are so rooted in superstition. They see a different god in every tree. If the wind blows, they say it is a witch moving; in the shimmering hot air, they see a ghost.

Augustine: And yet, we had reports of conversions.

Queen: Ah, but are they true conversions? A neighboring king keeps two altars, one for Christ and one for his pagan gods.

Augustine: That explains the strange cross we passed as we journeyed. Christ was not alone on the Cross!

Queen: No, indeed! The Germanic gods Wodin and Loki hang there with him.

King: And why should we change? Our gods have been with us for centuries.

Augustine: Be assured, my Lord, I come not to destroy. Pope Gregory knows that conversion must be gradual. He has advised me to blend Christian practices with local customs. I'm to remake the pagan temples into Christian churches.

Queen: Besides, dearest husband, look at how Christianity will enrich the lives of our people. Mass hymns and art that will lift our spirits to God will be available to us. Surely, our people will benefit from these treasures.

King: My dear Christian wife, our land would be peaceful if all my subjects were as good-hearted as you. Reverend Father, I cannot abandon the old beliefs that I have held. But since you are sincere in your desire to impart to all what you believe is true and excellent, we will not forbid you to preach and win anyone you can to your religion.

Exit.

In A.D. 597, Augustine baptized King Ethelbert and many of his people. The Church celebrates the Feast of Augustine of Canterbury on May 27.

Pope Gregory and the Empire

As Rome's power declined and barbarians attacked the Roman Empire, the Church stepped in and established leadership. One of the Church's most effective leaders, Gregory the Great, who became pope in A.D. 590, negotiated an agreement for peace with the barbarian invaders. Pope Gregory knew that to maintain a peaceful society, the barbarians would have to become Christians.

The Church's practice of celebrating feasts and honoring saints, the holy men and women who intercede for us in Heaven, encouraged new converts. Many Christian practices, which were rich in symbolism and tradition, naturally appealed to the barbarians because symbols, rituals, and feasts had been important in the barbarians' worship of pagan gods.

Already held together by strong leadership, the Church grew stronger by adopting the organization of the Roman legal system. The Byzantine emperor Justinian, whose rule began in A.D. 527, had made a collection of civil laws. The Church formed her own collection of laws, called **canon law** . The Church became the center for education, music, and art. People looked to the Church for spiritual and political leadership.

Pope Gregory's leadership helped the Church become the center of authority in place of the Roman government. Pope Gregory strove to unite the Church and state into one society. As the authority of the Church increased, the society of the Roman Empire became known as **Christendom**.

In the eighth century, as Rome faced another attack, Pope Leo III asked Charlemagne, the king of the Franks (peoples of what is now western Germany) to help stop the attack. Charlemagne turned back the attackers and united most of western Europe. Throughout his reign, Charlemagne had been devoted to the Church. On Christmas in A.D. 800, Pope Leo crowned Charlemagne Emperor of the Holy Roman Empire.

Christianity and Authority

In Christendom, people looked to the Church for leadership. Church authority and government authority were one. Things are very different today, but the basis for a just society was and continues to be the **natural law**. This is God's law, written upon everyone's heart. It is the foundation of the moral law for everyone that enables us to tell the difference between good and evil. Laws that are just and good arise from this understanding of morality that is part of human nature, which God created.

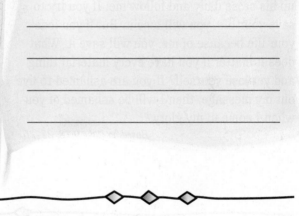

Activity

Would it be easier or harder to live a Christian life if the government and the Church were one? Give reasons for your answer.

_____

_____

_____

_____

_____

Faith Words

canon law Canon law is the collection of the laws of the Catholic Church.

Christendom Christendom is the name given to the growth of the Church in territory and in both temporal, or political, and spiritual authority resulting in the pope's authority exceeding that of the emperor and eventually kings.

natural law The natural law is the foundation of the moral life for everyone. It is part of human nature and allows people to know the difference between good and evil.

How do we practice natural law in our daily lives?

Hear & Believe

The Challenge of Discipleship

We do not live in a country where the government and the Church are one as they were in the Holy Roman Empire. Our society includes people of many faiths and beliefs, some of which directly conflict with Catholic faith and moral principles. This can make it difficult for Catholics to live out the Gospel.

Jesus knew that his followers would face times when living his teachings would go against the rest of society. He knew that we might face such struggles daily. In the following Scripture passage, Jesus told his disciples that it was important to hold fast to their beliefs and do what was right.

One day while Jesus was alone praying when the disciples came to him. He predicted his own Passion, telling the disciples that he was going to be rejected by many, and that he would suffer and be killed. He said to them, "If anyone wishes to be my disciple, he must deny himself and take up his cross daily and follow me. If you try to save your life, you will lose it. But if you lose your life because of me, you will save it. What does it matter if you have every material thing and yet lose yourself? If you are ashamed to live out my message, then I will be ashamed of you when I come in my glory."

Based on Luke 9:18, 22–26

Catholics today face many challenges to living their faith. Along with following the just laws of our society and government, we also have the primary responsibility to obey God's Laws and follow Jesus' teachings and example.

A Closer Look

Beowulf

Beowulf is the story about a heroic warrior, written about A.D. 700. The author drew upon both pagan and Christian elements to tell how Beowulf killed a monster, its mother, and a dragon to defend a kingdom. Pagan elements used in this story include sacrificing to idols, relying on omens, believing in fate, and taking revenge. Yet, Beowulf is a Christlike figure. Beowulf battled the evil monsters just as Christ battled the evils of sin. And, like Jesus, Beowulf gave up his life in order to save others.

Our Church Teaches

Natural law is the foundation of the moral life and of any law in society. Because society and government are based on human nature, they belong to an order God established. Civil laws and public authority should promote virtue, equality, justice, freedom, and the common good within the moral order God established. Everyone has a right to private property, but God also created our world for the good of all people.

We Believe

Civil laws and public authority are based on God's eternal natural law, and should promote virtue, equality, justice, and the common good.

Public authority is responsible for protecting the lives of individuals. In order to accomplish this, authorities are often faced with difficult decisions. All decisions to act in society's defense, such as the decision to go to war, must be justified and must ensure the common good. God is the ultimate authority of human society. We must not obey an authority that has created laws that are immoral; God's law must come first.

Activities

1. There are fundamental ideas of right and wrong in society that are based on the natural law. Give some examples of these.

_____

_____

_____

2. In the United States all people have the freedom to believe what they choose. What beliefs do some people hold that conflict with our Catholic Faith and moral principles?

_____

_____

_____

3. How can you remain faithful to your Catholic values when society promotes opposing values?

_____

_____

_____

4. Jesus said that it would be difficult to live out the Gospel. Give an example of a time when a Catholic might have to go against the government that establishes a law that is contrary to a Catholic moral teaching. How would you respond if you faced a similar situation?

_____

_____

_____

_____

_____

_____

_____

_____

How can society's values be transformed by the Gospel?

Respond
Charlemagne

Devotion to the Church was the driving force for Charlemagne, king of the Franks. He lived at a time when northern Europe was mostly pagan. In Rome the Church was being attacked by barbarians. Charlemagne decided to bring Christianity and order to all people. He succeeded due to his great ability to organize. He moved his armies with incredible speed and precision. By A.D. 800 he was the ruler of all of western Europe.

Charlemagne was a just leader and very protective of the Church. He had great sympathy for peasants and believed government should help, not oppress, people. He began many reforms to better the lives of his people. Making education and Christianity available to all was one of his main goals. He started schools that took not only the rich but also peasant boys. Charlemagne himself never stopped studying. He encouraged better farming methods and created monetary standards in order to help merchants. He sent out investigators to inspect local government and ensure justice for all people. He revived church music and art. In A.D. 768 Charlemagne built a beautiful cathedral at Aachen (in present-day Germany), where he is buried.

After Charlemagne died in A.D. 814, the Empire was divided among weak kings. This was the beginning of a conflict between kings and the popes that would last for centuries.

Activities

1. Charlemagne had the power to make changes in society that greatly benefited the people he ruled. If you had that power, what three specific things would you change in our society? How would these changes benefit people in our society?

_____

_____

_____

_____

_____

_____

2. Think of the TV shows you watch. On one TV screen below, write the name of a show whose characters seem to follow the natural law. On the other TV screen, write the name of a show whose characters do not. Then, on the appropriate screens, write examples of how the characters do or do not follow the natural law.

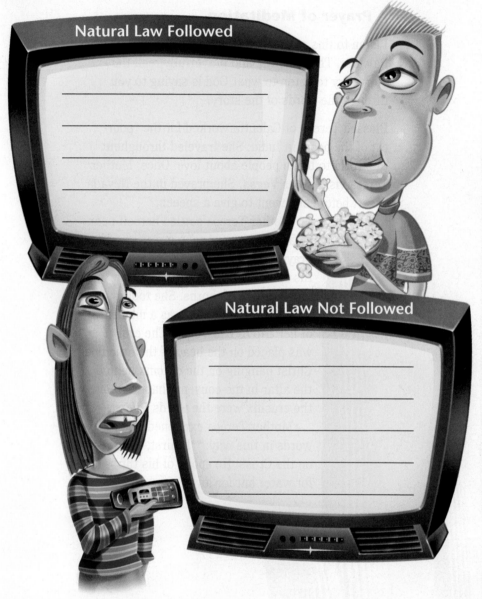

Natural Law Followed

_____

_____

_____

_____

Natural Law Not Followed

_____

_____

_____

_____

3. Some people think the Church should not attempt to influence the State. They think that the Church should not speak out on issues, such as abortion, the death penalty, and workers' rights. As a Catholic, what is your opinion?

_____

_____

_____

_____

*How do we
pray to better
love God?*

✝ Prayer Celebration

A Prayer of Meditation

Listen to this story about Blessed Teresa of Calcutta. Then silently and prayerfully read the story. Try to listen to what God is saying to you through the words of the story.

Blessed Teresa of Calcutta worked for the "poorest of the poor" in India. She traveled throughout the world to teach people about love. Once, Mother Teresa visited Las Vegas. She prayed in the Nevada desert before she went to give a speech.

Mother Teresa settled herself near a cactus plant for contemplation. After praying, she picked up a few long cactus spines. She easily twined them into a crown of thorns. She took this crown back to Calcutta as a memento of her trip to Las Vegas. The crown was placed on the head of the crucified Christ hanging on the crucifix behind the altar in the convent chapel. Above the crucifix were the words *I thirst*.

Mother Teresa explained Jesus' words in this way: " 'I thirst,' said Jesus on the Cross. He spoke of his thirst not for water but for love."

7 Chapter Review

A Write a brief summary of what you learned in this chapter, using words from the box.

Islam
Leo III
Justinian
Charlemagne
canon law
Holy Roman Emperor
leadership
Gregory the Great
barbarian

_____

_____

_____

_____

_____

_____

_____

_____

_____

B Complete the sentences.

1. Mardi Gras, a celebration held the day before Lent begins, is a social custom that has its roots in _____.

2. Civil laws and public authority should promote _____, equality, justice, freedom, and _____ within the moral order God established.

3. _____ is the ultimate authority of human society.

4. Civil society and authority are based on God's eternal _____.

5. Everyone has a right to private property but must also consider that God created our world for the good of _____.

C **Match** Column A with Column B by writing the correct number in the space provided.

A

1. natural law
2. canon law
3. Christendom
4. Beowulf
5. Augustine of Canterbury

B

___ the name given to a part of the world in which Christianity dominated

___ a hero of a medieval story who had Christlike traits

___ a Roman monk who baptized King Ethelbert of Kent

___ the collection of the laws of the Catholic Church

___ the law that is part of human nature, lasts forever, and allows people to know the difference between good and evil

D **Respond** to the following.

1. Jesus said, "If anyone wishes to come after me, he must deny himself and take up his cross daily and follow me" (Luke 9:23). How did Blessed Mother Teresa demonstrate what Jesus meant by this statement? How can a person your age respond to the same message from Jesus?

_____

_____

_____

_____

2. Charlemagne was a great leader who believed government should help people. Name some ways in which Christians can encourage their government to choose policies and enact laws that will improve society.

_____

_____

_____

_____

Get CONNECTED
with family and friends

Prayer for Understanding

Catholics have always faced the challenge of discerning between authentic faith and teachings and practices that do not reflect Christ's truth. Sometimes, when disagreements about beliefs and practices have arisen, they have caused schisms, or deep divisions, within the Church. Such divisions harm the unity of the Church. We must pray to understand others with humble hearts and open minds.

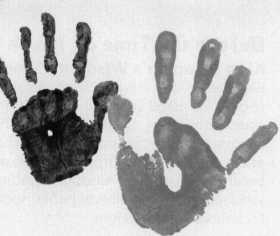

Activity

Allison, Maria, and Rachel were good friends. They enjoyed doing activities with a larger group of five other girls. Allison noticed that some girls in the group of friends gossiped about each other. Allison realized that, just as in the pulley system, some people try to pull themselves up by putting others down. What would you do to help end such divisions among your friends?

Do one of the following.

1. Invite someone new from your school or parish to do something with you and one of your friends. Try to find one skill that the person has and compliment the person.

2. Hands are a powerful symbol. They can be used to pray for peace or to inflict harm. With members of your family, come up with ways to promote peace and understanding at home and in the community. Then, using paint or food coloring, make prints of your hands on a suitable surface, such as a large piece of paper. Each person can then record their resolutions for peace on the handprints.

Trivia

- Church History
- Social Studies
- Arts & Culture
- People & Places

The term *Eastern Catholic Church* is used to describe traditions that originated in the eastern region of the Roman Empire. The term *Orthodox Church* refers to Eastern churches that are not Catholic—those not in communion with the pope, the Bishop of Rome.

Quotable Scripture

"Love your enemies, and pray for those who persecute you, that you may be children of your heavenly Father."

—Matthew 5:44–45

Get CONNECTED
with family and friends

✚ Scripture Background

Before the Time of Jesus

King Solomon's Wisdom   Solomon was the son of King David and Bathsheba. After David's death, Solomon inherited the throne. Early in his reign, God asked Solomon in a dream to name a gift he wanted. Solomon asked for wisdom. Solomon built the first Temple in Jerusalem and played an important part in Israel's development as a nation, but his reputation as a man of wisdom surpassed all his other accomplishments. Solomon became the patron of wisdom literature, inspiring a long tradition of scholars who wrote biblical books, such as Proverbs, the Song of Songs, Ecclesiastes, and Wisdom.

Read more about Solomon's dream and wise judgment in 1 Kings 3:5–28.

WEEKLY PLANNER

On Sunday

During the Penitential Act at Mass, pray for people about whom you have gossiped or whom you have rejected. Ask God to forgive you and bless them.

On the Web

blestarewe.com

Visit our Web site for the saint of the day and the reflection question of the week.

Saint of the Week

Saint Luke the Evangelist (1st century)

Luke, the writer of the Gospel of Luke and the Acts of the Apostles, has been identified as "the beloved physician" in Saint Paul's letter to the Colossians (4:14). According to legend, Saint Luke painted a portrait of the Blessed Virgin Mary during her lifetime. Saint Luke's symbol is the bull.

Patron Saint of: physicians, artists

Feast Day: October 18

A Prayer for the Week

Lord, help me change my ways when I reject or put down others. Give me courage to seek your forgiveness and make things right with people I have harmed in word or deed. Amen.

8 Prayer for Understanding

May the peoples praise you, God;
may all the peoples praise you!

Psalm 67:6

Share

One of the ways that people enter into prayer is by looking at an image or picture. Looking at an image of Christ on the Cross can remind us of Jesus Christ's suffering for us. Scenes from nature can remind us of the goodness of God. Whatever images we choose, reflecting on art can lead us into prayer as we remember the presence of God in our world.

Activity

Look thoughtfully at the three images on this page. On the lines provided, write what comes to mind when you look at each image. Then check the box next to the picture that most reminds you of the presence of God. Discuss your choice with the class.

Moses receives the tablets of Law by Marc Chagall. Engraving. Milan Museum of Fine Art. Collection of Meyer Chagall.

□ _____

_____

_____

□ _____

_____

_____

□ _____

_____

_____

What are some other ways that Christians enter into prayer?

125

Hear & Believe

Witness Spirituality Expressed Through Art

In the years after Jesus Christ founded his Church, the Apostles continued to spread his teachings throughout the Mediterranean. From Jerusalem to Rome to Alexandria, the disciples traveled far and worked hard to establish the Church in new cities and lands. Because of the distances between them, these local Churches developed their own leaders to guide them in the faith. Still, all shared the same faith, Tradition, liturgy, and **doctrine**.

From the beginning of the Church disagreements arose within the Church. In A.D. 1054 a disagreement resulted in a major break between the Church centered in Rome (the Catholic Church) and the Church centered in Constantinople (the Orthodox Church). In that split, known as a **schism**, the pope and the Patriarch of Constantinople, the leader of the Eastern church, excommunicated each other.

Differences in spirituality is one of the most important ways in which the Eastern Orthodox, or Greek Orthodox, Church and Roman Catholic, or Latin, Church have grown apart. The spirituality of the Catholic Church can best be described as being "immanent," or natural. Catholics in the West see and know God in Christ and in the physical world around them. This is evident in the sacred art of the Roman Catholic Church. For example, figures in Michelangelo's paintings in the Sistine Chapel in Rome look Italian, and sixteenth-century artists painted the Blessed Mother dressed in sixteenth-century clothing.

In the Church in the East, however, holy images are viewed as "transcendent," or going beyond the physical world. Such images are similar to "holy doors" entering into the mystery of Heaven, helping believers develop a deeper relationship with God. A holy image of Jesus, Mary, and the saints is known as an **icon**. For Christians in the East, icons are an important part of their spiritual life.

Sacred painting of Saint John the Baptizer by Spanish painter Bartolome Estaban Murillo, circa 1655. In the Western Church sacred art is "immanent," which means "natural." Catholics in the West see and know God in the physical world.

Sixteenth-century icon of John the Baptizer, Dmitrov, Russia. In Eastern churches icons are an important part of worship and liturgy. Icons are "transcendent"—that is, like "holy doors" that help believers enter the mystery of Heaven.

A Church Divided

In A.D. 800, relations between the East and West were harmed when Pope Leo III crowned Charlemagne Emperor of the Holy Roman Empire. Since the empire already had an emperor in Constantinople, this caused a greater rift. In the middle of the eleventh century, cultural, political, and theological differences also caused division within the Church. Differences in language and ways of celebrating the liturgy contributed to the division. Germanic invasions in the West and Islamic conquests in the East further deepened the divisions.

Reasons for the Division

Two of the greatest reasons for division within the Church, however, were theological. One had to do with the papacy and the other with the Creed. The Roman Church held to the doctrine that, as the successor of Peter, the pope was the head of the whole Church. As the head, he had a God-given right to rule the entire Church. On the other hand, the Orthodox Church held that all bishops succeeded Peter and, therefore, no one bishop could have power over the whole Church.

Disagreements about the Creed arose because there were different understandings of the Trinity. The Church in the West added the Latin word *filioque*, meaning "and the Son," to the statement in the Creed "the Holy Spirit proceeded from the Father." This addition emphasized the divinity of Jesus. The Church in the East protested. They believed that the addition suggested that God the Father was not the Creator of everything. The disagreement went on for several centuries, coming to a head in A.D. 1054. When the Eastern Church would not agree to the use of *filioque*, a papal ambassador excommunicated the Patriarch of Constantinople. In retaliation, the Patriarch excommunicated the pope.

The differences between the Roman Catholic Church and the Orthodox Church turned violent in A.D. 1204. While en route to Jerusalem, during the Fourth Crusade, Christians from the West attacked Constantinople, the capital of the Byzantine Empire and the spiritual center of Orthodox Christians.

Although the division between the East and West still exists, Pope Paul VI and Patriarch Athenagoras I of Constantinople lifted their Churches' mutual excommunication decrees in 1965 at the close of the Second Vatican Council.

Activity

Give an example of a time when distance made communication difficult and caused a break in a relationship. The example can be from your own life or from history.

_____

_____

_____

What might have helped heal the broken relationship?

_____

_____

_____

Faith Words

doctrine Doctrine refers to an official teaching or a body of official teachings of the Church.

schism The refusal of submission to the Roman Pontiff (the pope) or of communion with the members of the Church subject to him is called a schism.

icon An icon is a holy image of Jesus, the Virgin Mary, or the saints, often made out of gold leaf and other special materials.

How does the Church promote understanding and unity?

Hear & Believe

A Pope's Work of Reconciliation

The meeting between Pope Paul VI and Patriarch Athenagoras I in 1964 was an important first step in healing the rift between the Greek Orthodox Church and the Roman Catholic Church. As the time line below shows, this progress came after more than 900 years.

Pope Paul VI was born Giovanni Battista Montini in 1897. During his years as pope (1963–1978), Paul VI worked hard to promote peace and unity, both within the Church and around the world.

Paul VI steered the Church through the final years of the Second Vatican Council, after Pope John XXIII died. The Council brought about a renewal of Catholicism and encouraged the Church to establish dialogue with all Christians.

In his frequent travels, Paul VI often spoke of reconciliation and understanding. He visited the Holy Land, where he met with Patriarch Athenagoras I, and India, a country with a predominantly Hindu religious tradition. He wrote documents about the relationships between the Catholic Church and other religions. He also reached out to people who said they had no religion.

Paul VI was a strong advocate for developing communication among people of all faiths and political systems. During his historic visit to the United Nations in 1965, he called for all countries to work toward uniting humanity. It was his hope that unity among peoples and nations would mean an end to war.

Major Events: Eastern Church and Western Church

306	325	380	800	1054	1095–1099
Constantine crowned	Council of Nicaea	Christianity becomes official religion of Roman Empire	Charlemagne crowned	Schism between Christians in East and West	First Crusade

1147–1149	1204	1962–1965	1964	2001	2013
Second Crusade	Crusaders sack Constantinople in the Fourth Crusade	Second Vatican Council	Pope Paul VI meets Patriarch of Constantinople	Pope John Paul II visits Greece, an Orthodox Christian nation	Francis becomes Pope

Our Church Teaches

Despite differences in doctrine, the Orthodox Church and Catholic Church have much in common. They share faith in one God, one Savior, and one Baptism. Healing a Church divided for a thousand years is beyond the powers of humans alone. Through the power of the Holy Spirit, the Church carries out the mission of Christ, who wishes his Church to be one. The Church is the Temple of the Holy Spirit, who is the source of all unity, diversity, and life in the Church. The Holy Spirit draws us to the Father and we are one with Christ. In praying to the Father, our trust, humility, and will to become more holy grow. Catholics place their hope "in the prayer of Christ for the Church, in the love of the Father for us, and in the power of the Holy Spirit" (*Catechism of the Catholic Church* 822).

We Believe

God the Father sends the Holy Spirit to guide his Church. We pray to the Holy Spirit to unite all Christians.

Activities

1. Imagine that you are a newspaper reporter or editor in 1052. Write an editorial about the growing rift between the Church centered in Constantinople and the Church centered in Rome.

Universal Gazette

_____

_____

_____

_____

_____

_____

_____

_____

_____

_____

_____

2. When he became Pope, Giovanni Montini chose the name Paul VI to honor Saint Paul, the Apostle to the Gentiles. Why was that name an appropriate choice? How were the words and actions of Pope Paul VI similar to those of Saint Paul?

_____

_____

_____

_____

How can art enrich our prayer lives?

Respond

Creating an Icon

Icons have been called "holy doors" that open into Heaven and allow viewers to make a connection with God. They are more than pictures or decorations. They are meant for prayer. Most often painted on flat surfaces, icons are not meant to show what Jesus and the saints looked like but to portray the mystery of God.

An icon painter considers the making of an icon a prayer. The artist prepares by fasting and meditating, then selects a wooden panel and prepares it by applying several layers of a special glue, sanding it, and smoothing it. Next the artist traces the outline of the icon on the panel. Gold leaf is applied to halos or the background. After the gold leaf has dried, the painter is ready to paint the icon. The paint is made by mixing egg yolk, water, vinegar, and pigments ground from minerals. Several weeks after the painting is finished, a varnish is applied. Icon painters never sign the painting, for they believe the work is not their own but is from Heaven. Finally, a priest blesses the icon.

Painting an icon might take months. All the while, the painter prays and offers their work to God. Here is one iconographer's prayer:

"O heavenly Master, fervent architect of all creation, light the gaze of your servant, guard his heart and guide his hand, so that worthily and with perfection he may represent your image, for the glory and beauty of your Holy Church."

Father Andrei Davydov, pastor of the Cathedral of the Nativity of St. John the Baptist in Pskov, Russia, paints a religious icon of the Madonna and the infant Jesus. Father Davydov is one of the most famous icon painters in Russia.

Activities

1. Many symbols and works of art can lead us to prayer. These are often found in parish churches. Think about the artwork and symbols that are in your own church. Choose one, and tell how it leads you to think about God and to pray.

_____

_____

_____

_____

_____

_____

2. The Eastern Orthodox Church hymn "Thrice Holy" gives glory to the Father, Son, and Holy Spirit. It is sung before the Scripture readings in the Divine Liturgy, the Mass celebrated in the Eastern Orthodox Church. Pray this aloud with your group.

Holy God, Holy Mighty, Holy Immortal, have mercy on us. *(Say three times; bow and make the Sign of the Cross each time.)*

Glory to the Father, and to the Son, and to the Holy Spirit, now and ever, and unto the ages of ages. *(Bow and make the Sign of the Cross once.)*

Amen. Holy Immortal, have mercy on us.

3. The Gregorian chant "Parce Domine" is sung during Masses in the Lenten season. This version of the "Parce Domine" comes from a medieval hymnal. Pray this aloud with your group.

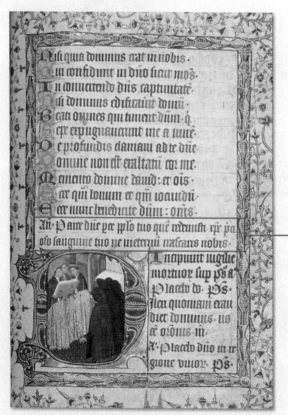

Spare your people, Lord.

Spare your people in your loving kindness.

Show us your mercy;

we have sinned against you, Lord.

How do we pray for understanding?

✝ Prayer Celebration

Praying with Saint Anselm

Saint Anselm (1033–1109), a monk and the Archbishop of Canterbury in England, wrote many letters, prayers, and theological documents. He argued, unsuccessfully, for unity of the Eastern and Western Churches.

Leader: Let us open our hearts to the Holy Spirit as we pray:

All: O merciful God, fill our hearts with the graces of your Holy Spirit. Fill our hearts with love, joy, peace, long-suffering, gentleness, goodness, faith, meekness, temperance.

Side One: Teach us to love those who are against us.

Side Two: Teach us to pray for those who do not respect us.

Leader: Father, you make your sun to shine on the evil and on the good and send rain on the just and on the unjust. Send the Holy Spirit to help us live as your people. Amen.

A **Complete** the sentences with words from the box.

1. A holy image of Jesus, the Virgin Mary, or the saints is known as an _____.

2. The spirituality of the Western Church is _____.

3. The spirituality of the Eastern Church is _____.

4. Vatican Council II encouraged the Church to establish _____ among all Christians.

5. The two major reasons for division between the Orthodox Church and the Roman Catholic Church had to do with the _____ and the _____.

> immanent
> Creed
> dialogue
> transcendent
> papacy
> icon

B **Fill in** the missing events in Church history.

306	325	380	800	1054	1095–1099
Constantine crowned	Council of Nicaea	_____	_____	_____	First Crusade
		_____	_____	_____	
		_____	_____	_____	
		_____	_____	_____	
		_____	_____	_____	

1147–1149	1204	1962–1965	1964	2001	2013
Second Crusade	_____	Second Vatican Council	_____	Blessed Pope John Paul II visits Greece, an Eastern Christian nation	_____
	_____		_____		
	_____		_____		
	_____		_____		
	_____		_____		

C **Match** Column A with Column B by writing the correct number in the space provided.

A

1. Divine Liturgy
2. "Thrice Holy"
3. doctrine
4. transcendent

B

___ going beyond the physical world

___ an official teaching of the Church

___ the Mass celebrated by Eastern Christians

___ the hymn sung before Scripture readings in the Eastern Church

D **Respond** to the following.

1. List some images that can help people enter into prayer.

_____

_____

2. Why were Pope Paul VI's actions important in promoting Christian unity?

_____

_____

_____

_____

E **Complete** the missing phrases from Saint Anselm's prayer:

O merciful God, _____, we pray you, with the graces

of your Holy Spirit, with _____, _____,

_____, long-suffering, gentleness, goodness, faith,

_____, temperance.

Teach us to love those _____;

to pray for those _____;

that we may be your children, our Father, who make your sun to shine

_____ and send rain

on the _____ and on the _____. Amen.

Faith in Action

Parish Maintenance Staff Working under the guidance of the pastor, a Catholic parish's maintenance staff serves the parish community in many important ways, such as by cleaning the classrooms, maintaining electrical equipment, and making necessary repairs. By keeping the environment clean, orderly, and safe, the maintenance staff creates a setting appropriate for worship and learning, and helps provide an environment where parishioners and visitors alike feel comfortable and secure.

 **In Everyday Life**

Activity Whether at home, at school, or around town, it takes the contributions of many people to keep things clean, tidy, and inviting. Name one thing you can do in each of these places to keep each in the best shape possible.

Place	What I Can Do
Home	
School	
Around town	

 **In Your Parish**

Activity Name one person you know who has done something extraordinary in your parish or at your school to make that setting more enjoyable for all who visit it. Tell how this person's work shows God's gifts at work in our lives.

_____

_____

_____

_____

Parish Priest Priests are co-workers with their bishops. They are called by God to serve the Church in a special way. They preside over the celebration of the Sacraments, they preach the Word of God, and they guide us on our path to holiness. In addition to these responsibilities, a pastor is entrusted with the pastoral care of the parish, acting as its shepherd under the authority of the diocesan bishop.

Activity Think about your home and the various tasks that must be completed to keep it comfortable for you and other members of your family. List at least three key tasks that must be completed. Then describe two things you can do to help, and tell how frequently you can do them. Set a goal for yourself to help out with these tasks on a regular basis.

_____

_____

_____

_____

In Your Parish

Activity It takes the work of many people to keep a parish running smoothly. Choose one of these people, such as the pastor, principal, director of religious education, or parish secretary, and write a brief note to this person acknowledging their hard work.

_____

_____

_____

_____

Faith in Action

Pastoral Care of the Sick Hospitals and nursing homes care for the sick and those who need special care. A visit from a priest, deacon, or a parish volunteer can go a long way toward reassuring the sick or elderly in these settings. These visits not only provide companionship, they also remind people who are ill or elderly of God's love for them.

In Everyday Life

Activity Design a get well card to cheer up a sick family member or friend. Be sure your card communicates to the recipient how much God loves him or her.

In Your Parish

Activity The following are some people who can bring God's love to the sick members of a parish community. Describe a way each person can do this.

Priests

_____

_____

Extraordinary ministers of Holy Communion

_____

_____

Youth group members

_____

_____

Faith in Action

Art Teacher In addition to learning math, science, social studies, and language arts, young people learn to appreciate the beauty of God's creation through the work of the art teacher. The art teacher guides students in learning to discover and observe the details in the world around them so that they can depict what they see in a variety of artistic forms.

Activity In the space below, describe two talents that you have and tell how you use each to help others.

_____

_____

_____

_____

_____

_____

Activity Name one talent that you have, such as drawing or singing well, and tell how you can use this talent to help your parish and to glorify God.

_____

_____

_____

_____

_____

_____

Using words or phrases from each box, write a brief summary of what you have learned in each chapter. Write your paragraphs in the space provided or on a separate sheet of paper.

Chapter 5

Leo the Great	Constantine	Creed	heresy
Ecumenical Council	Chalcedon	Arius	Nicaea

_____

_____

_____

Chapter 6

Paschal Mystery	Gothic cathedrals	Saint Justin Martyr	Eucharist
Eastern Church	Western Church	liturgy	Eastern Catholic

_____

_____

_____

Chapter 7

King Ethelbert	Pope Gregory	natural law	Canon Law
Charlemagne	Christendom	barbarians	Justinian

_____

_____

_____

Chapter 8

filioque	immanent	transcendent	icons
doctrine	schism	Pope Leo III	

_____

_____

_____

2 Unit Review

A **Write** the name of the person described by each clue.

1. I refused to sign the Nicene Creed. _____

2. I became Bishop of Alexandria and fought against Arianism. _____

3. I was Bishop of Hippo and one of the most important theologians of the fourth century. _____

4. I sent a letter to the Council of Chalcedon condemning the claim that Jesus Christ was not truly human. _____

5. My meeting with Patriarch Athenagoras I was a step in healing the rift between the Orthodox Church and the Roman Catholic Church. _____

B **Complete** each sentence by writing the letter of the correct answer from the box in the space provided.

a. Thessalonians	**e.** mosaics	**h.** basilicas
b. Beowulf	**f.** Eastern Catholic	**i.** reconciliation
c. Jesus	**g.** priests	**j.** grace
d. Resurrection		

1. Sunday was chosen as the Lord's Day because it is the day on which the _____ occurred.

2. The "overseers" that Saint Justin Martyr writes about later became known as _____.

3. The church buildings of the Eastern Church had colorful _____ depicting Bible scenes.

4. The first church buildings were _____.

5. The Sacraments were given to the Church by _____.

6. Anyone receiving the Eucharist must be in a state of _____.

7. In his frequent travels, Pope Paul VI often spoke of _____ and understanding.

8. The Catholic Church is made up of the Roman Catholic Church and the _____ Churches.

9. In a story written about A.D. 700, _____ is a Christlike figure who battled evil monsters and gave up his life in order to save others.

10. Paul warned the _____ not to be deceived by false teachings about Jesus' Second Coming.

Unit Review

C **Match** the correct answer in Column A with its question in Column B by writing the correct number in the space provided.

A

1. They attacked the Roman Empire as Rome's power declined.

2. The Church grew stronger by adopting the organization of this legal system.

3. This emperor made a collection of laws.

4. He wanted to unite the Church and State.

5. It was the center for art, education, and music.

6. He built the cathedral at Aachen.

7. She worked with the "poorest of the poor."

8. This social custom has its roots in Christianity.

9. To counter heresies, he convened the Council of Chalcedon.

10. He wrote "faith seeking understanding."

B

___ Who was Justinian?

___ Who was Saint Anselm?

___ Who was Blessed Mother Teresa of Calcutta?

___ Who were the barbarians?

___ Who was Leo the Great?

___ Who was Pope Gregory?

___ What is the Mardi Gras?

___ Who was Charlemagne?

___ What is Roman?

___ What was the Church in the Roman Empire?

D **Write** *E* next to the statements associated with the Eastern Church and *W* next to those associated with the Western Church.

___ **1.** Its spirituality is described as "immanent," or natural.

___ **2.** Holy images are viewed as "transcendent."

___ **3.** Its Fourth Crusade destroyed Constantinople.

___ **4.** The pope is the head of this Church.

___ **5.** Icons of Jesus and the saints are an important part of spirituality.

___ **6.** Members added a word to the Creed to emphasize the divinity of Jesus Christ.

___ **7.** Members believe that no one bishop can have power over the whole church.

___ **8.** The Patriarch is the head of this Church.

2 Unit Review

E **Match** the Faith Words in Column A with the definitions in Column B.

A

1. Ecumenical Council
2. Fathers of the Church
3. ritual
4. heresy
5. canon law
6. liturgy
7. Christendom
8. natural law
9. Paschal Mystery
10. icon
11. doctrine

B

___ a formal ceremony that has a set of rules

___ an official teaching or a body of official teachings of the Church

___ the official, public worship of the Church

___ the collection of the laws of the Catholic Church

___ God's plan for Salvation through the Passion, Death, Resurrection, and Ascension of Jesus Christ

___ a part of the world in which Christianity dominated

___ the law that is part of human nature, lasts forever, and allows people to know the difference between good and evil

___ a holy image of Jesus, the Virgin Mary, or the saints, often made out of gold leaf and other special materials

___ a false teaching of a church doctrine

___ a worldwide gathering of the pope and all the bishops

___ early leaders of the Church who helped develop authentic doctrine of the Church

F **Respond** to the following.

1. Explain why it is "meet and right" for you to thank the Lord in the Eucharistic Prayer of Hippolytus.

_____

_____

_____

2. Explain how the stonecutters and glassmakers who adorned the cathedrals of medieval Europe had the same purpose as the icon painters of the Eastern Church.

_____

_____

_____

_____

The Age of Faith and Beauty

The Church in medieval times expressed her deep faith through glorious cathedrals and elaborate worship. We are called to use the media of our time to proclaim our Catholic faith.

This is the day the Lord has made;
let us rejoice and be glad, alleluia.
Easter Sunday Antiphon, Liturgy of the Hours

It took many glassblowers, as this fifteenth-century painting shows, to make the beautiful windows in the chapel of Saint-Chapelle in Paris.

I Have Been Anointed

Words and Music by Steven C. Warner
Arranged by Peter M. Kolar

REFRAIN

I have been a-noint-ed with the song of the Lord! A song of love and com-pas-sion, a song to set me free! God is my rock of sal-va-tion! A bea-con for my soul! Hal - le - lu-jah! A-men! Hal - le - lu - jah! A-men. Praise to the

1., Final / Last time   2. To Verse

rock and the well-spring, cre-a-tor of my soul! Oh, soul!

VERSE

My heart knew dark-ness, My soul was filled with de-spair, Life-less and si-lent, no mu-sic an - y - where, and then my Lord and com-pan - ion, He filled my wait - ing

To Refrain

soul: Hal - le - lu - jah! Hal - le - lu - jah! For God has made me whole!

Get CONNECTED

with family and friends

Faith Expressed and Lived

After Christianity became the official religion of the Roman Empire, some people joined the Church to gain economic and political status. Others, however, wanted to live their faith as the early Christians did. Saint Benedict was one Christian who lived his faith in this way. He brought monasticism to the Church in the West. Monasticism is a way of living the Gospel simply, either alone or in a community, and centering one's actions on God.

Do one of the following.

1. Check the activities that your family does together.
   __ praying   __ celebrating happy events
   __ reading the Bible __ attending Mass

   Look at the unchecked activities. Discuss with your family how you might begin to do these or other God-centered activities together.

2. With your parents, other family members, or friends, discuss the lessons you have learned from one another about how to be a Catholic. How did you learn these lessons? After discussing these questions, write notes of thanks to one another for the lessons taught.

Activity

Christian families are the building blocks of the Church. They are the "mini-communities" of believers in Christ. Christian homes are the places where we begin to learn about God and how to be a disciple of Jesus Christ. In the Catholic Church, the home is known as the domestic Church, or Church of the home.

- Church History
- Social Studies
- Arts & Culture
- People & Places

Battle Abbey in Hastings, England, was established by William of Normandy to commemorate his victory in the Battle of Hastings in 1066. Although the abbey was destroyed during the reign of Henry VIII, visitors can still walk among its ruins, learn about the daily life of the monks, and stop for reflection and prayer.

Quotable Scripture

I will place my law within them, and write it upon their hearts; . . . says the LORD.

—Jeremiah 31:33–34

Get CONNECTED
with family and friends

✠ Scripture Background

In the Early Church

The Book of Revelation   The Book of Revelation is also known as the Apocalypse, because its symbolism, imagery, and mystic numbers were used to convey hidden messages to the early Church. Revelation is believed to have been written by John the Apostle to the early Church during a time of persecution. In this New Testament book, John reports his visions of the glorified Christ. Revelation has been subject to different interpretations by Christians, but all agree that it makes an unmistakable declaration about the final triumph of God.

Read about the Second Coming of Jesus in Revelation 22:6–21.

WEEKLY PLANNER

On Sunday

During silent reflection, think about God's presence with you at that moment and how he has been with you throughout the week.

On the Web

blestarewe.com

 Visit our Web site for the saint of the day and the reflection question of the week.

Saint of the Week
Saint Thomas Aquinas (1225–1274)

Thomas Aquinas secretly joined the Dominican Order, but his family kidnapped and imprisoned him to keep him from being a friar. He eventually rejoined the Order and was ordained. Thomas Aquinas is known as a brilliant thinker. His best known work is the Summa Theologica.

Patron Saint of: academics, booksellers
Feast Day: January 28

A Prayer for the Week

Lord, open our eyes to see you in all of creation, especially in one another. May we always find places where we can experience your comfort, love, and peace. Thank you for your goodness and love. Amen.

9 Faith Expressed and Lived

LET US PRAY

As the deer longs for streams of water,
so my soul longs for you, O God.

Psalms 42–43:2

Share

Brother Edward's days begin long before the sun rises. Like other monks in the community of brothers with whom he lives, Brother Edward wakes up early to pray in the chapel. Every day, he prays seven times with the other brothers who live in the community. When Brother Edward is not praying, eating, or sleeping, he spends his time working as a teacher in a high school run by his religious community.

This is not an easy life. But Brother Edward has chosen to live this kind of life so that he will be better able to develop his special relationship with God. By reducing noisy distractions in his life, Brother Edward is better able to hear the voice of God. Every time he prays, eats, sleeps, studies, or teaches, Brother Edward tries to remember that God is the most important part of his life.

Activity

Brother Edward lives in a special place where he can concentrate on developing his relationship with God. Do you have a special place where you can go to think about important things? Explain how being in that place helps you.

_____

_____

_____

Share your special place with others in your group.

How did the monks in the Middle Ages practice their faith?

147

Respond

Saint Thomas Aquinas

When Saint Thomas Aquinas was a young man, his classmates often called him "the dumb ox" because he was stocky and slow. Thomas's teacher, now known as Saint Albert the Great, knew better. "This ox will one day fill the world with his bellowing," he said. Indeed, Saint Thomas Aquinas has been called the most learned man who ever lived. Pope Pius XII said that studying Saint Thomas Aquinas's theology was the best way to understand Roman Catholic doctrine.

Thomas, born in 1225, was the seventh son of an Italian nobleman. When he was five-years-old, Thomas was sent to the Benedictine Abbey of Monte Cassino to be educated. He was a quiet, serious student who often asked his teachers, "Who is God?"

As a young man, Thomas shocked his parents by telling them he had decided to become a friar with the Dominicans, a mendicant order. This meant he would have to beg for his food. His family was furious, but Thomas would not change his mind. His family captured him and locked him in the family castle for a year. They tempted him with everything imaginable but could not get him to change his mind.

Thomas became a great teacher and writer. In Thomas's day, the works of the Greek philosopher Aristotle became very popular. Many in the Church feared that Aristotle's writings would undermine the teachings of the Church. Instead, Thomas eagerly read Aristotle's works and used them to help people understand their faith. He wrote the *Summa Theologiae*, a collection of essays in which he blended the works of many philosophers with the teachings of the Church. This work was a monumental intellectual achievement that constructed a new philosophy proving that reason and faith could complement each other. Saint Thomas was named a Doctor of the Church in 1567.

Saint Thomas Aquinas by Bernadino Mei (1615–1676), Siena, Italy

Activities

1. Saint Thomas Aquinas belonged to a religious order of priests and brothers called the Dominicans. Unlike Benedictine monks, who lived in monasteries, Dominicans traveled throughout the world and preached the Gospel. They took a vow of poverty so strict that they had to beg for their food as they journeyed.

   Read Luke 9:1–6. Discuss with a partner how the Dominicans in Thomas's time and today fulfill Jesus' instructions to the Apostles. Then imagine what it would be like to be a Dominican friar. Which part of that way of life would be most challenging for you? Which most appeals to you?

2. Monks and nuns who follow the Rule of Saint Benedict organize their days and nights around a schedule of labor, meals, study, and times for spiritual reading and prayer. In this way, monks and nuns follow Benedict's philosophy of *Ora et labora,* or "Pray and work."

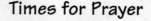

Times for Prayer

2 A.M.: Matins (Arise from sleep, pray many psalms, and read the Scriptures.)

5 A.M.: Lauds (Sing a hymn of praise at daybreak.)

Before dawn or after Lauds: Prime
(Read the Scriptures or the writings of the Holy Fathers.)

9 A.M., noon, and 3 P.M.: Terce, Sext, and None
(Pray short prayers and do short readings.)

6 P.M.: Vespers (Give praise and thanks at the end of the day.)

After supper: Compline (Pray before going to bed.)

On the chart below, make a schedule for your daily activities. Include time for prayer and study.

	Time	Activity
Morning	_____	_____
Afternoon	_____	_____
Evening	_____	_____

3. Listening to the Word of God is an important part of Benedictine prayer. Read the two quotations from Saint Benedict. Choose one, and write what you think it means.

"Idleness is the enemy of the soul."
"We should listen to Scripture with the ear of our hearts."

_____

_____

_____

_____

How do we pray for an increase in faith?

153

✝ Prayer Celebration

Divine Reading

"Idleness is the enemy of the soul," wrote Saint Benedict. "Therefore, the brothers should have specified periods for manual labor as well as for prayerful reading." The prayerful reading the monks did is known as *lectio divina*, or divine reading. It had four parts: reading and listening, meditating, praying through a loving conversation with God, and contemplating, or simply being with God.

Leader: Close your eyes, take several deep breaths, and be with God as you are guided through this prayerful reading.

Read/Listen: *(Leader reads twice, slowly and prayerfully.)*
As the deer longs for streams of water,
   so my soul longs for you, O God.
My being thirsts for God, the living God.

Psalms 42–43:2–3

Meditate: How often do you think of God during the day? How does your faith in God affect the way you act?

Pray: Pray for the strength to love God with all your heart, soul, and mind.

Contemplate: Sit quietly; feel God's love all around you.

All: Glory be to the Father and to the Son and to the Holy Spirit, as it was in the beginning is now, and ever shall be world without end. Amen.

Based on a prayer by Reverend Canon James T. Irvine

A **Check** the box next to the phrases that describe a way to nourish one's relationship with God. Note: Everything we do can nourish our relationship with God.

☐ singing the psalms

☐ doing hobbies

☐ saying grace before meals

☐ playing soccer

☐ studying Saint Thomas Aquinas's writings

☐ attending Mass

☐ reading Saint John's Gospel

☐ practicing the piano

☐ meditating on Jesus' Passion

☐ memorizing the multiplication tables

B **Circle** the letter of the best answer.

1. A monastery is _____.
   a. a punishment for sin
   b. a person who is considered a saint
   c. a lifelong residence for monks or nuns
   d. a gathering of all the bishops

2. Faith means _____.
   a. the assurance of things hoped for
   b. the conviction of things not seen
   c. believing in God
   d. all of the above

3. Lectio divina, or divine reading, combines reading with _____.
   a. prayer and penance
   b. prayer, meditation, and contemplation
   c. faith and good works
   d. poverty and obedience

4. Which of these places might help a person feel closer to God?
   a. a starlit night
   b. a shopping mall
   c. a church
   d. both a and c

5. As in Benedict's time, most Christians today _____.
   a. withdraw from the world
   b. attend Mass every day
   c. live in a society in which not everyone follows Jesus
   d. belong to religious orders

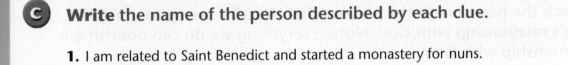

C **Write** the name of the person described by each clue.

1. I am related to Saint Benedict and started a monastery for nuns.

   _____

2. In the second half of the nineteenth century, we revived Gregorian Chant as a musical

   form for use at Mass. _____

3. I was considered slow and was once compared to an ox, but later I wrote essays

   about philosophy and religion. _____

4. Gregorian chant is named after me. _____

5. I wrote a rule for monastic life that many monks and nuns still practice today.

   _____

D **Respond** to the following.

1. Read and reflect on this selection from the Rule of Saint Benedict. Explain how it might apply to you.

   > Monks must remain busy, whether with manual work or in study
   > and prayer. Monks must remain silent, unless they have to speak.
   > The Abbot's orders must be obeyed without argument.

   _____

   _____

   _____

2. Explain how your conclusions about the passage above might nourish your faith.

   _____

   _____

   _____

   _____

Get CONNECTED with family and friends

Mass in the Cathedral

A description of Sunday Mass in a Gothic cathedral during the Middle Ages helps us understand some of the history behind our own liturgical celebrations. The art, architecture, and sensations we experience within the churches in which we worship help express our beliefs about the Eucharist. They also help us enter into the celebration of the mystery of the changing of the bread and wine into the Body and Blood of Jesus Christ.

Activity

Even though my grandfather died years ago, we still celebrate his birthday. Instead of having a party, all the relatives gather for a memorial Mass at my grandmother's church. Sometimes we go out for brunch afterward. I try to act like everything's fine, but, to be honest, I have some real problems with our celebration.

The Mass is always on a hot, humid day in August. The old-fashioned church that everyone thinks is so beautiful isn't air-conditioned. The way the liturgy is celebrated seems so outdated. And the hymns, which hardly anybody sings, seem to be from another century.

My dad says I should ask my grandmother and the other older relatives to talk about what this parish meant to them as they were growing up. He says that it might help me feel better about the Mass.

Do one of the following.

1. Ask your grandparents or older relatives to describe the churches they attended as children. Ask them to tell you what the celebration of Mass was like when they were your age.

2. Take a tour of your parish church. Find out when it was built. Try to learn as much as you can about its art, architecture, and sacred objects.

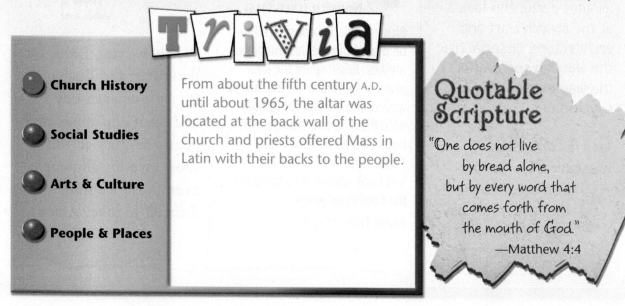

Trivia

- Church History
- Social Studies
- Arts & Culture
- People & Places

From about the fifth century A.D. until about 1965, the altar was located at the back wall of the church and priests offered Mass in Latin with their backs to the people.

Quotable Scripture

"One does not live by bread alone, but by every word that comes forth from the mouth of God."

—Matthew 4:4

Get CONNECTED
with family and friends

✝ Scripture Background

Before the Time of Jesus

Biblical Mountains   In the Bible, mountains have spiritual significance. From the Old Testament we learn that God made the Covenant with the Israelites on Mt. Sinai. Abraham went to Mt. Moriah to sacrifice his son (Genesis 22:2). Mt. Moriah (later called Mt. Zion) is also the site of the Temple built by Solomon (2 Chronicles 3:1). Mountains are also significant in the New Testament, most notably in the Sermon on the Mount (Matthew 5—7). Jesus' Transfiguration took place atop a mountain (Matthew 17:1–8). The Mount of Olives is the site of many important events in Jesus' life, including the Agony in the Garden (Matthew 26:36–46) and the Ascension (Acts of the Apostles 1:6–12).

Take a moment, look up, and read the Bible passages about mountains that are named above.

WEEKLY PLANNER

On Sunday
Arrive for Mass ten minutes early, and look at the church's art and architecture. Observe how the worship space affects the way people pray as a community.

On the Web
blestarewe.com

Visit our Web site for the saint of the day and the reflection question of the week.

Saint of the Week
Blessed Julian of Norwich (1342–1416)

Blessed Julian is considered to be one of the greatest medieval mystics. Julian spent the later years of her life as an anchoress—walled into a small room built onto the side of a church. Her book *Sixteen Revelations of Divine Love* is believed to be the first book written by a woman in the English language.

Feast Day: May 13

A Prayer for the Week

We thank you, Lord, for the gift of the Eucharist. Be with us each day and open our minds and hearts so that we will show love for all people, even those we find difficult to love. Amen.

10 Mass in the Cathedral

LET US PRAY

This is the day the Lord has made; let us rejoice and be glad, alleluia. *Easter Sunday Antiphon, Liturgy of the Hours*

Share

How do you spend a typical week? Of course, your days include attending school, doing homework, participating in sports or other activities, doing some chores around the house, and spending time with friends. On the weekend, though, you spend your time a little differently. You are a little less busy and have more time for leisure. How does Sunday differ from every other day of the week? What do you do—or not do—on Sunday that sets it apart as the Lord's Day?

Sunday is a special day. In the biblical account of creation in the Book of Genesis, this is the last and seventh day. It is the Sabbath on which God rested from the work of creation.

The Third Commandment tells us to keep the Lord's Day holy. Sunday is the Lord's Day for Christians. The first way Catholics live this Commandment is by participating in the celebration of Mass. We can also spend more time with our family, not doing chores that can be done on other days. We can take time to enjoy the gifts of God's creation and to appreciate his blessings in our lives.

Activity

Read the quote at the top of this page. Describe some ways that you might spend Sundays in a way that reflects the message of the antiphon.

_____

_____

_____

_____

_____

_____

How did Christians living in the Middle Ages express their love for God?

Hear & Believe

A Holy Day

Our responsibility and obligation to observe one holy day each week comes from the Ten Commandments. Moses brought the Hebrew people this message from God:

Remember to keep holy the Sabbath day. You have six days when you may do all your work. But the seventh day is dedicated to God. No work may be done on that day either by you, your family or servants, or anyone who works for you.

In six days the Lord created all that exists, but on the seventh day he rested. God has blessed the Sabbath day and made it holy.

Based on Exodus 20:8–11

For Jews this holy day is called the Sabbath; for Christians it is the Lord's Day. Sunday is the Lord's Day for Catholics and other Christians because it was the day of Jesus' Resurrection. Catholics set aside this holy day to remember and participate in Jesus' Sacrifice. At Mass, we share in the Body and Blood of Jesus, as the Apostles did at the Last Supper. The Gospel of Mark tells us:

While they were eating, Jesus took bread, blessed it, and broke it. He gave it to them and said, "Take this bread; this is my body."

Then he took a cup of wine, gave thanks, and gave it to the disciples. They all drank from it.

Jesus said to them, "This is the blood of the covenant, which will be shed for many."

Based on Mark 14:22–24

KEEP HOLY THE SABBATH

A Closer Look

The Fourth Lateran Council

Known as the Great Council, the Fourth Lateran Council was called by Pope Innocent III in 1215 and held at the Lateran Palace in Rome. The Council established seventy canons, or rules, for the Church. One rule directed Christians to receive the Eucharist at Easter. Another rule stated that people must individually confess their mortal sins in the Sacrament of Penance. In addition, priests were commanded not to reveal any sin a person disclosed in confession. Any priest found guilty of betraying the trust of the confessional would lose his priestly office and be confined to a monastery to do perpetual penance.

Our Church Teaches

Through Moses, God entered into the Covenant with the Hebrews and gave them his law in the Ten Commandments. The Hebrews kept the Third Commandment, "Keep holy the Sabbath day," by worshiping and honoring God as the source of all creation.

The Law of Moses was a preparation for the Gospel of Christ. The Commandment to observe the Sabbath received new meaning in Christ. At Mass we are made shar-

We Believe

At Mass, we offer thanksgiving to God the Father. The Eucharist recalls Christ's sacrifice and makes him truly present for us.

ers in Christ's Death and Resurrection. Sunday is the foremost holy day of obligation in the Church. We keep God's Commandment by participating in Mass on Sundays and holy days of obligation. By the power of the Holy Spirit and through the priest's repeating of the words Jesus said at the Last Supper, the bread and wine at Mass become the Body and Blood of Christ.

SIX DAYS YOU MAY LABOR AND DO ALL YOUR WORK,

Activities

1. List things that you and your family usually do on Sunday. How well do those activities follow the Commandment to keep holy the Lord's Day? Rate each activity on a scale of 1 to 5, with 1 meaning that Sunday is treated as an ordinary day and 5 meaning that Sunday is honored as the Lord's Day.

What We Do on Sunday	Rating
_____	1 2 3 4 5
_____	1 2 3 4 5
_____	1 2 3 4 5
_____	1 2 3 4 5
_____	1 2 3 4 5
_____	1 2 3 4 5
_____	1 2 3 4 5
_____	1 2 3 4 5
_____	1 2 3 4 5
_____	1 2 3 4 5

2. What changes could you make in order to truly celebrate Sunday as the Lord's Day? For example, instead of watching TV, you could do a service project with your family.

_____

_____

_____

_____

_____

BUT THE SEVENTH DAY IS THE SABBATH OF THE LORD, YOUR GOD.

(Exodus 20:9–10)

How did the design of Gothic cathedrals give honor to God?

Respond

The Gothic Cathedral

In A.D. 1144 the world's first Gothic cathedral was built next to a Benedictine abbey at Saint-Denis, near Paris, one of the most important monasteries in Europe. At that time Abbot Suger (1081–1151) was reported to have said, "The workmanship is greater than the value of the materials." Abbot Suger's reaction reflects the faith and devotion of those who labored to build the cathedral.

With their high-arching, rib-vaulted ceilings and elaborately decorated stained-glass windows, Gothic cathedrals were designed to remind people of God's power and grandeur. An important feature of the Gothic cathedral was its cruciform, or crosslike, shape. The cruciform design was first introduced in church construction during the construction of a basilica in A.D. 382 when Saint Ambrose ordered the building of transepts. Transepts are the sides of a church structure that make it look like the cross.

In the Gothic cathedral, the general public sat in the central area called the nave. The nave was bordered by aisles and two rows of columns. The nave—extending from east to west—reached all the way to the apse. Semicircular in shape, the apse, which is also known as the sanctuary, contained the altar. Monks sat in the choir area of the apse and prayed the Divine Office. On either side of the apse, and at right angles to the nave, were the transepts. These areas—extending from north to south—were generally reserved for members of the clergy. Behind the apse was the chantry chapel. It was reserved for the upper classes. The building of Gothic churches marked a great advancement in architecture, as well as an important contribution to the life of the Church.

The cruciform, or crosslike, shape of the Gothic cathedral is clearly visible in this overhead shot of the Cologne Cathedral in Cologne, Germany.

Activities

1. How do you think people of the Middle Ages felt when they entered a Gothic cathedral? Why?

_____

_____

2. How do you feel when you enter a church? What makes you feel this way?

_____

_____

_____

3. The three pictures on this page show different sections of a Gothic cathedral. Each section served a different purpose. Look closely at each picture. Then, in the space provided, draw a stained-glass window that would be appropriate for one of the sections. Use information provided in the captions to help you decide what to draw.

Stained-glass windows in the nave showed scenes from Scripture stories.

The transept area often was used for devotional services. It was reserved for members of the clergy. Stained-glass windows here often depicted saints.

Monks often sat in the choir area and prayed the Divine Office.

How might we pray as people longing to see the Lord?

165

✝ Prayer Celebration

A Meditation Prayer

Blessed Julian of Norwich lived in the Middle Ages. She was born around 1342 and was a mystic—a person who seeks to know God directly through spiritual insight. She also believed that love unites us with the Lord. Julian left living with her family and community in order to live as an anchoress. An anchoress usually lived alone in a room built onto the side of a church. Julian believed that the solitary life of an anchoress would allow her to focus on her spiritual life.

For a few moments, imagine that you have invited Jesus Christ to visit so you can directly express your love to him. Think about how you will respond to these questions. Then pray the prayer below. *(Pause.)*

Leader: Where will you meet? What special preparations will you make to get this place ready? How will you greet Jesus? What will you do to make him feel comfortable? How will Jesus answer your greeting? Tell Jesus why you are glad he is with you. Tell him why you love him. Invite him to visit you again.

Lord God our Father, in your compassion, you granted to Blessed Julian many spiritual insights of your love. Move our hearts to seek you above all things, for in giving us yourself you gave us all. We pray this through Jesus Christ our Lord, who lives and reigns with you and the Holy Spirit, one God, for ever and ever. Amen.

Describe how a Mass was celebrated in the Middle Ages. Use the words in the box.

| holy drama |
| symbolized |
| consecration |
| priest's actions |
| altar |
| elevation of the host |
| Communion |
| incense |
| Passion |

_____

_____

_____

_____

_____

_____

_____

B **Circle** the letter of the best answer.

1. The requirement to observe one holy day each week comes from the _____.
   a. Sermon on the Mount
   b. Beatitudes
   c. parables
   d. Ten Commandments

2. For Catholics, Sunday is a holy day set aside for _____.
   a. observing a day of rest
   b. sharing in the Body and Blood of Jesus
   c. honoring God as the source of creation
   d. all of the above

3. Someone who seeks to know God directly through spiritual insight is called _____.
   a. a saint
   b. a hermit
   c. an Apostle
   d. a mystic

4. One of the most well-known medieval mystics was _____.
   a. Blessed Julian of Norwich
   b. Alphonso
   c. Mary Magdalene
   d. Blessed Teresa of Calcutta

5. An anchoress lived a solitary life _____.
   a. in a convent
   b. in a room built onto the side of a church
   c. in the Vatican
   d. and ate only bread and water

Hear & Believe

Medieval Devotions

During the Middle Ages the practice of private devotions became more widespread. Two popular devotions that developed during this time period were the Stations of the Cross and the Rosary.

The Annunciation by Leonardo da Vinci (1452–1519), Uffizi, Florence, Italy

The Stations of the Cross. After Jesus' Death and Resurrection, people made pilgrimages to Jerusalem. Most likely, these pilgrimages included stops for meditation at the places where Jesus carried his Cross, was crucified, and was buried.

As Christianity spread, distance made pilgrimages difficult. In addition, since the seventh century, Muslim invaders had occupied Palestine and taken control of sacred Christian sites. Even so, Christians had a strong desire to remember Christ's Passion and Death. In the twelfth century, shrines were built outside of monasteries and churches to help people meditate on the suffering of Jesus. People meditated on stories, such as Jesus' falling under the weight of the Cross and Jesus' being condemned to death. This devotion became known as

the Stations, or Way of the Cross. Today, praying the Stations of the Cross is a devotion that is popular during Lent. There are fourteen Stations, but a Fifteenth Station, in memory of the Resurrection, is often added.

The Rosary. According to legend, Saint Dominic received the Rosary from the Blessed Mother to help him fight heresies. The word *rosary* comes from the Latin word *rosarium*, which means "rose garden." The Rosary that Christians pray has been described as a wreath of roses for Our Lady. The Rosary as we pray it today developed over a long period of time.

From the early days of Christianity, people used different methods to help them keep count of the

Our Church Teaches

Catholics often express their piety through popular devotions, such as reverencing relics, forming processions, making pilgrimages, praying the Stations of the Cross or the Rosary, or wearing medals. These devotions do not replace the liturgy, but flow from it and help the faithful deepen and express their faith. The liturgy is the official prayer of the Church; devotions extend the sacramental life of the Church and do not replace it.

We Believe

In devotions and in the liturgy, the Church reveres and worships God and recalls the saving events of the life of his Son, Jesus Christ.

The life, Passion, Death, and Resurrection of Christ are the central events and saving truths of our faith expressed through the Church's liturgy and recalled in the popular devotions of Catholics. Our personal conduct, in addition to our prayers and devotions, must show that we value these truths. Through devotions recalling these truths, we can grow stronger in our Catholic faith.

prayers they said. They used pebbles, precious stones, knotted string, and then stones or beads connected to the string.

At first, pious Christians would use the beads to pray the Lord's Prayer 150 times. The Lord's Prayer was prayed in three sets of fifty, and the sets of beads that helped them keep count were known as *Pater Nosters*, the plural Latin term for "Our Fathers."

In the twelfth century, the first part of the Hail Mary replaced the Lord's Prayer and the beads were called a "rosary." People recalled and meditated on scenes from the lives of Jesus and Mary as they prayed. In 1569, the Dominican Pope Pius V established fifteen mysteries to recall while praying the Rosary. In 2002, Pope John Paul II added five more mysteries.

Activities

1. The complete Rosary has twenty decades, divided into four sets of five mysteries. The Mysteries of the Rosary are events in the life of Christ or Mary that we meditate on while praying. Read the Sorrowful Mysteries, found on page 190. Choose one and write about its meaning for you.

_____

_____

_____

_____

_____

Who _____

_____

What _____

_____

When _____

_____

Where _____

2. Spend a few minutes imagining what it must have been like to be at the event described in one of the Stations on the Cross. Then imagine you are a reporter who must describe what you see and hear. Include reactions from one follower of Jesus and one non-Christian witness. Write your report at right.

How has praying the Rosary made a difference?

✝ Prayer Celebration

The Rosary

Devotion to Mary is an important part of the prayer life of the Church. From the earliest days of the Church, Mary has been honored as the Mother of God, and the faithful have turned to her for guidance and protection.

Leader: Let us meditate on one of the five Sorrowful Mysteries and reflect on how Mary brings us closer to Jesus.

Reader 1: The First Sorrowful Mystery: The Agony in the Garden. *(Pause.)* Dear Mary, help me place my trust in God.

Reader 2: The Second Sorrowful Mystery: The Scourging at the Pillar. *(Pause.)* Dear Mary, help me be more loving of others.

Reader 3: The Third Sorrowful Mystery: The Crowning with Thorns. *(Pause.)* Dear Mary, help me be more patient with myself and others.

Reader 4: The Fourth Sorrowful Mystery: The Carrying of the Cross. *(Pause.)* Dear Mary, help me be more obedient to God's will.

Reader 5: The Fifth Sorrowful Mystery: The Crucifixion and Death. *(Pause.)* Dear Mary, help me love God above all other things.

A **Write** a brief definition of each of the following.

1. The Sorrowful Mysteries _____

_____

2. Stations of the Cross _____

_____

3. popular devotion _____

_____

4. piety _____

_____

5. mendicant order _____

_____

_____

_____

B **Circle** the letter of the best answer.

1. Thomas à Kempis wrote that Christians should practice private devotions _____.
   a. to better set their sights on God
   b. instead of attending Mass
   c. after doing completely and faithfully all they are bound and commanded to do
   d. both a and c

2. There are _____ Mysteries of the Rosary.
   a. five
   b. ten
   c. fifteen
   d. twenty

3. Mendicant orders were started as a way to _____.
   a. make money for the Church
   b. help Christians return to a simple Gospel way of life
   c. give jobs to poor men and women
   d. convince people to leave their families

4. Private devotions today _____.
   a. help the faithful deepen and express their faith
   b. replace the liturgy of the Church
   c. are forbidden by the pope
   d. both a and b

C **Identify** the person described by each clue, using one of the names in the box.

> Father Titus Brandsma
>
> Saint Dominic
>
> Pope Pius V
>
> Blessed Pope John Paul II
>
> Thomas à Kempis

1. I established the first fifteen mysteries of the Rosary.

_____

2. I wrote *The Imitation of Christ* to encourage Christians to

remember Christ's sufferings and to practice private devotion. _____

3. I organized devotions, such as the Stations of the Cross, for concentration camp

prisoners. _____

4. Legend says that I received the Rosary from the Blessed Mother to help me fight

heresies. _____

5. I added five more mysteries to the Rosary. _____

D **Explain** the history of the Rosary.

_____

_____

_____

_____

E **Describe** the sights, sounds, and sensations Jesus might have experienced as he carried his Cross through the streets of Jerusalem on his way to be crucified.

_____

_____

_____

Faith in Action

Knights of Columbus The Knights of Columbus were founded in 1882 by Father Michael McGivney. The Knights were originally founded as an organization for Catholic men and provided assistance to widows and children. Charity is the first principle of the Knights of Columbus. Throughout its 125 year history, the organization has worked to help people who are suffering and in need by members raising funds and volunteering their time. With a common faith, the Knights of Columbus serve the Church and God's people in need.

Activity List an act of charity you can do this week for each of the following people.

A sibling or friend

_____

_____

A classmate

_____

_____

A parent or grandparent

_____

_____

Activity Think of a person in need in your community, your parish, or in a faraway place. Write one or two ways that you and members of your parish can help meet this need.

_____

_____

_____

_____

Faith in Action

Coaches and Athletics Instructors The development of students involves more than instruction in academic subjects. Students must also be given opportunities to develop emotionally, spiritually, and physically. Athletic instructors or coaches in Catholic parishes and schools tend to the latter. They help young people develop a spirit of teamwork, sportsmanship, and a commitment to living a physically healthy lifestyle. In doing so, coaches and athletics instructors encourage young people to respect and develop the gifts and talents God has given them.

In Everyday Life

Activity There are simple things you can do every day to keep yourself healthy in body and soul. First, name two things you can do to keep your body healthy. Then name two things you can do for the health of your soul.

Body:

_____

_____

Soul:

_____

_____

In Your Parish

Activity It takes many members of a parish community to plan parish events, such as a pancake breakfast or a parish carnival. Imagine that you are coordinating the team that is organizing a parish event. Name the event, then tell what skills you would expect from team members helping out with the event.

Event:

_____

Team members' essential skills:

_____

_____

_____

_____

Faith in Action

Godparents When a child is baptized a Catholic, the child's parents choose godparents to support the child as she or he grows in faith and in living the Commandments as Jesus taught. Godparents share openly about their own faith. They help their godchildren grow in the Christian faith and in commitment to Jesus and to the Catholic Church. They pray for their godchildren and support them as they prepare to receive and celebrate other Sacraments as well. God gives godparents special graces to help them make a positive difference in the lives of their godchildren.

In Everyday Life

Activity When you were baptized you became a member of the Catholic Church. Because of Baptism, you belong to a faith family that extends to all parts of the world. Write a sentence that expresses what it means to you to be a member of the Catholic Church.

_____

_____

In Your Parish

Activity Imagine that you are godparent to a younger cousin. In the space, tell what that cousin would say if they were to write a note thanking you for a way you have been helpful in your role as godparent.

Dear _____ ,

Thank you for _____

_____

_____

_____

_____ .

✝ Prayer Celebration

Praying with Saint John of the Cross

Saint John of the Cross wrote beautiful poetry praising God. He believed that joy comes only from God who alone should be our desire. Together, pray this poem of Saint John.

All: In the name of the Father, and of the Son, and of the Holy Spirit. Amen.

Leader: That eternal spring is hidden, for I know well where it has its rise, although it is night.

All: I know that nothing else is so beautiful, and that the heavens and the earth drink there, although it is night.

Leader: This eternal spring is hidden in this living bread for our life's sake, although it is night.

All: This living spring that I long for, I see in this bread of life, although it is night.

Adapted from The Collected Works of St. John of the Cross

212

A **Complete** the following sentences.

1. Martin Luther challenged the **d**_____ of the Church and questioned

   the **a**_____ of the pope.

2. The Catholic Church teaches that **S**_____ and **T**_____ are

   two ways that God's Revelation is transmitted, or comes, to us.

3. Luther accepted only **t**_____ Sacraments and not **S**_____

   Sacraments celebrated by the Catholic Church.

4. Churches that have separated from the Catholic Church share elements of

   g_____ and **t**_____.

5. Only in the Catholic Church is found the fullness of the means of **S**_____.

6. We pray that all Christians will be **o**_____ as Christ prayed

   to his Father.

7. Jesus told his followers that their **f**_____ would be strengthened by

   their **a**_____.

8. Jesus compared those who put his words into practice to a wise person who builds a

   house on a firm **f**_____ of rock.

9. Saint John of the Cross wrote beautiful **p**_____ praising God.

10. Saint Thomas More refused to take an oath stating that the king of England had

    a_____ over the **C**_____ in England.

Respond

A Penitential Celebration

The revised Rite of Penance, a document describing the ways the Church celebrates the Sacrament of Penance and Reconciliation today, includes examples of penitential celebrations. Penitential celebrations help us prepare to participate in the Sacrament of Reconciliation. They are not celebrations of the Sacrament.

Activity

Below is an outline to help you plan a penitential celebration for your class. In the spaces provided, name prayers, readings, and songs you would like to include in the penitential celebration.

Opening Song: Choose a song or hymn that everyone knows from Sunday Mass. Try to suggest one that mentions Baptism.

Collect: Write a prayer that reminds us that we are baptized into Christ and called to be his disciples. Ask the Holy Spirit to guide us in understanding the message of the Gospels.

Scripture Reading: Choose one or two Bible readings about forgiveness or healing.

Reflection: Write your thoughts about the Scripture readings. Invite other members of the group to share their reflections on the Scripture.

Examination of Conscience: Plan a period of silence for reflecting on past behavior and how to better live as a Catholic. Choose a New Testament reading to precede the period of silence that encourages sorrow for sin and turning back to God. You may also choose to read the Ten Commandments (see pages 421–424).

Prayer of Contrition: Pray an act of contrition together. You can find one in the Catholic Prayers section of this book on page 438 or write one of your own here.

How might we pray for God's forgiveness?

✝ Prayer Celebration

A Prayer for Mercy

All: In the name of the Father, and of the Son, and of the Holy Spirit.
Amen.

Hear, Lord, the prayers we offer from contrite hearts.
Have mercy on us as we acknowledge our sins. *(Pause.)*
Lead us back to your way of holiness.
Protect us now and always from the wounds of sin.
May we forever keep safe in all its fullness
    your life-giving gift of grace, which your mercy now restores.

Leader: We ask this through our Lord Jesus Christ, your Son, who lives
and reigns with you and the Holy Spirit, one God for ever and ever.

All: Amen.

Based on the Rite of Penance

A **Complete** the sentences with words from the box.

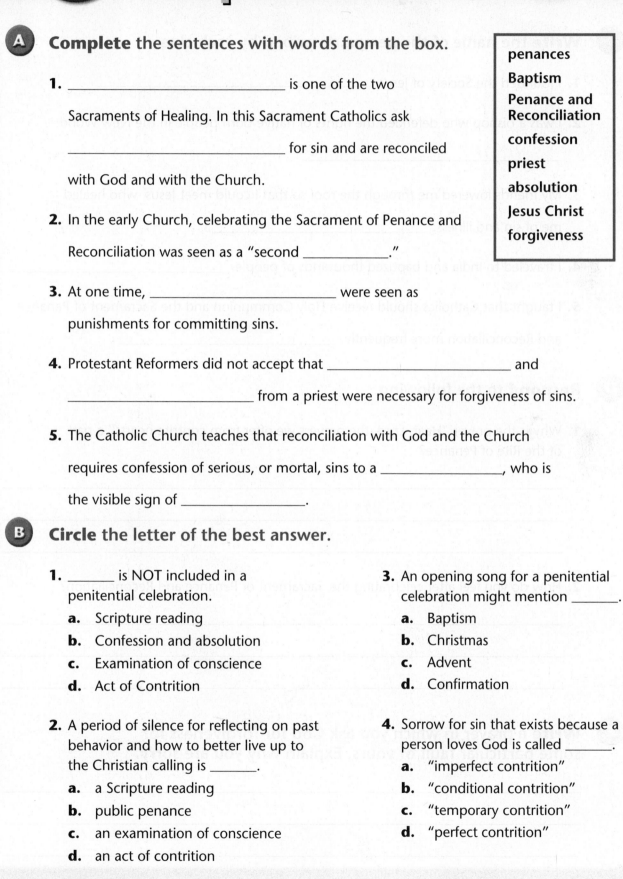

penances

Baptism

Penance and Reconciliation

confession

priest

absolution

Jesus Christ

forgiveness

1. _____ is one of the two Sacraments of Healing. In this Sacrament Catholics ask _____ for sin and are reconciled with God and with the Church.

2. In the early Church, celebrating the Sacrament of Penance and Reconciliation was seen as a "second _____."

3. At one time, _____ were seen as punishments for committing sins.

4. Protestant Reformers did not accept that _____ and _____ from a priest were necessary for forgiveness of sins.

5. The Catholic Church teaches that reconciliation with God and the Church requires confession of serious, or mortal, sins to a _____, who is the visible sign of _____.

B **Circle** the letter of the best answer.

1. _____ is NOT included in a penitential celebration.
   a. Scripture reading
   b. Confession and absolution
   c. Examination of conscience
   d. Act of Contrition

2. A period of silence for reflecting on past behavior and how to better live up to the Christian calling is _____.
   a. a Scripture reading
   b. public penance
   c. an examination of conscience
   d. an act of contrition

3. An opening song for a penitential celebration might mention _____.
   a. Baptism
   b. Christmas
   c. Advent
   d. Confirmation

4. Sorrow for sin that exists because a person loves God is called _____.
   a. "imperfect contrition"
   b. "conditional contrition"
   c. "temporary contrition"
   d. "perfect contrition"

C **Write** the name of the person described by each clue.

1. I founded the Society of Jesus. _____

2. I was a bishop who defended the rights of native-born people in the New World.

_____

3. My friends lowered me through the roof so that I could meet Jesus, who healed

me of sin and illness. _____

4. I traveled to India and baptized thousands of people. _____

5. I taught that Catholics should receive Holy Communion and the Sacrament of Penance

and Reconciliation more frequently. _____

D **Respond** to the following.

1. Why is the prayer "Hear, Lord, the prayers we offer from contrite hearts" a part
of the Rite of Penance?

_____

_____

_____

2. How do you feel after celebrating the Sacrament of Penance and Reconciliation?

_____

_____

_____

E **Write** a prayer in which you ask God for forgiveness for
some particular fault of yours. Explain why you are sorry.

_____

_____

_____

Get CONNECTED
with family and friends

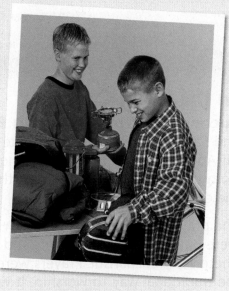

Morality and Salvation

God first loved us and his love is a pure gift. We do not earn God's love through our own efforts. His love is unconditional. God gave us the gift of free will to accept his love. Our conscience helps us know what is morally right and wrong. God's gift of grace helps us make decisions to live as followers of Jesus. These decisions positively affect others and ourselves.

Activity

Mark has been my close friend since kindergarten. He's fun to be with, knows all about famous ships and camping out, and can fix things. When my friends make fun of Mark, I get upset. They don't want him to be in our group. Sometimes they threaten to exclude me, too. The kids tease Mark because he needs to use a walker and has a speech defect. They don't understand that he has cerebral palsy. Mark's mom said that his brain didn't get enough oxygen when he was born and that's why he uses a walker.

People often make fun of or exclude someone because they lack an understanding of the person's situation. Do one of the following.

1. Watch a popular TV show with friends. Consider whether the characters treat each other with respect, and if they do not, discuss alternative behaviors.

2. Discuss with your family why it is morally wrong to tease or exclude people who seem different from us.

- **Church History**
- **Social Studies**
- **Arts & Culture**
- **People & Places**

The Protestant Reformation in the sixteenth century led to the establishment of new Christian denominations. Today there are more than 300 different Christian denominations in the United States.

Quotable Scripture

Give thanks to the LORD, who is good, / whose love endures forever.

—Psalm 106:1

Get CONNECTED
with family and friends

✝ Scripture Background

In the Early Church

Eucharistic Prayers Among Early Christians   All four Gospels and Saint Paul tell us that Jesus ate a final meal, the Last Supper, with his Apostles on the night before he died. These accounts contain words from that meal that form part of the Eucharistic Prayers that are part of the celebration of Mass today.

The prayers said at the celebration of the Eucharist in the early Church were based on these accounts and on Jewish traditions and worship. These early Eucharistic Prayers were spontaneous, because that was the traditional way to worship. It was not until the third century that formal Eucharistic Prayers were developed by the Church.

Read one Gospel account of the Last Supper in Mark 14:12–26.

WEEKLY PLANNER

On Sunday
During Mass express thanks to God for your health, family and friends, freedom, and all the gifts of creation.

On the Web
blestarewe.com

 Visit our Web site for the saint of the day and the reflection question of the week.

Saint of the Week
 Saint Catherine of Siena (1347–1380)

Catherine of Siena chose at a young age to dedicate her life to God and lived a life of solitude. At age 23 she experienced a vision in which she received a command to enter the public life of the world. Through her persuasion, the papacy was restored to Rome, after twenty-seven years of residence in Avignon, France.

Feast Day: April 29

A Prayer for the Week

All-knowing and all-loving Lord, help us be open and honest with you, with each other, and with ourselves. Help us know and have the courage to do what is right. Amen.

15 Morality and Salvation

LET US PRAY

For just as a body without a spirit is dead,
so also faith without works is dead.

James 2:26

Share

In 2001 Pope John Paul II visited Greece on a pilgrimage to retrace the footsteps of Saint Paul the Apostle. Paul came to Greece in A.D. 51 while traveling the Mediterranean region to spread the Gospel. While in Greece, the pope met with the leader of the Greek Orthodox Church, Archbishop Christodoulos. This was a historic meeting.

It was the first meeting between the leaders of the Roman Catholic Church and the Greek Orthodox Church since the Schism of 1054, when the Church divided into East and West. The relationship between the Church in the East and the Church in the West was made worse when Crusaders from the West sacked Constantinople, the seat of the Orthodox Church, on their way to the Holy Land during the Fourth Crusade in 1204.

During his visit, Pope John Paul II offered an apology on behalf of the Roman Catholic Church. Referring especially to the events of 1204, the pope said, "For the occasions past and present, when sons and daughters of the Catholic Church have

sinned by action or omission against their Orthodox brothers and sisters, may the Lord grant us the forgiveness we beg of him." The pope also prayed the Lord's Prayer with Archbishop Christodoulos. This prayer, which Jesus taught his first disciples, remains a point of unity for all Christians.

Activity

Individuals and groups respond differently when faced with conflict. Pope Saint John Paul II recognized that Christians are called to respond to conflicts as peacemakers. In your opinion, how can individuals and groups respond peacefully to situations of conflict that divide people?

_____

_____

_____

_____

_____

_____

How has the Church responded to conflict and division in the past?

Hear & Believe

Witness   The Choice of Heaven

By the middle of the sixteenth century, Protestant Reformers had won many supporters who joined with them. The Protestant Reformation begun by Martin Luther had swept like wildfire through Europe. Luther inspired others to speak out against the beliefs and practices of the Catholic Church. One of the strongest voices of the Protestant Reformation belonged to John Calvin (1509–1564).

The following passage is a meditation from *An Introduction to a Devout Life* by Saint Francis de Sales (1567–1622). Through such writings, Francis de Sales was able to defend Catholic doctrine against the teachings of Calvin.

Imagine that you are in the open country. . . . You see Heaven open above [with all its pleasures]. . . . Then you see hell open below [with all its torments]. . . . While imagining yourself in this situation:

1. Be aware that in reality you are between Heaven and hell. The one and the other is open to receive you, according to the choice you make.

2. Realize that the choice which is made of the one or of the other in this world will last forever in the next.

3. Even though the one and the other is open to receive you, according to the choice you make, yet God—who is ready to give you either the one by his justice or the other by his mercy—desires very earnestly that you should choose Heaven. Your Guardian Angel urges you to do this with all his power, offering you on God's behalf a thousand graces and a thousand helps to assist you in the ascent.

4. Jesus Christ looks at you lovingly, from the heights of Heaven, and gently invites you: "Come, dear one, to everlasting rest in the arms of my goodness. In the abundance of my love, I have prepared for you never-ending delights." See, with the eyes of your spirit, our Lady inviting you with a mother's love: "Courage my child. Do not despise my Son's desires, nor my great concern for you, since with him I long for your eternal salvation." Look at the Saints who earnestly request you, and a million faithful who gently invite you, only desiring to see one day your heart united to theirs to praise God forever. They assure you that the way to Heaven is not as difficult as the world claims it to be: "Be daring, our dear friend. Whoever examines well the path of devotion, by which we have come here, will see that we have reached [this place] by means of delights immeasurably more enjoyable than those of the world."

Saint Francis de Sales, 1608

Saved by Faith Alone?

John Calvin was born into a devout Catholic family. Calvin began studying philosophy and theology when he was only fourteen. By the time he was twenty-seven, however, he had left the Catholic faith and joined the Protestant Reformers. Just as Martin Luther, Calvin believed that people could achieve Salvation only through having faith and that Christian teaching should be guided only by the Scriptures.

Calvin also taught that God decided which people would be saved before they were born and that a person has no real part in their being saved. This teaching of Calvin, known as **predestination**, is contrary to the teaching of the Catholic Church. The Catholic Church teaches that God creates each person with a **free will** and gives each person the grace to respond to the gift of Salvation in Jesus Christ.

When Francis de Sales was ordained bishop of Geneva, Switzerland, in 1602, many of the city's churches and government offices had been taken over by Calvin's followers. Most Catholics in the region either had become followers of Calvin or had been driven from the city. For a brief time in his life, Francis de Sales had himself feared that God had predestined *him* for damnation.

Because Geneva was mostly Calvinist, Francis had to keep his office in Annecy, France. From where he ministered to the people of his diocese. His writings and attitude impressed many Protestants so much so that they returned to the Catholic faith.

Defending Catholic Doctrine

During the difficult period of the Reformation, the Church used the Inquisition to defend her doctrine. In the thirteenth century, Pope Gregory IX had set up Inquisition courts to investigate people accused of heresy or refusing to deny that what they were teaching was against the doctrines of the Catholic faith. The Inquisition handed down punishments to people found guilty of heresy. The punishments included fines, imprisonment, or if the crime was severe enough, **excommunication.**

Activity

What role does the gift of free will play in God's plan of Salvation? Discuss this question with a partner.

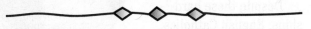

Faith Words

predestination Predestination is the teaching that states that God determines whether someone is saved or damned before they are born.

free will Free will is the ability to choose to do what is morally right or what is morally wrong.

How do we choose Salvation?

Hear & Believe

Choosing the Path of Salvation

In 1534, King Henry VIII declared himself to be the head of the Church in England, because the pope would not annul his marriage with Queen Catherine. Henry VIII responded by declaring himself the head of the Church in England. He then required all English citizens to swear the Oath of Supremacy, acknowledging the English monarch as the supreme head of the Church of England. He also made it a crime to practice or teach the Catholic faith. Catholics could be punished for the crime of recusancy, for refusing to attend the services of the Church of England.

Despite these hardships, English Catholics, known as recusants, followed their consciences and remained true to their Catholic faith. One recusant, Blessed Margaret Pole, was godmother to Henry VIII's daughter Mary. At one time Henry had called her the saintliest woman in the kingdom. But because of her opposition to the king's marriage to Anne Boleyn, Margaret was banished from the royal court.

Margaret's son Reginald was a cardinal in the Catholic Church. He left England for Italy, where he spoke and wrote against the king's behavior. Henry took his revenge on Margaret, who he had arrested, questioned, imprisoned, and treated harshly. Reginald's protests made little difference, and his mother was condemned to death.

On May 28, 1541, at the age of seventy-two, after a two-year imprisonment in the Tower of London, Margaret died for her faith. According to reports, her last words were, "Blessed are they who suffer persecution for justice's sake, for theirs is the kingdom of heaven." Margaret Pole was beatified by Pope Leo XIII in 1886. The Catholic Church honors her as Blessed Margaret Pole and celebrates her life and martyrdom on May 28.

Our Church Teaches

In the Ten Commandments God reveals his will. For example, the First Commandment forbids testing God, showing disrespect for Sacraments and sacred objects and people dedicated to God. If we knowingly and freely choose to do evil, we sin. The more we follow God's will, the greater our freedom becomes.

When we are faced with making a choice between good or evil, our conscience helps us know the difference. We should always follow our conscience and choose what is good. Sometimes fear can lead someone to make the choice for evil. If our conscience is not well informed, we can also make the incorrect choice out of ignorance. We can form our conscience by learning Church teachings, listening to the Sacred Scripture and Tradition, seeking the advice of parents or other adults, and praying for the guidance of the Holy Spirit.

We Believe

Grace is a gift from God. Grace and our conscience help us know and choose what is right.

Activities

1. What do Blessed Margaret Pole's last words tell you about the kind of person she was and how she made her decisions?

_____

_____

_____

2. Margaret followed her conscience. We too are called to follow our conscience when making decisions.

Name a specific moral decision a person your age might have to make.

_____

What do teachings of the Catholic Church say about this decision?

_____

What Scripture passage guides you in making this decision?

_____

Who among your parents, teachers, and friends could give you good guidance?

_____

What might you ask of the Holy Spirit to help you to make a good decision?

_____

What decision would you make?

_____

What helps Catholics understand the doctrines of the faith?

Respond

Doctors of the Church

Some of the saints have been declared Doctors of the Church. Their writings help people understand the doctrine and faith of the Church. Saint Robert Bellarmine (1542–1621) and Saint Catherine of Siena (1347–1380) are two Doctors of the Church.

Saint Robert Bellarmine was born in Montepulciano, Italy. He entered the Jesuit order, was ordained a priest in 1570, became a cardinal in 1599, and was ordained an archbishop in 1602. He spent a great deal of time confronting theological controversies and heresies for the Church. As a consultor of the Holy Office, he examined Galileo's writings. In 1616, Bellarmine warned Galileo not to defend the theories of Nicolaus Copernicus, whose scientific theories were incorrectly believed to be in conflict with Scripture.

Saint Robert Bellarmine

Bellarmine was also a respected teacher and defender of the faith against Protestantism. He was canonized in 1930 and declared a Doctor of the Church in 1931. His feast day is September 17.

Saint Catherine of Siena was born in Italy in the fourteenth century. As a young child she

Saint Catherine of Siena

had visions of Jesus Christ. When she was 16, Catherine became a member of the Third Order of Saint Dominic, or Dominicans. She visited many regions of Italy, where she was known for her ability to keep peace between cities and within the Church.

For seventy-four years, Popes had not been living in Rome but in Avignon, France. Saint Catherine's persuaded Pope Gregory XI to return to Rome from Avignon in 1377. Saint Catherine was also respected for her wisdom in answering difficult theological questions and for her spiritual writings, such as the *Dialogue of St. Catherine*. In it, she wrote, "The soul, who is lifted by a very great and yearning desire for the honor of God and the salvation of souls, begins by exercising herself . . . in the ordinary virtues, remaining in the cell of self-knowledge, in order to know better the goodness of God towards her. . . . [O]nly when she has attained love, can she strive to follow and to clothe herself with the truth."

Saint Catherine was canonized in 1461 and declared a Doctor of the Church in 1970. Her feast day is April 30.

Activities

1. The Doctors of the Church, or great teachers of the Catholic Church, helped others understand the faith and doctrine of the Church. Who in your everyday life helps you understand and follow the teachings of the Catholic faith? How?

_____

_____

_____

_____

_____

2. Saint Francis de Sales wrote about the need to always make a conscious choice to follow Jesus. When have you been called to make this choice? Circle Yes or No following each question below. If your answer is Yes, recall how you responded to the temptation. You will not be asked to share your responses.

Have you ever been tempted to . . .
cheat on a test? **Yes   No**

_____

copy someone's homework? **Yes   No**

_____

tell a lie? **Yes   No**

_____

not help someone in need? **Yes   No**

_____

ignore people you don't like? **Yes   No**

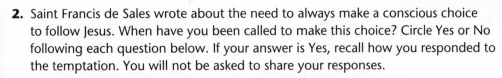

3. How important are the following freedoms? Rate each item by marking an X under Very Important, Somewhat Important, or Not Important. Discuss the reasons for your responses as a class.

The freedom to . . .	Very Important	Somewhat Important	Not Important
pray anytime or anywhere you want.			
tell others about the Catholic faith.			
confess your sins to a priest.			
learn more about your religion.			
read the Bible.			
learn more about saints and other Catholic heroes.			
discuss moral questions with friends.			

How do we pray to stay close to Jesus?

235

✝ Prayer Celebration

A Prayer for Trust

Saint Teresa of Jesus (Teresa of Ávila) said that mental prayer was nothing but friendly and frequent conversation with Jesus, who loves us. She wrote, "If you are happy, look upon your Risen Lord. . . . If you are sad, . . . look upon Him bending under the weight of the cross." She urged us to simply be with Jesus.

The following prayer was found in Saint Teresa's prayer book after she died. As you pray her prayer together, keep an image of Jesus Christ in your mind.

Nada te turbe,	Let nothing disturb you,
Nada te espante;	Let nothing frighten you;
Todo se pasa;	All things are passing;
Dios no se muda!	God never changes!
La paciencia	Patient endurance
Todo lo alcanza;	Gains all things;
Quien Dios tiene	Who possesses God
Nada le falta;	Needs nothing else;
Sólo Dios basta.	God alone is enough.

A **Write** a brief summary of what you learned about Catholics in England during the time of King Henry VIII, using words from the box.

> King Henry VIII
> divorce
> Oath of Supremacy
> Church of England
> recusants
> Margaret Pole

_____

_____

_____

_____

_____

_____

B **Circle** the letter of the best answer.

1. The ability to choose to do what is morally right or what is morally wrong is known as _____.
   a. Original Sin
   b. temptation
   c. free will
   d. grace

2. _____ is the teaching that God determines whether our souls are saved or damned before we are born.
   a. Original Sin
   b. Predestination
   c. Free will
   d. Total depravity

3. To help keep doctrine faithful to Scripture and Tradition, the Church _____.
   a. relied on the Inquisition
   b. started the Reformation
   c. built more monasteries
   d. moved the pope's residence to Avignon

4. In the Ten Commandments God reveals his _____.
   a. glory
   b. will
   c. grace
   d. mercy

5. The more we follow God's will, the greater our _____ becomes.
   a. freedom
   b. grace
   c. Salvation
   d. forgiveness

C Write the name of the person described by each clue.

1. I was known for my counsel to popes and was declared a Doctor of the Church.

_____

2. I made a pilgrimage following in the footsteps of Paul the Apostle and offered an apology

for occasions when sons and daughters of the Catholic Church have sinned against their

Orthodox brothers and sisters. _____

3. I taught that people could achieve Salvation only through having faith and that

Christian teaching should be guided only by the Scriptures. _____

4. I was a famous teacher and defender of the faith against Protestantism. I

examined Galileo's writings and warned him not to defend the theories of

Nicolaus Copernicus. _____

5. I wrote *An Introduction to a Devout Life* to defend Catholic doctrine against the

teachings of Calvin. _____

D Respond to the following.

1. What does Saint Teresa of Ávila's (Teresa of Jesus') prayer tell you about her belief in God?

_____

_____

2. Rewrite Saint Teresa's prayer. Apply it to your life.

_____

_____

3. How do conscience and grace help us do God's will?

_____

_____

Get CONNECTED
with family and friends

Seeking a Common Prayer

Catholicism has a rich tradition of prayer that brings us closer to God and to one another. In this chapter, you will examine prayer and its role in Catholic life. You will also learn about the growth of the Catholic Church in America and its relationship to other Christian denominations. God's plan for humanity is that all people may be one.

Activity

My friends and I feel like we are being pulled in all directions. It's hard for us to know who is in, who is out, and who is making the rules. The "social power brokers" at school put pressure on us to wear the right clothes, say the right things, and act a certain way. We just wish that we could be ourselves and still be accepted.

Jesus does not play by the rules of the "in" crowd. Jesus loves us for who we are. He does not judge us by our looks, popularity, intelligence, or athletic ability. We are always welcome to accept his love. We can do this through prayer, either alone or with others.

Do one of the following.

1. Get together with your friends and name each other's special qualities. Pray that each of you will use these qualities to have a positive effect on others.

2. Encourage family members to write petitions on note cards. Place the cards in a bowl. Invite each person to select a card and pray each day for the request on the card.

 Trivia

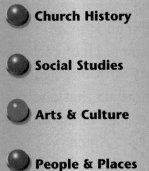

- Church History
- Social Studies
- Arts & Culture
- People & Places

Gerard Manley Hopkins, a Jesuit priest and poet who lived in the nineteenth century, had a unique way of expressing his thoughts and deep appreciation for God in nature. His poem "Pied Beauty" praises God for the beauty of the natural world he created.

Quotable Scripture

Do not let the sun set on your anger.

—Ephesians 4:26

Get CONNECTED

with family and friends

✠ Scripture Background

In the Time of Jesus

Mustard Seed   The mustard plant is one of the many plants mentioned in the Bible. Few plants grew as large as the mustard plant in such a short time. A fully-grown mustard plant could reach ten feet tall and was a favorite of birds. Some varieties grew wild, while others were cultivated for their flavorful seeds. Its seeds were used in foods and for medicinal purposes. Jesus told the parable of the Mustard Seed to illustrate how God's kingdom, from small beginnings, will grow to welcome and shelter all people in peace and justice.

Read the parable of the Mustard Seed in Mark 4:26–34.

WEEKLY PLANNER

On Sunday

While praying the Lord's Prayer at Mass, remember all Christians who also pray the words that Jesus taught us.

On the Web

blestarewe.com

Visit our Web site for the saint of the day and the reflection question of the week.

Saint of the Week

Saint Rose Philippine Duchesne (1769–1852)

Rose Duchesne became a religious sister in France at age nineteen and later helped establish religious communities in France. At age forty-nine, Rose became a missionary to the United States. She spent the last years of her life working among Native Americans, teaching and ministering to them.

Feast Day: November 18

A Prayer for the Week

Holy Spirit, help us celebrate what we have in common with all Christians. Help each of us pray with one heart and mind so that one day we may all be united in Christ. Amen.

16 Seeking a Common Prayer

Let everything that has breath
give praise to the LORD!   *Psalm 150:6*

Share

"The immense multitude of people of every origin is called to give glory to God. . . . Like [Saint] Paul, the disciples of Christ face a great challenge: they are to transmit the Good News by expressing it in a manner suited to each culture, without losing its content or altering its meaning. Do not be afraid to bear witness to this joyful news among your brothers and sisters, by your word and by your whole life: God loves everyone and calls them to be one family in love, for they are all brothers and sisters!

"This joyful news should inspire all Christ's disciples to seek ardently the paths of unity."

Pope John Paul II, homily for Mass,
Damascus, May 6, 2001

You probably have several friends who are Christian but not Catholic, and you may be aware of differences between your practices and doctrines and theirs. The worship and prayer of different Christian communities, however, have many of the same roots.

Activity

What ways of hearing, following, and spreading Christ's message do all Christians share? Circle all the ways that apply. Then add two examples of your own.

praying

studying the Scriptures

worshiping God

giving aid to people who need it

trying to live by Jesus' example

following the Ten Commandments

teaching Christ's message to others

_____

_____

_____

_____

What is
religious
pluralism?

November 10, 1791

We pray Thee, O God of might, wisdom and justice, through Whom authority is rightly administered, laws are enacted, and judgment decreed, assist with Thy holy spirit of counsel and fortitude the President of the United States, that his administration be conducted in righteousness, and be eminently useful to Thy people over whom he presides; by encouraging due respect for virtue and religion; by a faithful execution of the laws in justice and mercy; and by restraining vice and immorality.

Let the light of Thy divine wisdom direct the deliberations of Congress, and shine forth in all the proceedings and laws framed for our rule and government, so that they may tend to the preservation of peace, the promotion of national happiness, the increase of industry, sobriety and useful knowledge; and may perpetuate to us the blessing of equal liberty.

Catholicism in the New World

The above prayer is by John Carroll, a Jesuit priest from Maryland who became the first Catholic bishop in the United States in 1790. Charles Carroll, his cousin, signed the Declaration of Independence in 1776. The appointment of John Carroll as the first bishop and the selection of Baltimore, Maryland, as the first American diocese came at a time when the Catholic Church in the United States was just beginning to grow. But the country established by the Constitution wasn't always a place where Catholics could freely and openly participate in public life.

The settlers who came to America and settled the thirteen colonies along its eastern coast between 1607 and 1733 were primarily people of the Reformation. Mostly Puritans and Pilgrims seeking a life free from the restrictions of the established Church of England, these settlers also distrusted Catholics and the Catholic Church. With the exception of Maryland and Pennsylvania, the colonies forbade the practice of Catholic faith. Catholics had to prove their loyalty.

John and Charles Carroll became examples of loyal Catholic citizens who were dedicated to the growth of the new nation. Once the Constitution separated the Church from the State, and the First Amendment to the Constitution provided freedom of religion to all, Catholics were permitted to practice their faith freely. As bishop of Baltimore, John Carroll was able to organize the Catholic Church in the United States. Today, there are approximately 450 Catholic bishops, more than 190 dioceses, and over 77 million Catholics in the United States.

Missions in the Americas

In many parts of the New World, Catholicism spread through the missionary work of the Church. Christopher Columbus brought Spanish Franciscans with him on his second voyage to America in 1493. These missionaries spread the Gospel to the native peoples. Beginning in 1539, Spanish Franciscan missionaries worked in the southwestern United States. Many cities, such as San Diego, began as missions. Junípero Serra, a Franciscan, settled nine Catholic missions in California. Jesuits from France brought Christianity to California and Canada. Latin America, settled by people from Spain and Portugal, also became Catholic. The missionaries also provided for the physical care of the native peoples.

Religious Influences in America

American democracy made religious pluralism, or the free existence of a variety of religions in society, possible. Freedom of religion meant that all Christian **denominations** could flourish in the United States.

Before the Bible was available in the **vernacular**, the language of the people, Latin was the language of the Bible and the liturgy—a language that only the clergy and educated laypeople could read or understand. In the seventeenth and eighteenth centuries, as the division between Christians in Europe widened, preaching the Word of God in the vernacular was vital to the life of Christians and became the ordinary way to educate Christians in the faith. This tradition of public preaching remains vital in the Church and has influenced religious life in the United States. For example, Archbishop Fulton J. Sheen (1858–1979) continued this tradition by preaching on network television in the 1950s.

The Catholic Church, however, teaches that in addition to hearing the Word of God participating in the sacramental life of the Church and assenting in faith to the Tradition of the Church are necessary for Salvation.

Worship and Prayer

Almost all Christian faith communities have liturgical calendars and seasons, celebrate sacred rites, and devote themselves to prayer. The Catholic Church's official public daily prayer is the **Liturgy of the Hours**, which has its roots in Jewish prayer and was developed by early monastic communities.

GO TO *the Liturgical Year Calendar on page 318 to learn more about the Catholic Church's liturgical seasons, celebrations, and holy days of obligation.*

Activity

What contributes most to your spiritual life? Rank the following items from 1 to 6, with 1 being the most important.

Hearing the homily at Mass _____

Reading Scripture _____

Receiving the Sacraments _____

Learning Church Tradition _____

Praying _____

Other: _____

Faith Words

denomination A denomination is an individual, organized religious body that is a form of a particular faith.

vernacular The vernacular is the language that is native to the people of a region or a country.

Liturgy of the Hours The Liturgy of the Hours is the Church's official prayer for certain times of the day and night. It is also called the *Divine Office*. It consists of psalms, readings, hymns, and prayers.

Why is Christian unity important?

Hear & Believe

From Secrecy to Survival

Because the American colonies in the 1700s were under English rule, Catholics in the New World were subject to the same harsh laws as Catholics in England. In many places, Catholics had to pay double taxes on property and were forbidden to hold worship services.

At that time, the Catholic Church was an underground Church. A few brave priests came from Europe to minister to Catholics in the colonies. Father Ferdinand Farmer (1720–1786), a Jesuit, whose real name was Steinmeyer, was among them. Father Farmer traveled constantly, bringing the Sacraments to Catholics in New Jersey, New York, Philadelphia, and Maryland. He baptized, witnessed marriages, and celebrated Mass in secret with small groups. There were no church buildings and few supports for these missionaries. At the time of Father Farmer's death in 1786, there were only twenty-four priests in the United States.

Eventually, thanks to the religious pluralism ensured by the U.S. Constitution, the Catholic Church thrived in the United States. Although

religious pluralism is better than religious oppression, Catholics today work for the unity of all Christians. As we read in this passage from Ephesians, even in the Church's early days, there were calls for all Christians to be one.

You are members of God's household built on the foundation of the Apostles and prophets. Christ, its cornerstone, holds you together as the Lord's holy temple, being built into a house of the Spirit.

Based on Ephesians 2:19–22

A Closer Look

The Book of Common Prayer

In 1549 the *Book of Common Prayer,* based on the Catholic Church's prayer and liturgy, was authorized for use in the Church of England. Thomas Cranmer, Archbishop of Canterbury, had compiled it. After several revisions, it now contains Scripture, prayers, and rites of worship and is used by Anglicans and Episcopalians in 163 countries.

Our Church Teaches

Christ meant his Church to be one Body, unified in him. But as the Church grew, certain disagreements damaged the unity of the Church. Large Christian communities left the Catholic Church and were formed during the Reformation. Guided by the Holy Spirit we must work toward uniting all Christians. The Holy Spirit leads all in worship,

We Believe

The Holy Spirit works through all Christians to bring them to the truth of the Gospel.
We pray to the Holy Spirit to unite us.

prayer, and good works. All who have been baptized into Christ are brothers and sisters in Christ and are called to be one in him. The Holy Spirit calls us to work for the unity of Christians. The Lord's Prayer is the most perfect prayer for all Christians. It is the prayer all Christians have embraced since the beginning of the Church.

Activities

1. Both the Christians of the first century and Catholics in the United States in the eighteenth century were persecuted for their faith. List some hardships that each group endured.

_____

_____

_____

What finally helped each group flourish?

_____

_____

_____

2. List some of the effects of religious freedom in today's world.

_____

_____

_____

Conflicts based on religious intolerance can cause uncertainty and fear. How can your faith help you deal with those feelings?

_____

_____

What religious sister aided the growth of the Church in the United States?

Respond

Saint Rose Philippine Duchesne

Nine million Catholics immigrated to the United States between 1820 and 1920. Many were poor and had no or little formal education. Some opposition toward Catholics increased at this time, but this was also a period of growth for the Catholic Church. Many parishes were established, formed by people of the same nationality or language. An immigrant saint, Rose Philippine Duchesne, established schools and convents in the United States around this time.

Rose Philippine Duchesne left France for the United States in 1818, at the age of forty-nine, to lead a group of Catholics in missionary activity west of the Mississippi. She had already proven her courage and strength during a period of religious persecution in France. In the middle of the French Revolution, during which convents were destroyed and Catholics killed, Rose had helped shelter priests and care for political prisoners.

Born in Grenoble, France, in 1769, Rose came from a prominent family. Against the wishes of her father, she joined the Visitation Sisters when she was seventeen, but the convent was shut down in 1792 during the French Revolution. When the Revolution ended, Rose returned to the convent to reestablish the community of sisters, spent several years doing charitable works, and took her religious vows as a member of the Society of the Sacred Heart in 1804.

In the United States, Mother Duchesne opened schools and orphanages for the children of pioneers and for Native American people and the first Sacred Heart convents in America. In 1841, Mother Duchesne was sent to a mission at Sugar Creek in present-day Kansas. The Potawatomi Indians who lived there called her "the woman who prays always." While she suffered much the last years of her life, her missionary spirit and single-mindedness never weakened. She died in 1852 at age eighty-three.

Mother Duchesne was canonized in 1988. "With missionary courage," commented Blessed Pope John Paul II, "this great pioneer looked to the future with the eyes of the heart—a heart that was on fire with God's love." Her feast day is November 18.

Activities

1. Why were the schools and convents that Rose founded so vital for the growth of the Church in the United States?

_____

_____

_____

_____

_____

_____

_____

2. Rose Philippine Duchesne stayed focused on spreading Christ's message through missionary work. What Christian activities would you like to focus on? In the space below, write a prayer of petition. Write down the time each day that you will remind yourself to pray the petition asking God to help you to achieve this goal.

Time of day to pray this prayer: _____

3. Read the following story about preaching as a way of spreading Christ's message. Then complete the activity.

"You got to feed on God's Word!" the preacher's voice booms as the camera shows the congregation, nodding in agreement and shouting, 'Amen!' "

Besides listening to the Bible proclaimed, in what other ways do people hear the Gospel message? On the lines below, write two examples.

_____

_____

_____

_____

How do we pray as one family of God?

Prayer Celebration

A Prayer for Christian Unity

Jesus prayed to his Father that everyone "may be brought to perfection as one, that the world may know that you sent me, and that you loved them even as you loved me" (John 17:23). Jesus' prayer calls all Christians to be one in belief and worship. Let us pray for the fulfillment of Jesus' prayer.

All: In the name of the Father, the Son, and the Holy Spirit. Amen.

Leader: God, the one Father of all, you know our ways and have brought us together. From wherever we come, in Christ, your Son, our separated ways are united. In you we are linked together.

Reader 1: Lord Jesus, you are "the way." Give us courage to leave behind our self-centeredness and walk on the way to unity for the glory of your name.

All: Glory be to the Father and to the Son and to the Holy Spirit, as it was in the beginning is now, and ever shall be world without end. Amen.

Reader 2: Lord Jesus, you are "the truth." May we seek your truth from every corner of the earth for the glory of your name.

All: Glory be to the Father and to the Son and to the Holy Spirit, as it was in the beginning is now, and ever shall be world without end. Amen.

Reader 3: Lord Jesus, you are "the life." Guide us to find that unity which will give us your life in its fullness for the glory of your name.

All: Glory be to the Father and to the Son and to the Holy Spirit, as it was in the beginning is now, and ever shall be world without end. Amen.

Based on the Order of Worship for an Ecumenical Service, Prayer for Christian Unity 2001, *Pontifical Council for Promoting Christian Unity*

16 Chapter Review

A **Complete** the sentences with words from the box.

1. With the exception of Maryland and Pennsylvania, the American colonies forbade the practice of
_____.

2. The first diocese in the United States was
_____.

3. An individual, organized body that is a form of a particular faith is a _____.

4. The Church's official daily prayer for certain times of the day and night is the _____.

5. The U.S. Constitution ensures the practice of _____, or the free existence of religion in society.

6. In Ephesians we read that through Jesus, the Church would be built into a
_____ of the Holy Spirit.

7. The _____ calls us to pray and work for the unity of all Christians.

8. In colonial America the Catholic Church was forced to worship
_____.

9. The language that is native to a region or country is the _____.

10. In many parts of the New World, Catholicism spread through _____.

religious pluralism
Catholicism
underground
Holy Spirit
missionary work
Baltimore
vernacular
denomination
house
Liturgy of the Hours

B **Explain** why the Lord's Prayer is a good prayer to promote Christian unity.

_____

_____

_____

C **Match** Column A with Column B by writing the correct number in the space provided.

A

1. John Carroll

2. Junípero Serra

3. Father Farmer

4. Charles Carroll

5. Rose Philippine Duchesne

B

___ Jesuit priest who faced many hardships to minister to Catholics in colonial America

___ signed the Declaration of Independence

___ established schools, convents, and orphanages in the United States

___ ministered to Catholics in the western United States and established nine missions

___ was the first Catholic bishop in the United States

D **Describe** why the unity of all Christians is something to strive for. What can we do to promote this unity?

_____

_____

_____

_____

_____

E **Write** a prayer in which you ask God to take away one of the divisions in Christianity. Be specific about which division and what you are asking God to do about it.

_____

_____

_____

_____

Faith in Action

Altar Servers Altar servers carry the cross and processional candles at Mass. They hold the Roman Missal, or book of prayers used at Mass, for the priest when he is not at the altar. They assist at receiving the bread, wine, and water at the Preparation of the Altar and Gifts and pour the water for the priest to wash his hands. Altar servers participate with the assembly in making prayer responses and singing songs and are models of grace and reverence. Learning responsibility and organization, they serve Jesus in many ways as they grow in their faith and love for God.

In Everyday Life

Activity What are some roles you have or have had, such as babysitter, camp counselor, or older brother or sister, that have given you special responsibilities? Name at least two roles and describe the responsibilities that came with each.

1. _____

   _____

2. _____

   _____

In Your Parish

Activity If you have ever served as altar server or simply observed the actions of altar servers at Mass, you can surely identify qualities that are essential for the role. For example, if the altar server is inattentive to the priest, they may not be ready to assist him as needed. Therefore, it is important for an altar server to be attentive. Name at least two other qualities an altar server must have and tell why each is important.

_____

_____

_____

_____

Faith in Action

Peter's Pence On the Sunday nearest to the Solemnity of Saints Peter and Paul, Apostles (June 29), Catholic parishes around the world take up a special collection to support the pope's charitable and missionary works. This tradition started about a thousand years ago in England. Each family gave one penny, or pence, to the pope to help needy people in all parts of the world. Peter's Pence reminds us that we belong to one worldwide Church called to bring God's love to all people.

In Everyday Life

Activity When a group of people work together to achieve a goal, each person's contribution, no matter how small, helps the group reach the goal. Name a time when you helped out in a small way to achieve a goal as part of a group or a team. Tell how it felt to be part of this effort and achieve success.

_____

_____

_____

_____

_____

In Your Parish

Activity Throughout the world there are many people in need. The Church comes to the aid of these people in many ways, providing food, clothing, medicine, education, and other services. In the space below, name one place in the world where charitable work is needed. Then name one way that you can contribute to the Church's work of helping the poor in that place.

Place:

_____

How I can help:

_____

_____

_____

In the empty shapes that surround each of the four chapter titles, write words or phrases that you learned in the chapter. Use the words or phrases in the box below.

Book of Common Prayer	Protestant Reformation	vernacular
predestination	free will	pagan missions
Martin Luther	Counter-Reformation	Saint Francis de Sales
Inquisition	California missions	Bishop John Carroll
Rite of Penance	Scripture and Tradition	
indulgences	Bartolomé de Las Casas	

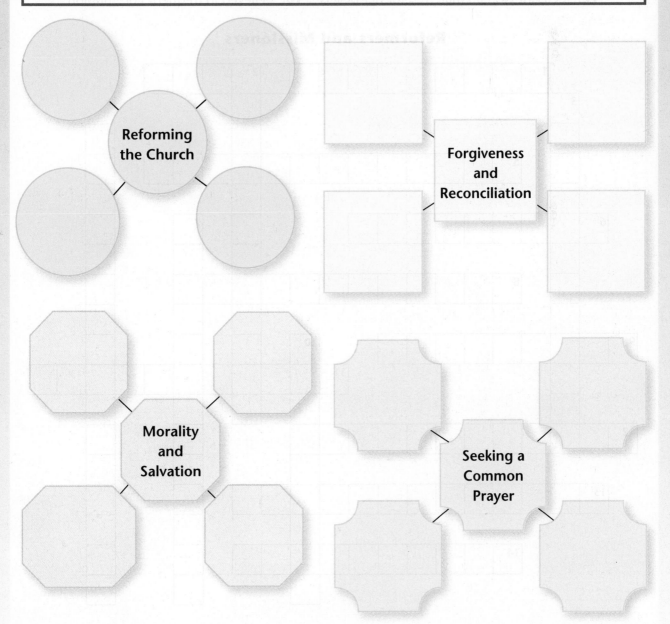

Reforming the Church

Forgiveness and Reconciliation

Morality and Salvation

Seeking a Common Prayer

4 Unit Review

A **Complete** the crossword puzzle.

Across

1. Spanish Carmelite friar
5. settled nine California missions
6. executed Thomas More
8. posted ninety-five theses on the castle church door
9. Teresa of Ávila's (Teresa of Jesus') order
11. first Catholic bishop in the United States
12. recusant woman martyred for her beliefs

13. preached the Gospel in India
14. reformer Bishop Batholomé _____

Down

2. "the woman who prays always"
3. ministered to Catholics in colonial America
4. founded the Society of Jesus
7. reformed her religious order
10. believed in frequent communion

Reformers and Missioners

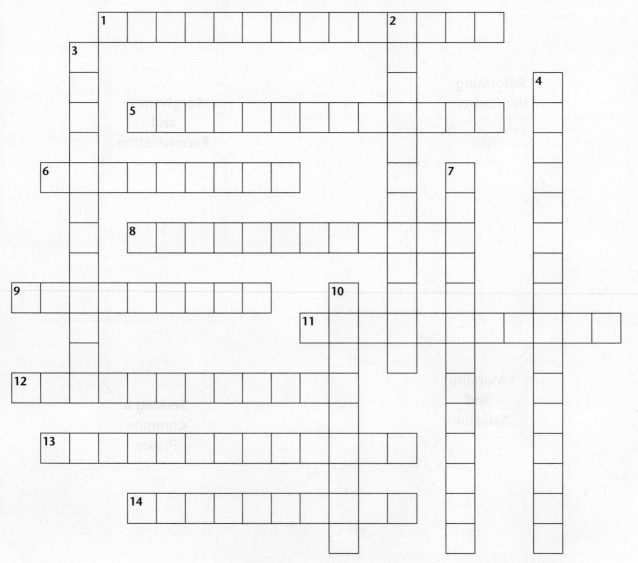

B **Circle the word or phrase that best completes the sentence.**

1. Jesus established his Church _____.
   a. to conquer the Romans
   b. to continue his mission of Salvation
   c. to exclude people with different beliefs
   d. to establish a national religion

2. Jesus cured the paralytic to show _____.
   a. his power to baptize
   b. his power to forgive sins
   c. his power to raise the dead
   d. his power to feed the multitudes

3. In Greece in 2001, Blessed Pope John Paul II _____.
   a. retraced Peter's footsteps
   b. rejected Orthodox Christian beliefs
   c. apologized to the Orthodox Church
   d. reunited the Orthodox Church to Rome

4. It is necessary to have _____ to understand God's Revelation.
   a. Scripture and Tradition
   b. Scripture alone
   c. Confirmation and Holy Orders
   d. Baptism and Eucharist

5. Catherine of Siena and Robert Bellarmine had all these in common except _____.
   a. both were members of religious orders
   b. both were Doctors of the Church
   c. both wrote about difficult matters of doctrine and faith
   d. both were martyrs

C **Match the Faith Words in Column A with the definitions in Column B.**

A

1. indulgence
2. Purgatory
3. Protestant Reformation
4. Sacrament of Penance and Reconciliation
5. denomination
6. predestination
7. free will
8. vernacular
9. Liturgy of the Hours

B

___ the teaching that God determines whether our souls are saved or damned before we are born

___ the language that is native to a region or country

___ a final purification from sin after death

___ a sixteenth-century movement aimed at reforming some doctrine and practices of the Catholic Church

___ a Sacrament of Healing in which Catholics ask forgiveness for sin and are reconciled with God and the Church

___ the Church's official prayer for certain times of the day and night

___ the freedom to choose to do what is morally right or what is morally wrong

___ an individual, organized religious body that is a form of a particular faith

___ the removal of all or some of the temporal punishments that we must suffer in Purgatory for our sins

D Fill in the correct word to complete each sentence.

1. The early Church saw _____ as a "second Baptism."

2. During the Counter-Reformation, the Church defended itself against the attacks of the _____.

3. The _____ helped to renew and reform the Catholic Church.

4. God always finds a way to forgive his people who cry out to him with _____ hearts.

5. In the Sacrament of Penance and Reconciliation, the _____ is the visible sign of Jesus Christ.

E Respond to the following.

Teresa of Ávila (Teresa of Jesus) wrote, "If you are happy, look upon your Risen Lord. . . . If you are sad, . . . look upon him bending under the weight of the cross."

1. Write a prayer of contrition to Jesus bending under the weight of the cross.

_____

_____

_____

2. Write a prayer for Christian unity to the Risen Lord.

_____

_____

_____

3. Write the prayer of Teresa of Ávila (Teresa of Jesus) that you learned in this unit.

_____

_____

_____

Returning to the Roots of Christianity

Grounded in the Gospel of Jesus Christ, the Catholic faith is expressed in new ways in every age to meet the challenges of contemporary life. We are called to be part of this renewal of the Gospel in our age.

Be heralds of hope. Be messengers of joy. Be true workers of justice.
Blessed Pope John Paul II

The brilliant baptistery of Sacré Coeur in France expresses in art the same faith shown by Blessed Mother Teresa's care of the poor.

Send Down the Fire

Marty Haugen

with family and friends

Modern Ecumenical Councils

The Second Vatican Council is the most recent of three Ecumenical Councils held since the Reformation. Each Council was called to respond to the needs of the Church and to reaffirm her doctrine and moral teaching. In 1545, the Council of Trent initiated a number of reforms that are part of our Catholic heritage today.

Activity

Michelle's parents want to know where she is and who she is with at all times. One day, she told her parents she was going to spend the afternoon at a friend's house. Instead, Michelle and her friend met up with two boys at the mall. Michelle's older sister saw them and told her mother. Michelle's parents were unhappy. Michelle, in turn, was angry with her sister.

Even in the happiest of families and among the best of friends, conflicts occur. If they are resolved properly, however, conflicts can actually help relationships grow stronger. But conflicts that remain unresolved can damage family happiness and shatter friendships.

Do one of the following.

1. How do you and your friends deal with conflict? Note the strategies that best resolve conflicts.

2. Identify a conflict in your family that remains unresolved. Get together with family members to develop a strategy for resolving the conflict.

Church History

Social Studies

Arts & Culture

People & Places

Antonio Gaudí (1852–1926) was one of the most famous modernist architects of the twentieth century. Gaudí's work was inspired by his deep faith in God and his love of nature. His most famous work is the unfinished church *La Sagrada Família* in Barcelona, Spain.

Quotable Scripture

"You are the light of the world... Just so, your light must shine before others, that they may see your good deeds and glorify your heavenly Father."
—Matthew 5:14, 16

Get CONNECTED
with family and friends

✝ Scripture Background

In the Early Church

The City of Corinth   During the first century A.D., many people passed through the city of Corinth in Greece. Merchants stopped at this busy seaport when traveling between Rome and Asia Minor. The city of Corinth was well-known throughout the Mediterranean world as a commercial center. Unfortunately, Corinth was also known for its corruption and immorality. Paul took on the challenge of establishing the Church in this prosperous city. After he left Corinth, Paul continued to guide the Church in Corinth through his writings.

Read 1 Corinthians 12:12–26 for Paul's message to the Corinthians about unity and variety of gifts within the church.

WEEKLY PLANNER

On Sunday
Make a special effort to extend the Sign of Peace to someone you do not know.

On the Web
blestarewe.com

 Visit our Web site for the saint of the day and the reflection question of the week.

Saint of the Week
Saint Francis Xavier
(1506–1552)

Saint Francis Xavier is known as the "Apostle of the Indies and Japan" because of his missionary work in India and Japan. He is credited with baptizing thousands in the Far East. With Saint Ignatius Loyola, he founded the Society of Jesus, or the Jesuits.

Feast Day: December 3

A Prayer for the Week

Teach us, Lord, to respect others as your children, learn from our differences, bring peace where there is conflict, and cherish your love. Amen.

17 Modern Ecumenical Councils

Put on then, as God's chosen ones, . . . heartfelt compassion, . . . and patience, bearing with one another and forgiving one another.

Colossians 3:12–13

Share

Jeanine watched as her mother piled ingredients into a big bowl. Mom began to mix flour, salt, sugar, eggs, milk, and yeast together with her hands.

"You haven't measured anything," said Jeanine. "How do you know how much to put in?"

"The recipe is in my head and in my heart," Mom said. "I know from the feel of the dough when it is right. My mother taught me, just as I am now teaching you."

Activity

Traditions such as lessons, stories, or rituals are passed on from generation to generation. What traditions have been shared by the generations in your family?

_____

_____

What can you learn about your family from its traditions?

_____

_____

_____

Just as a family passes on its cherished traditions, the Catholic Church passes on the traditions of her faith and practices.

How does our Church family pass on its traditions?

263

Scripture   The Parable of the Sower

Jesus told parables to help his followers understand and live out his teachings. In these parables, Jesus spoke of shepherds and fishermen, travelers and weddings, seeds and birds, sons and fathers. He spoke about things that were familiar to his listeners. This helped his listeners better understand his message and help it take root in their hearts and lives. Jesus told this parable to a crowd that had gathered around him as he sat by the sea.

"A farmer went out to sow some seed. Some seed fell on a footpath, where it was quickly eaten by birds. Some fell on rocky ground. The seed sprang up right away, but the sun scorched it and it died. Other seed fell among thorns, began to grow, but the thorns choked it. But some seed fell on good soil and produced much fruit."

Jesus then explained what the parable meant.

"The seed on the footpath is like a person who hears God's Word but does not really accept it and evil drives it out. The seed on the rocky ground is like a person who hears and understands God's Word but never makes it part of his or her life. The seed in the thorns is like a person who hears the Word of God and begins to live it but lets other concerns crowd it out. The seed in the good soil is like a person who hears the Word of God, understands it, and lives it. The faith of such a person continues to grow and flourish."

Based on Matthew 13:3–9, 18–23

The Church sows the seeds of faith among people of all backgrounds and cultures. It reaches out to people by speaking to them in their own languages, using symbols and customs they understand. In this way, the Church's seeds of faith can land on fertile soil, where they will thrive.

Our Church Teaches

The Sacred Tradition of the Church and Sacred Scripture reveal God's Word to us and guide the Church in carrying out God's will. The Church always makes its Sacred Tradition of faith, worship, moral teaching, and spirituality available to people of every time and culture. The Holy Spirit always guides the Church to meet this chal-

We Believe
Through the guidance of the Holy Spirit, Ecumenical Councils make decisions that help the Church grow.

lenge. The actions and structures of society do not always reflect the Gospel vision of life. The Church works to shed the light of the Gospel on society so that the freedom and dignity of human life are respected. The Holy Spirit always calls and guides the Church to renew herself and face the challenges of each new age.

Activities

1. In what ways and through whom is the Word of God shared with you? How can you become more like the good soil so that God's Word can take root in your life and guide you?

_____

_____

_____

_____

_____

2. Some of the problems and influences in the world today can be like the footpaths, rocky soil, and thorns that keep the seeds of faith from flourishing. What are some hazards that prevent God's Word from taking root in people's lives today? List three on the lines below. Next to each hazard, write one way the Church can work to overcome the hazard.

Hazards in the World Today	How the Church Can Overcome Them
_____	_____
	_____
	_____
_____	_____
	_____
	_____
_____	_____
	_____
	_____

How does the Church prepare for the needs of the future?

✝ Prayer Celebration

A Prayer for Peace

Group 1: Remove from us all that could endanger the cause of peace, and transform us into witnesses of truth, justice, and brotherly love.

Group 2: Enlighten those who preside over the destiny of nations so that, while ensuring the legitimate welfare of their fellow citizens, they uphold the priceless blessing that is peace.

Group 3: Give us the strength to overcome divisions, to reinforce the bonds of mutual love, to understand others, and to forgive those who have caused us harm.

All: Then, because of you, all peoples on Earth will form a real community of love, and peace will forever blossom in their midst.

Based on a prayer of Blessed Pope John XXIII

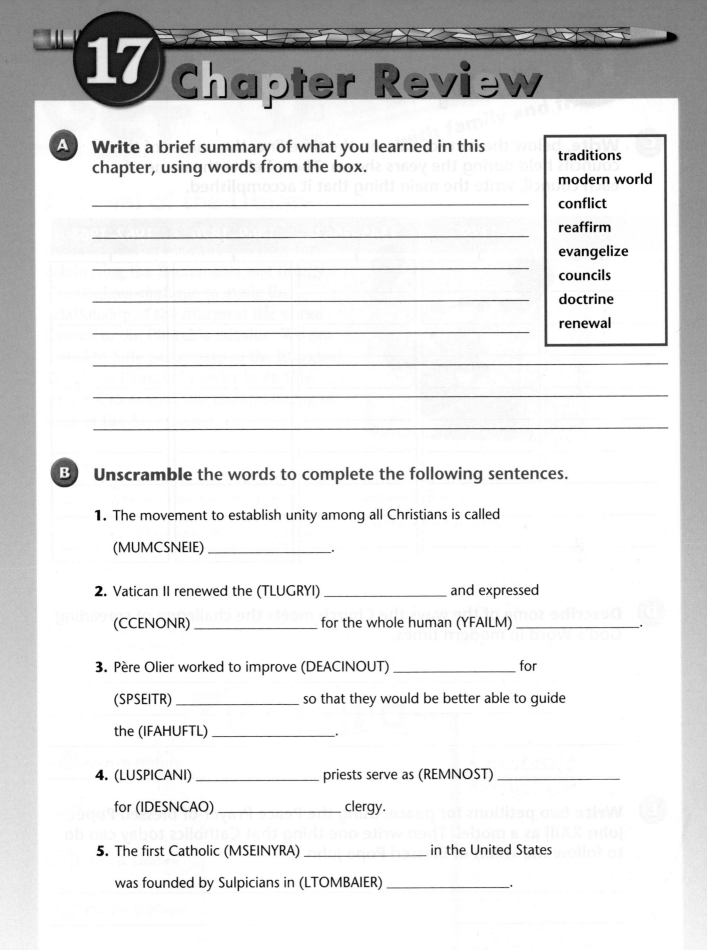

A **Write** a brief summary of what you learned in this chapter, using words from the box.

traditions
modern world
conflict
reaffirm
evangelize
councils
doctrine
renewal

_____

_____

_____

_____

_____

_____

_____

B **Unscramble** the words to complete the following sentences.

1. The movement to establish unity among all Christians is called

(MUMCSNEIE) _____.

2. Vatican II renewed the (TLUGRYI) _____ and expressed

(CCENONR) _____ for the whole human (YFAILM) _____.

3. Père Olier worked to improve (DEACINOUT) _____ for

(SPSEITR) _____ so that they would be better able to guide

the (IFAHUFTL) _____.

4. (LUSPICANI) _____ priests serve as (REMNOST) _____

for (IDESNCAO) _____ clergy.

5. The first Catholic (MSEINYRA) _____ in the United States

was founded by Sulpicians in (LTOMBAIER) _____.

Hear & Believe

✝ Scripture The Christian Community

Vatican II stressed the role the community has in the celebration of the Sacraments In the following letter from James to the early Church, we read about the role of community in the Sacrament of Anointing of the Sick.

If you are suffering, pray. If you are joyful, praise God. If you are sick, ask the presbyters of the Church to visit and anoint you in the name of the Lord. You will be healed and if you have sinned, your sins will be forgiven. Confess your sins and pray for one another.

Heartfelt prayers by holy people are very powerful. Remember that Elijah prayed that no rain would fall, no rain fell on the land. When he prayed for rain, rain came.

If any one among you strays from the truth, other members of the community should bring them back so that they can be saved.

Based on James 5:13–20

We grow in our relationship with God in the community, in the company of others. As a community of healing and prayer, we continue Jesus' work.

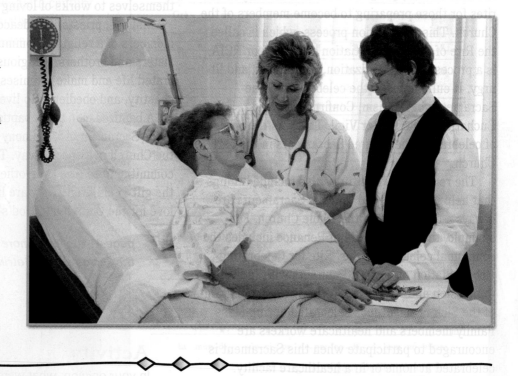

Our Church Teaches

The liturgy is a source of prayer for us. The rite of each Sacrament involves signs, words, or objects that help us pray. Besides participating in the liturgy on Sunday, we keep the Lord's Day holy by spending time with family, visiting the sick, helping the poor, and praying.

Other sources of prayer include the Scriptures and the Theological

We Believe
The Word of God, the liturgy of the Church, and the virtues of faith, hope, and love are sources of prayer.

Virtues of faith, hope, and charity (or love). They are the graces behind the Cardinal Moral Virtues of temperance, prudence, justice, and fortitude. We grow in these virtues when we work hard at practicing them in spite of temptations that might come our way.

 page 416 to learn more about virtues.

Activities

1. Three sources of prayer are the Word of God, the liturgy of the Church, and the Theological Virtues of faith, hope, and love. Name three other things that help you pray.

_____

_____

_____

Pick one of the items you added, and explain how it helps you pray.

_____

_____

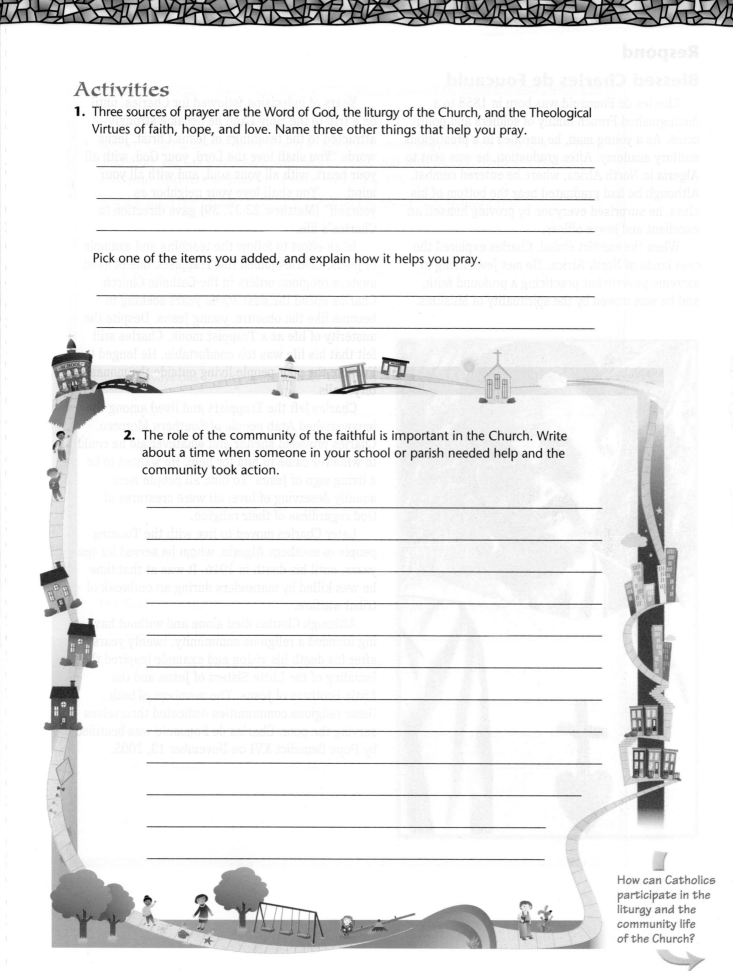

2. The role of the community of the faithful is important in the Church. Write about a time when someone in your school or parish needed help and the community took action.

_____

_____

_____

_____

_____

_____

_____

_____

_____

_____

_____

How can Catholics participate in the liturgy and the community life of the Church?

† Prayer Celebration

A Prayer of Praise

With your class, pray or sing the Gloria, the Church's great hymn of praise to God. Use the prayer postures created by your class.

Gloria

Refrain:

GLORY TO GOD IN THE HIGHEST, AND ON EARTH
PEACE TO PEOPLE OF GOOD WILL.

Verse:

1. We praise you, we bless you, we adore you,
   we glorify you, we give you thanks for your great glory,
   Lord God, heavenly King.
   O God, almighty Father.

2. Lord Jesus Christ, Only Begotten Son,
   Lord God, Lamb of God, Son of the Father,
   you take away the sins of the world, have mercy on us;
   you take away the sins of the world, receive our prayer;
   you are seated at the right hand of the Father,
   have mercy on us.

3. For you alone are the Holy One,
   you alone are the Lord,
   you alone are the Most High Jesus Christ,
   with the Holy Spirit,
   in the glory of God the Father.
   Amen.

Text ICEL, ©2010 Music: *Mass of Creation*, Marty Haugen,
© 1984, 1985, 2010 GIA Publications, Inc.

A **Complete** the sentences about Vatican Council II, using words from the box.

> Latin
> liturgy
> language
> community
> Sacraments
> mission
> Church
> assembly
> Scripture readings
> Second Vatican Council

1. The _____ approved reforms that created a renewal of the Church's _____.

2. Vatican II revised the rites for the celebration of the _____ to emphasize celebrating them as a _____.

3. A change was approved in the _____ of the Mass, which no longer had to be _____.

4. Vatican II affirmed that the whole _____ shares in Christ's _____ to live as priest, prophet, and servant of God.

5. As a result of Vatican II, the number of _____ at Mass was increased, and the priest faced the _____ during Mass.

B **Circle** the letter of the best answer.

1. A process of faith formation that includes education and participation in the life of the Catholic Church is called _____.
   a. apprenticeship
   b. catechesis
   c. discipleship
   d. mentoring

2. _____ is NOT one of the three main functions of priests emphasized by the Second Vatican Council.
   a. Preaching
   b. Administering Sacraments
   c. Translating the Bible
   d. Leading the Church

3. Diocesan priests promise to live a life of celibacy and of _____ to their bishop.
   a. obedience
   b. faith
   c. fortitude
   d. temperance

4. James's letter to the early Church recommended the members of the Church live a life of _____.
   a. patience, love, and gratitude
   b. modesty, humility, and faith
   c. virtue, penance, and devotion
   d. prayer, healing, and forgiveness

Get CONNECTED
with family and friends

✠ Scripture Background

In the Time of Jesus

The Passover Meal The Jewish Passover commemorates the freeing of the Israelites from Egypt. The name *Passover* comes from the Scripture passage "I will pass over you; . . . no destructive blow will come upon you" (Exodus 12:13). Passover was and is the Jewish festival of freedom and redemption. The Last Supper celebrated by Jesus and his disciples was a Passover meal. But Jesus gave Passover a new meaning offering up his Body and Blood—setting us free from slavery to sin, achieving our Redemption so we might have eternal life in Heaven.

Read an account of Jesus' last Passover meal, the Last Supper, in Matthew 26:17–30, Mark 14:2–26, or Luke 22:7–20.

WEEKLY PLANNER

On Sunday

At Mass, listen for prayers about justice for the poor or about peace among nations. Silently add your own prayers for people who need help in your community.

On the Web

blestarewe.com

 Visit our Web site for the saint of the day and the reflection question of the week.

Saint of the Week

Saint Anne
(1st century B.C.)

According to legend, Anne and her husband, Joachim, prayed to God for many years for a child. An angel appeared to Anne and told her she would have a child who would be blessed by the world. Anne gave birth to the Blessed Virgin Mary.

Patron Saint of: Quebec, grandparents

Feast Day: July 26

A Prayer for the Week

Lord, open our eyes to people who are poor and suffering and help us see your presence in their midst. Teach us to share our blessings with those in need. Amen.

19 The Moral Struggle of a New Age

LET US PRAY

If anyone is in need, do not turn away from them.
Freely and generously help them meet their need.

Based on Deuteronomy 15:7–8

Share

People in developed nations are accustomed to having boundless resources—such as water, fuel to power their cars and warm their homes, and nutritious food that is available in abundance. For most of us living in wealthy nations, it is hard to imagine a lifestyle where sanitary drinking water is a rare luxury, where few people can even dream of owning a car, and where meals often consist of little more than a bowl of rice or mashed cornmeal.

People in prosperous nations must strive to share the Earth's resources with their less wealthy neighbors living in poor nations. It is a matter of justice for all people to have what they need to survive and live in dignity.

Activity

List five ways in which people in our country can consume fewer of the world's resources.

1. _____

2. _____

3. _____

4. _____

5. _____

What are some social problems?

Get CONNECTED
with family and friends

✠ Scripture Background

Before the Time of Jesus

Signs of God's Presence   In the Old Testament, God sometimes revealed himself through forces of nature, such as fire, lightning, or storms. Moses experienced God's presence through the burning bush and later as a pillar of fire leading the Israelites through the wilderness. These dramatic sights signaled God's presence and revealed his power and authority.

Read Exodus 19:16–25 to find out how God made his presence known to Moses and the Israelites on Mount Sinai.

WEEKLY PLANNER

On Sunday

On the way to church, invite family members to name something for which they are thankful. After you receive Holy Communion, remember to thank God for all your family's gifts.

On the Web

blestarewe.com

 Visit our Web site for the saint of the day and the reflection question of the week.

Saint of the Week

Mary, Mother of God

The Church celebrates the Solemnity of Mary, the Holy Mother of God, on January 1. Throughout the Church year we celebrate many events relating to Mary, but on this day we celebrate her role as the Mother of the Savior. On this day Catholics around the world also traditionally join in praying for peace.

A Prayer for the Week

Lord, help us open our minds and hearts to recognize you in the people, places, and events of our daily lives. May our awareness of your presence strengthen our faith and trust in you. Amen.

20 A Prayer for the Church

May the LORD give might to his people;
may the LORD bless his people with peace!

Psalm 29:11

Share

Every day, God blesses us. He provides for our needs and gives us moments of opportunity and wonder. We, in turn, bless God for the blessings he gives us. We are all familiar with morning and evening prayers and blessings before and after meals. In such blessings, we give thanks for the gifts of the day and express our hope that we will use our gifts for the good of all. Blessings are an important part of the worship and prayer life of the Church.

Activity

Write a blessing for one of the daily activities listed below. Be sure that your blessing includes elements of thanksgiving and hope.

rising	washing	dressing
going to school	studying	taking a test
helping someone	coming home	being with friends
	going to sleep	

_____

_____

_____

_____

_____

_____

_____

_____

_____

How has the Church been blessed throughout the centuries?

Hear & Believe

What's Next?

During the past year, you have learned a lot about the Catholic faith. You have grown in your knowledge of what it means to live as a Catholic, to be filled with the Holy Spirit, and to follow Jesus. You have deepened your understanding of the Catholic Church, its history, and its goals for the future. You have learned more about the Sacraments of the Church, the liturgy, and other Christians. You have heard stories from Scripture and accounts of people who have lived according to the Gospel. The knowledge you have acquired can help you make good decisions. But knowing lots of facts isn't enough. You also have to live what you have learned.

Jesus' Apostles knew a lot about him. They heard him preach, witnessed his miracles, and experienced his love and concern for all. But Jesus told his followers that it was important to translate their knowledge into actions. At the Last Supper, he advised them:

"Do not let your hearts be troubled. You have faith in God; have faith also in me.

"As the Father loves me, so I also love you. Remain in my love. . . . This is my commandment: love one another as I love you. . . . You are my friends if you do what I command you. . . . It was not you who chose me, but I who chose you and appointed you to go and bear fruit."

John 14:1; 15:9, 12, 14, 16

All of those who follow Jesus are called to put his message into action. All Christians share this mission to go forth and bear fruit. We do this together as the Church, with the grace of the Holy Spirit.

The Last Supper by Fra Angelico. Museo di Marco dell'Angelico, Florence, Italy/Bridgeman Art Library

A CLOSER LOOK

A Life of Prayer

Many men and women serve the Church by joining contemplative religious communities and dedicating their lives to prayer. They separate themselves from the world to concentrate on praising God and praying for our future life in God's kingdom.

Our Church Teaches

Throughout the years, the Church has been blessed by the gifts and talents that many have devoted to building up the People of God. God has given us charisms, or gifts that we are to use to build the Church, marked by strong faith, a desire for justice, and a love of God celebrated in worship.

Christ is our model of respect for ourselves and for all humanity. Modeling ourselves after him will help us

We Believe

In prayer, we ask God for the grace to become true followers of Christ, people who respect all human dignity.

achieve purity of heart—a modesty and decency that comes from within and helps us protect our integrity and the integrity of others. Patiently working at being modest and decent will help us achieve purity of heart. With patience, prayer, and effort, we can overcome the temptation to gossip about others or harm their reputation. We must show awareness of the dignity of all other people in all our words and actions.

Activities

1. What are three things you have learned about the Catholic faith during the past year?

_____

_____

_____

How can you use what you have learned to take action or make changes in your life? In this space, write about putting what you have learned into action.

_____

_____

_____

_____

_____

_____

2. Think about how you can help build up the Church. In the space below, write or draw your ideas.

For what does the Catholic Church pray?

✝ Prayer Celebration

A Prayer for the Church

Leader: Lord God, hear the prayers of your faithful. Help us always to be grateful for your goodness and hopeful for your mercy.

We pray for vocations . . .
(Pray individual prayers from page 304.)

We pray for our nation . . .
(Pray individual prayers from page 304.)

We pray for peace . . .
(Pray individual prayers from page 305.)

We pray for families . . .
(Pray individual prayers from page 305.)

Leader: God our loving Father, we ask these blessings through our Lord Jesus Christ, your Son, who lives and reigns with you and the Holy Spirit, one God, for ever and ever.

All: Amen.

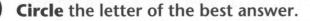

20 Chapter Review

A   **Circle** the letter of the best answer.

1. As we continue Christ's mission, we rely on _____ to lead us.
   a. the news media
   b. the Holy Spirit
   c. elected government officials
   d. someone else

2. In prayers of _____, we give thanks for the gifts of the day and express our hope that we will use our gifts for the good of all.
   a. blessing
   b. petition
   c. contrition
   d. intercession

3. Respecting human dignity means defending and caring for human life _____.
   a. in early childhood
   b. when people are old and sick
   c. whenever it is convenient
   d. at all stages

4. Jesus told his followers that it was important to translate their knowledge into _____.
   a. songs
   b. poetry
   c. actions
   d. writing

5. The Church of the future should be marked by _____.
   a. strong faith
   b. a desire for justice
   c. love of God celebrated in worship
   d. all of the above

B   **Match** Column A with Column B by writing the correct number in the space provided.

A

1. contemplative religious communities

2. alms

3. purity of heart

4. blessings

5. human embryo

B

___ a human being in the early stages of life

___ men and women who separate themselves from the world to concentrate on praising God and praying for our life in the Kingdom of God

___ donations of time, money, or goods to people in need

___ a modesty and decency that comes from within

___ an important part of the worship and prayer life of the Church

A **Fill in** the correct word or words to complete each sentence.

1. Grace before meals is a prayer of _____.

2. Blessed Pope John XXIII wanted Vatican II to open the "Church's _____" to the modern world.

3. Through the guidance of the _____, Ecumenical Councils make decisions that help the Church grow.

4. At the Second Vatican Council the rites for all the _____ were revised to invite greater participation and devotion.

5. A _____ should provide a loving environment.

B **Circle** the letter of the best answer.

1. Just as a family passes on cherished _____, the Catholic Church passes on the _____ of her faith and practices.
   - **a.** photos . . . evidence
   - **b.** traditions . . . traditions
   - **c.** traditions . . . records
   - **d.** recipes . . . results

2. The Second Vatican Council changed the _____ of the Triduum liturgies.
   - **a.** time
   - **b.** meaning
   - **c.** dates
   - **d.** place

3. One of the ways that we show concern for others is by _____.
   - **a.** celebrating Penance and Reconciliation
   - **b.** reading about poor people
   - **c.** giving alms
   - **d.** writing to politicians

4. Social justice requires people with material wealth to _____.
   - **a.** invest it wisely
   - **b.** write a will
   - **c.** save for a rainy day
   - **d.** share with people in need

5. "To go forth and bear fruit" means _____.
   - **a.** to plant a garden
   - **b.** to put Jesus' message into action
   - **c.** to give away one's possessions
   - **d.** to heal the sick

Unit Review

C **Complete** the crossword puzzle.

Across

3. started Vatican II

8. reported on the unjust actions committed by the El Salvadoran government

Down

1. founded the Sulpicians

2. said, "Unless your work is interwoven with love, it is useless."

3. wanted richer nations to share their resources

4. proclaimed *Gaudium et Spes*

5. lived a life of poverty and simplicity in North Africa

6. subject of a parable about spreading God's Word

7. wrote a letter to early Christians advising community, prayer, and healing

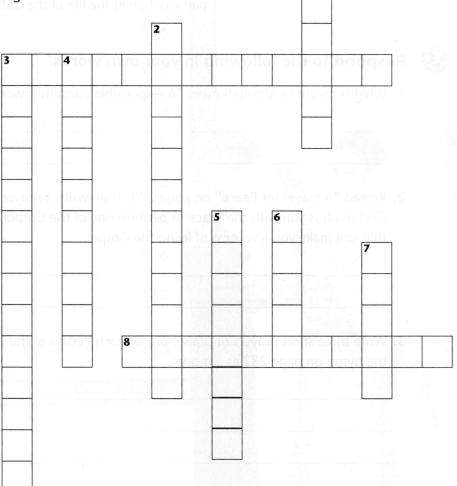

The Liturgical Year

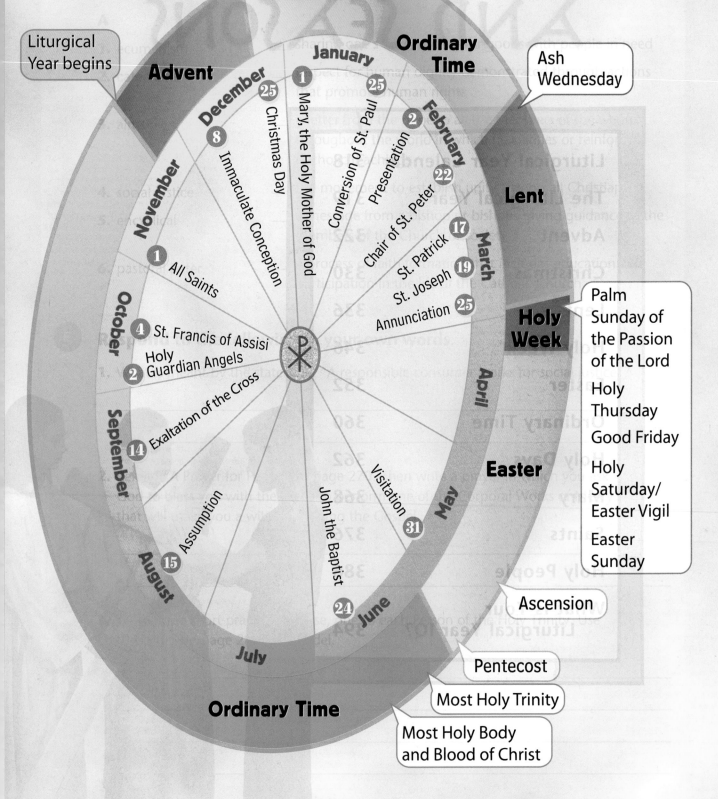

Christmas

Holy Family
Epiphany
Baptism of the Lord

Ordinary Time

Ash Wednesday

Advent

Liturgical Year begins

November

December

January

February

25 — Christmas Day

8 — Immaculate Conception

1 — Mary, the Holy Mother of God

25 — Conversion of St. Paul

2 — Presentation

22 — Chair of St. Peter

Lent

March

17 — St. Patrick

19 — St. Joseph

25 — Annunciation

1 — All Saints

4 — St. Francis of Assisi

2 — Holy Guardian Angels

14 — Exaltation of the Cross

October

September

August

15 — Assumption

July

June

24 — John the Baptist

31 — Visitation

May

April

Holy Week

Palm Sunday of the Passion of the Lord
Holy Thursday
Good Friday
Holy Saturday/Easter Vigil
Easter Sunday

Easter

Ascension

Pentecost

Most Holy Trinity

Most Holy Body and Blood of Christ

Ordinary Time

318

The Liturgical Year

As we gather for Eucharist each Sunday we notice that throughout the year the color of the priest's and deacon's vestments changes. We may see green, white, purple (or violet), or red. Hymns and readings change too. All these changing elements help us recognize the solemnity, feast, or season of the liturgical year we are celebrating. The liturgical year is the cycle of seasons and feasts the Church celebrates each year.

Sunday. Sunday is the weekly celebration of the Resurrection. It is the Lord's Day. From the days of the early Church, Sunday has been ranked as the first holy day of all.

Advent and Christmas. During the liturgical seasons of Advent and Christmas, we prepare for and celebrate the Incarnation and Nativity and the announcement of Jesus as the Savior of the world.

Lent, Easter Triduum, and Easter. During Lent the elect (unbaptized) and candidates (baptized) prepare for their initiation into the Church. All the faithful join with them and renew their own baptismal promises. The whole Church prepares for the celebration of Christ's Passion, Death, and Resurrection. Holy Thursday, Good Friday, and the celebration of Easter Vigil/Easter Sunday are the most important days of the liturgical year. We call these days—which begin with the celebration of the Evening Mass of the Lord's Supper on Holy Thursday and conclude with Evening Prayer on Easter Sunday—the Easter Triduum, or simply the Triduum, a term which means three days.

Ordinary Time. The longest part of the liturgical year is called Ordinary Time. The word *ordinary* comes from a Latin word meaning "number." On these numbered weeks of the year—for example, the Thirteenth Sunday in Ordinary Time—we listen to the events of the public ministry of Jesus and respond to his invitation to live as his disciples.

Solemnities, Feasts, and Memorials. The Church also celebrates a yearly cycle of feasts. These include the holy days of obligation and other days, such as the Solemnity of Our Lord Jesus Christ, King of the Universe, and days remembering Mary, the Apostles, and the other saints.

Advent

Mary said, "Behold, I am the handmaid of the Lord.
May it be done to me according to your word."

Luke 1:38

Waiting and Trusting

During the four weeks of Advent, the **Church** prepares to celebrate the birth of Christ while also anticipating his Second Coming. The **liturgy** for the first three Sundays of Advent focuses on the themes of penitence and preparation for the Second Coming of the Messiah, Jesus Christ. The readings for the liturgy include messianic prophecies of Isaiah and John the Baptist and readings about Jesus Christ as the fulfillment of these prophecies.

The liturgy for the final week of Advent centers on the approaching birth of Christ and places special emphasis on the role of Mary. In Luke's Gospel, the angel Gabriel tells Mary, "The Lord is with you" (Luke 1:28), meaning that Mary is full of **grace** and is to become the mother of God's Son. In an exceptional way, Mary is united to the Son and the Father. After learning she will be the mother of God's Son, Mary visits Elizabeth, her elderly relative. Elizabeth, who had never had a child, has become pregnant in her old age. This is a further sign to Mary that nothing is impossible for God.

The Church focuses on the role of Mary during Advent because she plays an integral and unique role in the mystery of the Incarnation and God's plan of Salvation. Mary shows us that the way we receive Christ into our hearts is by saying yes to God and trusting in him completely. Mary's example of waiting and trusting illustrates the true spirit of Advent.

The Advent Wreath

The observation of a preparatory period before Christmas dates back to the fourth century, and the custom of lighting candles on a wreath during this period originated in Germany in the Middle Ages. A wreath is itself an ancient symbol of glory. Each of the four candles on an Advent wreath represents one of the four weeks of Advent. The pink candle, lit on the Third Sunday of Advent, signifies our hope and joy about the coming of our Messiah. On that Sunday, also known as Gaudete Sunday, the priest can wear rose-colored vestments. During the other three weeks, his vestments are violet.

The three violet candles signify penance—not so much the penance of Lent but a sorrowful longing for Christ's presence.

In addition to representing the glory of Christ's coming, the wreath, with its ring shape, symbolizes God's eternal nature. Its green hue is also a sign of hope and everlasting life.

A Time to Reflect

During the Advent Season—the time when we prepare to welcome Christ into our hearts at Christmas—we reflect on our relationship with God. We should ask whether we are following the example of Mary, who said yes to God when he called her to be the Mother of Jesus. Mary is a perfect model of a person who always trusted God and who was thankful for all of his blessings.

> Almighty and merciful God, may no earthly undertaking hinder those who set out in haste to meet your Son, but may our learning of heavenly wisdom gain us admittance to his company. Amen.
>
> *Collect from the Second Sunday of Advent, Roman Missal*

Activity

Take a few moments to consider the following questions.

- Is deepening my friendship with God a priority in my life?
- Do I thank God for all the blessings in my life?
- Do I try each day to have a little more trust in God?
- Do I set aside time each day to spend with God in prayer?

On the lines below, write a covenant with God telling him how you will answer his call this Advent season to be his faithful child and deepen your relationship with him.

_____

_____

_____

_____

_____

✝ Prayer Celebration for Advent

True to Your Promises

Leader: In the name of the Father, and of the Son, and of the Holy Spirit.

All: Amen.

Leader: Let us pray.
O God, the maker and keeper of promises,
you promised long ago to send this world a savior.
In Jesus you fulfilled that promise.
As the day draws near to celebrate his coming,
give us willing hearts to welcome him again.
Turn our thoughts to the ways of your peace
so that he may find us ready and waiting,
in joyful expectation, truly prepared.
We ask this through Christ, our Lord.

All: Amen.

Reader 1: A reading from the Letter of James.
(Read James 5:7–8.)
The word of the Lord.

All: Thanks be to God.

Leader: *Quietly reflect on these questions.*
What are your positive or negative experiences of waiting?
(Pause.)
What does it mean to be patient as we wait for Christmas?
(Pause.)

Leader: During Advent, we keep vigil. As we patiently await the coming of Christ, we watch for signs of his nearness. Let us pray that he may come soon.
(After each invocation is prayed, you or one of your classmates will light a vigil candle and place it on a center table or in a candelabra. Then all will read the O Antiphon together.)

Reader 2: There is so much foolishness in the world. It is hard to know the way to be happy. What seems important today may be forgotten tomorrow. Teach us to treasure things that are lasting.

All: O Wisdom, O holy Word of God, you govern all creation with your strong yet tender care. Come and show your people the way to Salvation.

Reader 3: It is not easy to be free. We can become slaves to selfishness, anger, or violence. We can be imprisoned by other people's unfair judgments. Rescue us, and lead us to freedom.

All: O Sacred Lord of ancient Israel, who showed yourself to Moses in the burning bush, who gave him the holy way on Sinai mountain; come, stretch out your mighty hand to set us free.

Reader 4: The powerful and the mighty of this world are as nothing compared to you. Help us know that by your power we can change the world. Through your words and teachings, may we learn the ways of God.

All: O Flower of Jesse's stem, you have been raised up as a sign for all peoples; kings stand silent in your presence; the nations bow down in worship before you. Come, let nothing keep you from coming to our aid.

Reader 5: Death is a fearful thing. But you have broken the chains of death and given us eternal life. You hold the key that unlocks our spirit. Release us from fear.

All: O Key of David, O royal Power of Israel controlling at your will the gate of heaven: come break down the prison walls of death for those who dwell in darkness and the shadow of death, and lead your captive people into freedom.

Reader 6: Winter days are dark and cold. At times we feel tired and troubled and alone. Shine your love on us. Warm us and bring us your light.

All: O Radiant Dawn, splendour of eternal light, sun of justice: come, shine on those who dwell in darkness and the shadow of death.

Reader 7: Buildings are built and torn down. Nations rise and fall. Relationships grow and falter. But Christ is the one sure foundation. Teach us to trust you above all.

All: O King of all the nations, the only joy of every human heart; O Keystone of the mighty arch of man, come and save the creature you fashioned from the dust.

Reader 8: Justice and peace are your gifts. In a world of corruption and violence, we turn to you. Reign over us, so that we may know the joy of your kingdom.

All: O Emmanuel, king and lawgiver, desire of the nations, Savior of all people, come and set us free, Lord our God.

O Antiphons excerpted from the Liturgy of the Hours

Christmas (Nativity of the Lord)

We have seen his star in the East and have come with gifts to adore the Lord.

Based on Matthew 2:2

A Child Is Born to Us

The first reading at Midnight Mass on the Nativity of the Lord (Christmas) is always, Isaiah 9:1–6. The message in these verses explains why the Church reads this passage at the beginning of the celebration of Christmas. In verse 5, Isaiah announces, "For a child is born to us; a son is given us." This child, Isaiah says, will be called the "Prince of Peace." Since the earliest days of the Church, Christians have understood these six verses of Isaiah as a prophecy of the birth of Jesus.

Of these six verses, only verse 5 refers to the birth of a baby. The others are clearly about a mighty king. In fact, even in verse 5, Isaiah may not have been talking about a baby at all. Some scholars think that the words "a child is born to us" refer to the enthronement of a king. Isaiah may have borrowed these words from a ceremony used by ancient Israelites to enthrone a new king after the death of his father. When the new king sat on the throne for the first time, his subjects understood that now he was to become God's son—God's favorite. The new king, even though he was an adult, was considered God's "child."

Who is this mighty king that Isaiah is describing? The other verses describe him and the effects he will have on others. He will inherit the kingdom of David, Israel's greatest king. His reign will bring peace and justice to the fortunate people over whom he rules. He will be like a light for people who have been living in darkness. He will bring joy to those freed from slavery. This king will liberate his people. Although this passage was written perhaps seven centuries before the birth of Christ, it nevertheless beautifully describes the impact Jesus had and continues to have on people.

Isaiah 9:1–6 is a good passage to read at Midnight Mass because the celebration of Christmas is much more than the story of the birth of Jesus. Christmas celebrates the whole mystery of who Jesus is: the Incarnation of the Son of God. "And the Word became flesh / and made his dwelling among us, / and we saw his glory" (John 1:14). The Scriptures for the season of Christmas point out many ways that Christ is the Revelation of God in our midst. Isaiah's prophecy shows that Jesus comes to be a just and peaceful Savior and to bring light for all people.

Mosaic of Jesus Christ with the Virgin and St. Minias
San Miniato al Monte, Florence, Italy/Bridgeman Art Library

Imagine the Future

The Israelites spent years imagining what the Messiah would be like. We know now that what they imagined and what Jesus was really like were not always the same. Great things often have humble beginnings. A mighty oak begins as an acorn you can hold in the palm of your hand. A newly hatched chick gradually becomes a proud hen or rooster. Butterflies of many colors all begin in small white cocoons. Likewise, humans gradually develop the gifts and abilities they have been given—often with amazing results. Unlike plants and animals and insects, however, humans have choices in deciding their future. They can imagine the future, and, through the gift of free will, they will influence who they will become.

Imagine your own future. What are some of your hopes and dreams? Reflect on the questions below, and answer them to the best of your ability.

Activity

No one knows the future, but anyone can dream. Sometimes those dreams become a reality. Imagine that you have unlimited possibilities and resources. Then answer the questions below.

1. What kind of job will you have when you are an adult?

_____

_____

2. If you could create one thing in your lifetime that would benefit others, what would it be?

_____

_____

3. Imagine that at the end of your life the three people who knew you best in the world are talking about you. What do you hope they will say?

_____

_____

> Grant us, we pray, O Lord our God, that we, who are gladdened by participation in the feast of our Redeemer's Nativity, may through an honorable way of life become worthy of union with him. Who lives and reigns for ever and ever. Amen.
>
> *Prayer after Communion, Christmas, Mass during the Night, Roman Missal*

The Solemnity of the Epiphany of the Lord

The word *epiphany* means "showing, appearance, or revelation." The Solemnity of the Epiphany of the Lord, celebrated on the first Sunday after January 1, recalls God's Revelation of himself through his Son, Jesus Christ, the **Messiah**. This appearance occurred to the people of Israel as well as to the Magi, who represented all humanity.

The Magi were wise and priestly men living in ancient Persia. The Gospel of Matthew relates the story of how these ancient astrologers followed a star to the place of Jesus' birth in Bethlehem. Matthew probably drew upon an ancient tradition in which a new star was said to appear whenever a ruler was born.

Matthew's story of the Magi symbolizes the idea that all people are called to worship Christ. The Magi came from the East. They were Gentiles, not Jews. This conveys an important part of the Christmas message: the Son of God, Jesus, came to save not only the Jews, but all people.

The three gifts the Magi presented to the infant Jesus are also symbolic: gold for a king, frankincense for God, and myrrh for one who was to die. These gifts reveal three parts of Jesus' identity. The gold shows us his royal kingship; the frankincense shows us his divinity; the myrrh foretells his suffering and Death.

An ancient custom that takes place on Epiphany is the proclaiming of the dates of feasts for the coming liturgical year. A deacon, priest, lector, or cantor may sing this proclamation. The singing takes place either after the Gospel reading, within the homily, or after the homily. Below is the text of the proclamation. The asterisk indicates where the proper date (*) and month (**) are inserted for the current year.

My brothers and sisters, the glory of the Lord Jesus has been made manifest and will continue to be revealed in our midst until he comes again. In the rhythms and alternations of time let us recall and live the mysteries of our **salvation**. Central to the entire liturgical year is our celebration of the TRIDUUM OF THE LORD, crucified, buried and risen, which culminates on EASTER SUNDAY, the * of **. Every SUNDAY, when we recall this **Paschal Mystery**, holy Church makes present this great event in which Christ has conquered sin and death. From Easter derive all other celebrations: Ash Wednesday, the beginning of the season of Lent, the * of **; the **ASCENSION** OF THE LORD, the * of **; **PENTECOST**, the * of **; and the FIRST SUNDAY OF ADVENT, the * of **. Likewise, in the feasts of the Holy Mother of God, of the apostles and saints, and in the commemoration of the faithful departed, the Church, in its pilgrimage here on earth, proclaims the Paschal mystery of the Lord. To Christ who is, who was, and who is to come, the Lord of all time and history, be endless praise now and forever!

From the Roman Pontifical

On Epiphany, when this proclamation is made, some parishes bless calendars and distribute them to the congregation. This proclamation of the important feasts of the Church makes it clear that the whole liturgical year revolves around the celebration of Christ's Resurrection.

Activity

For many of us, our birthday is one of the most important days of the year. We may impatiently count the days before its celebration, then look back and relive the excitement after it is over.

Reread the Epiphany proclamation. The feasts mentioned are extremely important to Catholics. The Church counts the days by celebrating special feasts and seasons from the Epiphany until the Triduum, the holiest three days of the year.

The Three Wise Men.

> O God, who on this day revealed your Only Begotten Son to the nations by the guidance of a star, grant in your mercy that we, who know you already by faith, may be brought to behold the beauty of your sublime glory. Through our Lord Jesus Christ, your Son, who lives and reigns with you in the unity of the Holy Spirit, one God, for ever and ever. Amen.
>
> *Collect from the Epiphany of the Lord, Roman Missal*

Using a new church calendar or one of your own, find the dates of this year's feasts. Write them on the lines below.

1. The First Sunday of Advent

_____

2. Ash Wednesday, the beginning of Lent

_____

3. Triduum of the Lord

_____

4. Ascension of the Lord

_____

5. Pentecost Sunday

_____

6. When is your birthday? How close is it to the Epiphany?

_____

_____

7. Which important church feast day is your birthday close to?

_____

✝ Prayer Celebration for Christmas

A Prayer Offering

Leader: In the name of the Father, and of the Son, and of the Holy Spirit.

All: Amen.

Leader: Let us pray. O God, Father of all, you revealed Jesus, your Son and our Savior, to the nations. You helped seekers find him through the guidance of a star. Lead us by the light of faith so that we may find Christ and live in his friendship forever.

All: Amen.

Reader: A reading from the holy Gospel according to Matthew.

All: Glory to you, O Lord.

(Read Matthew 2:1–12.)

Reader: The Gospel of the Lord.

All: Praise to you, Lord Jesus Christ.

Leader: The Magi came from faraway lands to find Jesus in Bethlehem. They had a long and dangerous journey. Yet they reached their destination. They presented their gifts of gold, frankincense, and myrrh to Jesus with reverence and joy.

What gift do you bring to Jesus? Is it a particular ability or talent? Is it a personal quality, such as kindness or truthfulness? What can you place before him today?

Think of your own gift—not gold, frankincense, or myrrh, but a gift of yourself that you can offer to Jesus in prayer right now. Write it on a slip of paper, and when you are done, quietly place it in this box.

(Place your gift in the box. When all are finished, the leader will close the box and hold it up in a gesture of offering. Then the leader will pray the following prayer.)

Leader: O God, Father of all, you have given us many gifts. What can we give you in return, except the gift of ourselves? Accept this offering presented to your Son, Jesus Christ. Send the Holy Spirit to lead and guide us on the journey of life. Keep us safe, so that one day we may come into your presence and rejoice with your saints forever. We ask this through Christ, our Lord.

All: Amen.

Leader: May almighty God bless us,
Father, Son, and Holy Spirit.

All: Amen.

Leader: Go in peace.
All: Thanks be to God.

Lent

A clean heart create for me, God;
renew in me a steadfast spirit.

Psalm 51:12

Praying the Liturgy of the Hours

The **Liturgy of the Hours** is the official public daily prayer of the Church that fulfills the Lord's command to pray at all times. (See Luke 18:1–8.) The beauty of sunrise and sunset, the brightest noontime, and the darkest night are all gifts that call us to prayer. Time itself is a creation of God and is sacred. Therefore, the prayers of the Liturgy of the Hours celebrate fixed times of the day and night: morning, midday, evening, and night. Laypeople, as well as priests and deacons, may preside at celebrations of the Liturgy of the Hours. Cantors and other musicians may help lead the singing. Incense and candles are sometimes used in evening or nighttime celebrations.

Each celebration of the Liturgy of the Hours begins with an introduction and a hymn. The praying of psalms (from the Book of Psalms in the Bible) then follows. The psalms are the heart of the Liturgy of the Hours. They express the joy,

gratitude, sorrow, and suffering of God's faithful people. As the people pray the psalms, they enter into the spirit of each of these ancient biblical songs and make the psalms their own prayer. A short reading from Scripture follows. The passage may come from the Old or New Testament, but not from the Gospels.

Next comes the most joyful part of the service, the time when everyone stands and sings a canticle, or song, based on Scripture. For Morning Prayer, the canticle is the Song of Zechariah, the father of John the Baptizer. This song, from Luke 1:68–79, is particularly appropriate because John the Baptizer prepared the way for Jesus, and at the start of a new day we prepare to meet Jesus again. For Evening Prayer, the canticle is Mary's song, the Magnificat (see Luke 1:46–55). Her great hymn of praise sums up the joy of being a disciple. We can identify with Mary, who is the Mother of Jesus and our Mother, too. The canticle for Night Prayer consists of the touching words of the elderly prophet Simeon, in which we hear him say, "Now, Master, you may let your servant go in peace / . . . for my eyes have seen your salvation" (Luke 2:29–30). At the very end of the day, like Simeon, we are glad to have seen God's promises fulfilled in Jesus. After a closing prayer, the service ends with a blessing and dismissal.

In monasteries, monks and nuns pray the Hours as many as ten times daily. Parishes and schools that celebrate the Liturgy of the Hours do so perhaps once or twice a day. Individuals and families may pray the Hours, too. During special seasons, such as Lent, more people may take advantage of the opportunity to pray the Liturgy of the Hours together.

How Do You Spend Your Day?

Time is precious. Each day is a gift. Yet sometimes we are not grateful for the time we have been given. Some days seem to drag on in boredom, while others go by much too fast. We often waste time or try to do too many things in a short time.

The rhythms of nature remind us that in God's world there is always the right amount of time. Day follows night. The moon and the sun mark the months and the seasons. God's creation calls us to balance rest and activity, waking and sleeping, work and play. Along with these activities, we must also make time for prayer—prayer in which we thank God for all the wonderful gifts of his creation, including the gift of time.

Lent is a springtime season when new life is emerging in nature. All things seem possible. The Lenten season can remind us to look at how we spend time and to plan our days so that we regularly spend time with God in prayer.

Activity

Think about the time of day that is your favorite, and then answer the following questions.

1. Reserve time for prayer during your favorite part of the day. When will you pray?

   _____

2. You can pray in your room, outdoors, or anyplace else where you can pay attention to God without interruption. Where will you pray?

   _____

3. Find something to help you focus your prayer, such as a passage of Scripture or an image of Jesus or Mary or one of the saints. Keep it nearby. What will help you focus on prayer?

   _____

4. Talk to God in your own words, or use the words of Scripture or a prayer book. How will you pray?

   _____

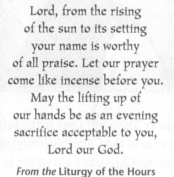

Lord, from the rising of the sun to its setting your name is worthy of all praise. Let our prayer come like incense before you. May the lifting up of our hands be as an evening sacrifice acceptable to you, Lord our God.

From the Liturgy of the Hours

A Penitential Season

The season of Lent begins on Ash Wednesday and concludes with the Evening Mass of the Lord's Supper on Holy Thursday, the beginning of the Easter Triduum. Lent is the primary penitential season of the Church's liturgical year. During this season, Christians are called to respond to the Gospel and to experience a change of heart as they prepare for the joyous celebration of Easter. Lent is a time of repentance, spiritual renewal, and conversion.

On Ash Wednesday, church members receive ashes marked on their foreheads in the sign of a cross. Ashes were worn as a sign of penance in the Jewish faith tradition and in the early Church. Palm branches from the previous Palm Sunday of the Lord's Passion are burned and blessed for this **ritual**. As individuals come forward to be signed with ashes, the priest, deacon, or pastoral associate says, "Repent, and believe in the Gospel" or "Remember that you are dust, and to dust you shall return" *(Roman Missal)*. These words remind the faithful of the Lenten themes of humility, sorrow for sin, and the need for God's forgiveness. The ashes are a sacramental, or sacred sign, signifying that all people need God's love and mercy.

During Lent we acknowledge that every Christian is a penitent. All of us sin and are in need of God's forgiveness. Traditional forms of Lenten penance include prayer, fasting (eating only one full meal per day), abstinence (not eating meat), almsgiving (charity to one's neighbor), and more frequent participation in the Sacraments.

In the Middle Ages, Lenten practices were quite severe. The forty days of Lent were all fast days. Only one meal a day, after evening prayers, could be eaten. No meat or meat products, cheese, milk, or eggs were allowed. On Wednesdays and Fridays, penitents, often barefoot, would process from one church to another. Persons guilty of serious sin did public penance.

Today, Catholics in the United States between the ages of eighteen and sixty are required by Church law to fast on Ash Wednesday and Good Friday. Catholics over fourteen years of age are required to abstain on Ash Wednesday, Good Friday, and all the Fridays of Lent. The emphasis during Lent is on becoming more Christlike through prayer, personal penance, and doing good works.

Turn Away From Sin

The Season of Lent invites us to take an honest look at who we are. We examine our conscience. We evaluate our good and bad points, and we rate how our actions "measure up" against the way Jesus taught us to live. We decide how to make changes and grow to become more like Christ.

> O God, author of every mercy and of all goodness, who in fasting, prayer and almsgiving have shown us a remedy for sin, look graciously on this confession of our lowliness, that we, who are bowed down by our conscience, may always be lifted up by your mercy. Amen.
>
> *Collect from the Third Sunday of Lent, Roman Missal*

Activity

Think about your behavior during the past month. What did you do right? What needs improvement?

What I did right

_____

_____

How I could improve

_____

_____

What I need to do in order to become more like Christ

_____

_____

What I will do to accomplish this

_____

_____

_____

✝ Prayer Celebration for Holy Week

The Reproaches

Leader: In the name of the Father, and of the Son, and of the Holy Spirit.

All: Amen.

Leader: Let us pray.
Loving God, your kindness knows no end.
Despite our failures and sinfulness,
you are always there for us, ever faithful.
You sent prophets to guide your people.
You sent your only Son to be our Savior.
Help us realize how deep your love for us is
and respond gratefully to that love always.
We make this prayer through Christ our Lord.

All: Amen.

Reader 1: A reading from the Passion according to Matthew.
(Read Matthew 26:20–25.)
The Gospel of the Lord.

All: Praise to you, Lord Jesus Christ.

Reader 2: The history of God's people is full of God's generous goodness to those he loves. Yet they turn away. They choose to sin. They are unfaithful. Whenever we turn away from God, we too are unfaithful. When we choose to sin, we turn our back on God and his love.

Reader 3: On Good Friday we are reminded that *all* sinners share the responsibility for the death of Jesus—Judas Iscariot, Pontius Pilate and Herod, the Roman soldiers, the Jewish Sanhedrin, the mob, the disciples who ran away. *All* sinners share this responsibility.

Reader 4: Because we are sinners, we, too, have brought Christ to his Cross.

(Pause and reflect on the suffering of Christ.)

Leader: During the Good Friday liturgy, we pray the "Reproaches." They tell of God's saving actions throughout history. Let us pray these words, remembering his goodness to us all the days of our lives.

Sides 1 and 2:	My people, what have I done to you?
	Or how have I grieved you? Answer me!
Side 1:	Because I led you out of the land of Egypt,
	you have prepared a Cross for your Savior.
Side 1:	Holy is God,
Side 2:	Holy and Mighty,
Side 1:	Holy and Immortal One, have mercy on us.
Sides 1 and 2:	Because I led you out through the desert forty years
	and fed you with manna and brought you into a land
	of plenty, you have prepared a Cross for your Savior.
Side 1:	Holy is God,
Side 2:	Holy and Mighty,
Side 1:	Holy and Immortal One, have mercy on us.
Sides 1 and 2:	What more should I have done for you and have not done?
	Indeed, I planted you as my most beautiful chosen vine
	and you have turned very bitter for me, for in my thirst
	you gave me vinegar to drink and with a lance you pierced
	your Savior's side.
Side 1:	Holy is God,
Side 2:	Holy and Mighty,
Side 1:	Holy and Immortal One, have mercy on us.

Reproaches I, Good Friday, Roman Missal

Leader:	God, Father of mercy, help us understand the meaning of your
	Son's Passion. Let us see the bitter fruit of all human sin.
	Turn us from the path of disobedience,
	and deepen our commitment to following your ways.
	We ask this in the name of Jesus the Lord.
All:	Amen.

✝ Prayer Celebration for Easter

Rejoice in the Good News

Leader: Jesus Christ is risen! That's the Good News of the Easter Season. Let us celebrate, rejoice, and give thanks.

All: Let us celebrate, rejoice, and give thanks.

Group 1: I will bless the LORD at all times;
    praise shall be always in my mouth.
My soul will glory in the LORD
    that the poor may hear and be glad.

Group 2: All you peoples, clap your hands;
    shout to God with joyful cries.
For the LORD, the Most High, inspires awe,
    the great king over all the earth.

Group 1: Sing joyfully to God our strength;
    shout in triumph to the God of Jacob!
Take up a melody, sound the timbrel,
    the sweet-sounding harp and lyre.

Group 2: The promises of the LORD I will sing forever,
    proclaim your loyalty through all ages.

Group 1: LORD, God of hosts, who is like you?
    Mighty LORD, your loyalty is always present.

Group 2: Sing to the LORD a new song;
    sing to the LORD, all the earth.
Sing to the LORD, bless his name;
    announce his salvation day after day.
Tell God's glory among the nations;
    among all peoples, God's marvelous deeds.

Psalms 34:2–3; 47:2–3; 81:2–3; 89:2, 9; 96:1–3

All:	Alleluia! Give thanks to the LORD, who is good, whose love endures forever.
Group 1:	Let the house of Israel say: God's love endures forever.
Group 2:	Let the house of Aaron say, God's love endures forever.
Group 3:	Let those who fear the LORD say, God's love endures forever.
All:	Alleluia! Give thanks to the LORD, for he is good, whose love endures forever.
Group 1:	I will give thanks to you for you answered me you have been my savior.

Group 2:	The stone the builders rejected
	    has become the cornerstone.
	By the LORD has this been done;
	    it is wonderful in our eyes.

Group 3:	This is the day the LORD has made; let us rejoice in it and be glad.
All:	Alleluia! Give thanks to the LORD, for he is good, whose love endures forever.

Psalm 118:1–4, 21–24, 29

Leader:	Almighty God, you gave us new life when you raised Jesus from death. Help us feel the power of this life every day of our lives. We ask this through Christ, our Lord.
All:	Amen.

Holy Days

*O God, you are my God—
for you I long!*

Psalm 63:2

The Conversion of Saint Paul, the Apostle

As you learned in unit 1, Paul shaped the life of the Church in a dramatic way. He was a preacher, a leader, and a man of great faith. His letters, which so well express the Christian faith, were adopted as part of the Bible. They are still read in the liturgy today. Who was this extraordinary person?

Paul was born in the Roman city of Tarsus, near the beginning of the Christian era. He was a devout, Greek-speaking Jew. He was also a Pharisee who believed that the followers of Christ distorted and threatened the true Jewish faith. He persecuted Christians. Saul, as he was called, first appears in the Acts of the Apostles as a dangerous man and a ruthless opponent of Christianity. When the crowd stoned Stephen, the first Christian martyr, Saul approved of their actions. Stephen's persecutors laid their cloaks at Saul's feet. (See Acts 7:58.) At that time Saul thought he was serving God by persecuting Christians.

In A.D. 32 Saul was on his way to the city of Damascus to arrest Christians when, suddenly, a blinding light stunned him. He heard a voice saying "Saul, Saul, why do you persecute me?" Saul asked, "Who are you?" The voice answered, "I am Jesus, whom you are persecuting." Jesus ordered Saul to go to the city, where he would be told what to do. Still blinded by his vision, Saul had to be led

The Conversion of Saint Paul by Daniele Crespi

by the hand. Yet he did what the Lord asked (based on Acts 9:1–9). After three days, Saul's blindness lifted.

Saul had experienced a conversion—a spiritual turnaround or a change of heart. As a new follower of Christ, Saul used his Roman name, Paul. At first, the Christians were suspicious of Paul. Eventually they accepted his story and embraced him as a brother.

Paul's conversion is one of the best-known stories in Christian history. He became a fervent Christian. He established the Church in many places and preached to Jews and non-Jews alike. Everywhere he went, he spread the Good News of the crucified and Risen Jesus. His own history made him keenly aware that God's grace can touch and change any person, no matter how misguided. "Christ Jesus came into the world to save sinners," Paul wrote. "Of these I am the foremost" (1 Timothy 1:15).

Paul suffered much and was harshly beaten and thrown into prison for preaching Christ. He faced great dangers to travel to faraway places to teach about Jesus. Yet he persevered through everything, strengthened by the Holy Spirit. Paul was martyred outside the city of Rome in about the year A.D. 67. The Church celebrates his conversion on January 25.

Conversion: A Work of the Holy Spirit

Conversion to Christ can be sudden and dramatic, as the conversion of Paul was, or it may be a more gradual process. Conversion to Christ is a lifelong process and can also happen many times in a person's life. Conversion happens whenever God calls a person away from sin, or to deeper faith in Jesus Christ, and the person responds. It happens when a person is inspired to greater love for God and neighbor.

True conversion is sparked and guided by the Holy Spirit. It can never be forced. Conversion of heart also leads to new ways of thinking and acting. When people experience conversion, they act differently. Something blossoms within them. Like Paul, they are given strength and enthusiasm for doing God's work.

Activity

Many movies, books, television programs, and real-life situations involve the story of someone's conversion or change of heart. Sometimes a conversion helps someone overcome addiction or turn away from a life of crime. Think of an example of conversion, and answer the following questions.

1. How did the person change?

_____

_____

2. What actions showed that the person had experienced a change of heart?

_____

_____

3. How was the Holy Spirit active in the conversion? List as many ways as you can.

_____

_____

_____

_____

_____

_____

O God, who taught the whole world through the preaching of the blessed Apostle Paul, draw us, we pray, nearer to you through the example of him whose conversion we celebrate today, and so make us witnesses to your truth in the world. Amen.

Collect from the Conversion of Saint Paul, the Apostle, Roman Missal

The Immaculate Conception of the Blessed Virgin Mary

The Church has always held the highest regard for Mary, the Mother of Jesus. The dogma of the Immaculate Conception states that Mary was conceived and born without Original Sin and remained free from all personal sin throughout her entire life. God gave this privilege only to Mary because she was to be the Mother of Jesus.

Devotion to Mary the Immaculate Conception has a long history in the Church. In 1476, Pope Sixtus IV approved a feast to celebrate the Immaculate Conception.

In 1830, Saint Catherine Labouré had a vision of Mary as the Immaculate Conception. In this vision, Mary asked that Catholics wear a medal displaying her image and the prayer "O Mary, conceived without sin, pray for us who have recourse to thee." In 1854, Pope Pius IX proclaimed the Solemnity of the Immaculate Conception a Holy Day of Obligation to be celebrated on December 8.

In 1858, Mary, as the Immaculate Conception, appeared as a vision to fourteen-year-old Bernadette Soubirous in Lourdes, France. Today many people travel to Lourdes to ask Mary's intercession for healing their illnesses and disabilities.

In 1959 the National Shrine of the Immaculate Conception was dedicated in Washington, D.C. This is the largest Catholic church in the country and one of the largest churches in the world. Mary, as the Immaculate Conception, is the patroness of the United States of America.

When we celebrate the Immaculate Conception, we celebrate our own Salvation from sin. Although we are often weak and sinful, we are a community of believers, the followers of Jesus, journeying toward the Kingdom of God. As God worked through Mary, so he works through us to accomplish his will. His grace is always stronger than the power of sin.

Human Life Is Sacred

The Solemnity of the Immaculate Conception of the Blessed Virgin Mary reminds us that human life does not begin at birth but at conception. God loves us and is with us from the moment of our conception. Therefore, all life is sacred from the moment of conception. Each human life is precious and needs to be protected. Every human being, healthy or sick, has the right to be born and respected throughout life, until the time of natural death.

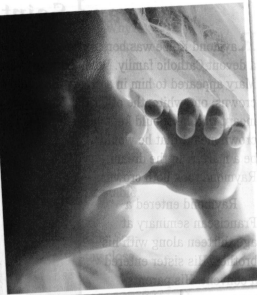

Activity

In the space below, write a letter to God about why you are grateful you were born.

Dear God,

_____

_____

_____

_____

_____

_____

_____

_____

Yours truly,

> O God, who by the Immaculate Conception of the Blessed Virgin prepared a worthy dwelling for your Son, grant, we pray, that, as you preserved her from every stain by virtue of the Death of your Son, which you foresaw, so, through her intercession, we, too, may be cleansed and admitted to your presence. Amen.
>
> *Collect from the Immaculate Conception of the Blessed Virgin Mary*

Our Lady of Perpetual Help

A picture is worth a thousand words. This is certainly true of pictures of the Blessed Mother. Some images accent Mary's holiness. Others stress her motherly love. Some inspire awe for the Queen of Heaven. The image of Our Lady of Perpetual Help, first painted by an unknown artist in Crete in the fourteenth or fifteenth century, presents a portrait of Mary that is gracious and kind. It shows a woman whose steady gaze and upturned hands offer continual consolation and protection.

The image of Our Lady of Perpetual Help is an icon. Icons are a special kind of religious art. They are valued by the Church in the East as gifts from God, as windows to Heaven. Their creators, who are called iconographers, follow very strict rules when they are working on their art. The materials, forms, and colors iconographers use are meant to express spiritual ideas. The icon of Our Lady of Perpetual Help is filled with symbols of important spiritual concepts. The details of this painting can help us understand Mary's role in our Salvation.

Background The golden background symbolizes Heaven and the joy shining through.

Dark blue mantle Blue symbolizes motherhood.

Red tunic Red symbolizes virginity.

Star in Our Lady's veil A star traditionally guides sailors. Mary, known as Star of the Sea, guides us on our journey of life.

Golden crown This feature was added in 1867 because of the many miracles associated with Mary as "Our Lady of Perpetual Help."

Mary's features Mary's eyes are large and compassionate; they look directly at the viewer of the icon. Her mouth is small, for she speaks gently. Her hands lovingly support Christ and all who come to her through him.

The child Jesus The palms of his hands are turned downward, showing that he has entrusted his graces to Mary's safekeeping. His eyes are turned upward, gazing at the signs of his coming persecution.

Greek initials for "Mother of God" are located above Mary's head. This is Mary's title.

Michael the Archangel This angel stands to Mary's left and is identified by his Greek initials. He holds the lance that pierced the side of Christ as he hung on the Cross. He also holds the sponge soaked in sour wine.

Gabriel the Archangel This angel stands to Mary's right and is also identified by his Greek initials. He holds the other instruments of Christ's Passion: the Cross and nails.

Greek initials for "Jesus Christ" are located to the right of the Christ child. This identifies the child in Mary's arms as Jesus.

Falling sandal of Jesus The exact meaning of this symbol is unknown. It may show the child's knowledge of his coming persecution and his haste to be gathered into his mother's arms.

Portraits of Mary

Through the centuries, Christian artists all over the world have created images of Mary. She has been shown with the features of every ethnicity and wearing the clothing of every age. Such images proclaim that Mary is the Mother of us all because she is the Mother of our Savior.

Activity

Recall what you know about Mary. What kind of portrait of her would you paint? In your portrait of Mary, what symbols would you use? Design your symbols in the space below, and explain the meaning each symbol has for you. (Remember that the colors you choose also have meanings.)

Remember, O most gracious Virgin Mary,
that never was it known that anyone who fled to your protection, implored your help, or sought your intercession was left unaided.
Inspired by this confidence, I fly unto you,
O Virgin of virgins, my mother;
To you do I come, before you I stand, sinful and sorrowful.
O Mother of the Word Incarnate, despise not my petitions, but in your mercy hear and answer me. Amen.

The Memorare

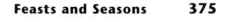

Saint John Nepomucene Neumann

Some people think that a saint must be a "super-hero." They believe that saints must have superhuman strength and virtue. Finally, people sometimes believe that everything "extraordinary" that saints did was easy for them.

John Neumann would disagree. He understood that saints aren't superhuman. They are ordinary people who keep on trying to imitate Christ and to love others. They work hard at following Christ, and they never give up.

John Neumann was born in Bohemia in 1811. He became known for his determination and willingness to work hard. Although John felt that God was calling him to be a priest, the Church in Bohemia would not ordain him. This was because at that time the Church in Bohemia had more priests than were needed. However, John did not quit his seminary studies. Instead, he studied diligently and became fluent in many languages. Then he traveled to New York and was ordained there.

Father Neumann's first assignment was to work with Native Americans and German, French, and Irish immigrants in upstate New York. After four years as a missionary there, John joined a religious community known as the Redemptorists. He took religious vows and continued working as a missionary in Maryland, Virginia, Ohio, and Pennsylvania.

At age forty-one, John was ordained bishop of Philadelphia. His motto as bishop was a simple one: "Passion of Christ, strengthen me." During the next seven years, John worked relentlessly to bring the Word of God to the people of Philadelphia. He supervised the building of ninety-eight Catholic elementary schools and eighty new churches. He even wrote a catechism that was widely used in Catholic schools for more than thirty-five years.

Unfortunately, Bishop John died of a heart attack at age forty-eight. Canonized in 1977, he is the first bishop in the United States to be named a saint. His feast day is January 5.

Lucas

AN 1738

ABRIDGED CATECHISM

OF THE

NATIONAL COUNCIL.

FOR PERSONS WHO MAY NOT BE ABLE TO LEARN THE LARGER ONE.

PUBLISHED WITH THE APPROBATION OF
RIGHT REV. JOHN N. NEUMANN, D.D.,
BISHOP OF PHILADELPHIA.

PHILADELPHIA:
PUBLISHED BY H. & C. McGRATH,
207 MARKET STREET.

Going the Extra Mile

What is the longest race you have ever run? What is the greatest distance you have ever hiked? The celebration of the Feast of Saint John Neumann (January 5) reminds us of what it means to go the extra mile for others. Saint John traveled by ship across the Atlantic to serve Catholic immigrants in the New World. Once ordained, he often walked twenty miles a day to reach the faithful people in his territory. He was known for his generosity to the poor. After being ordained a bishop, John Neumann continued to give away his best clothing to people in need. The clothes he kept for himself were old and often needed repair.

The Church calls us to be generous in serving others: to feed the hungry, shelter the homeless, and clothe the naked. Such work is not easy, nor is it always comfortable. It's tempting to think that we're not important enough to do this work or that someone else could do it better. Imagine what would have happened if Jesus or any of the saints had given in to this temptation! How much goodness would have been lost to our world!

Activities

1. Bishop John Neumann's motto was "Passion of Christ, strengthen me." How might this motto have helped him in his ministry? How could adopting this motto help you?

_____

_____

2. Think of some practical ways that young Catholics your age can serve the poor in their parish or local community. Record your ideas here.

Feed the hungry _____

Shelter the homeless _____

Clothe the naked _____

Choose one of the ideas you listed above. Then make a plan to "go the extra mile" to offer your help. Write about your plan on the lines below.

_____

_____

> O God, who called the Bishop Saint John Neumann, renowned for his charity and pastoral service, to shepherd your people in America, grant by his intercession that as we foster the Christian education of youth and are strengthened by the witness of brotherly love, we may constantly increase the family of your Church. Amen.
>
> *Collect from Feast of Saint John Neumann, Bishop, Roman Missal*

Father Jerzy Popieluszko

Poland has been a Catholic country since 966. Throughout Poland's history, the Church has worked to help the Polish people keep their identity. This has been especially true whenever Poland has been taken over by foreign powers.

Poland faced such a takeover at the end of World War II. Although the country was officially independent, it had a Communist government. The Russian army, which occupied Poland when the war ended, installed this government. The Communists were atheists who were bitterly hostile to the Church. With the Russian occupation, a forty-five-year battle began between the Catholic Church and the Communist Party. One hero of this struggle was Father Jerzy Popieluszko.

Father Jerzy did not look like anyone's idea of a hero. He was short and slender, with an acne-scarred face. He looked younger than he really was. He was shy and spoke in a soft voice, even to the crowds who came to hear him preach. Throughout his life Father Jerzy suffered from many illnesses. When he had studied for the priesthood, he was not a great student. But he was simple, sincere, friendly, and a hard worker.

In August 1980, Poland's factories were swept by strikes. The workers at these plants wanted a better life. They wanted to form trade unions to protect their interests. After several weeks, the government reluctantly gave in. The workers' new union, called "Solidarity," grew fast. By 1981, one-third of Poland's people belonged to it.

There was a big steel mill at the edge of Father Jerzy's parish. When the mill was occupied by striking workers, he went there to celebrate Mass. When the strike ended, he continued to minister to the steelworkers and their families.

Solidarity operated legally for about a year. Then, in December 1981, the Communist government cracked down on the union. It closed the union's offices and arrested thousands of Solidarity members. Father Jerzy attended trials to keep track of who had been arrested. He collected food and clothes to give to the families of those in prison. He also collected money to buy gift packages for jailed union members.

Most importantly, Father Jerzy kept alive the Poles' hope for a better life. People came from all over to hear him preach at Sunday Mass. Some would stand on the roofs of their cars in the street behind the church, listening to his voice over loudspeakers.

The government sent dozens of secret police to follow Father Jerzy and report on everything he did. He was jailed briefly. He had the chance to leave Poland but refused. Late in 1984, he was kidnapped by a trio of secret police officers and beaten to death. His shattered body was dumped in a reservoir, where it was found two weeks later. Father Jerzy was thirty-seven when he died.

Stand by Me

No one likes to be abandoned. When we are in a conflict, we want our friends to stay with us and support us. When we are hurt or in need, we want people to acknowledge our pain and help us. Whenever we struggle with a difficult problem, we need to know that we are not alone.

Solidarity was the name of the Polish workers' union that Father Jerzy supported. It is also a common noun meaning "fellowship." When a group has solidarity, it means that every member can count on the others to stand by them and help one another in time of need.

The *Catechism of the Catholic Church* speaks about human solidarity. People must stand with one another and work together to build a just and peaceful world. The Catechism describes the principle and virtue of solidarity as "a direct demand of human and Christian brotherhood" *(Catechism of the Catholic Church, 1939).*

Activity

Many groups of people struggle and are in need. Our brothers and sisters around the world and even in our own neighborhood may be homeless, hungry, living alone, or sick. How can you experience solidarity with them?

1. Identify a group you would like to "stand by." This may be people in a town hit by a natural disaster, homeless people you know of, or people living with AIDS. It could also be people struggling with war or famine in a faraway corner of the globe, or any other group in need. Find out more about this group. Write your findings here.

_____

_____

2. Make a commitment to pray for this group, recognizing that these people are your brothers and sisters. Write your prayer commitment here.

_____

_____

3. Do something to help. You might take part in a food or clothing drive or a similar activity. Or you might send a note of support and encouragement. Write what you will do.

_____

_____

O God, who gave one origin to all peoples and willed to gather from them one family for yourself, fill all hearts, we pray, . . . for the just advancement of their neighbor, that, through the good things . . . each human person may be brought to perfection, every division may be removed, and equity and justice may be established in human society. Amen.

Collect for the Progress of Peoples, Roman Missal

The Carmelites

The Carmelites, a religious order of men and women, are located all over the world. They serve the Church by teaching, preaching, missionary work, and parish life. Prayer, contemplation, and community life are important to all Carmelite groups. However, some Carmelites devote themselves totally to a cloistered, or secluded, way of life.

The Carmelites began with men who had left Europe and retreated to Palestine to live a life of prayer and solitude. They gathered on Mount Carmel, in present-day Israel. During the twelfth century, these hermits received a rule of life from Albert Avogadro, the ordained leader of the Church in Jerusalem. Under Albert's direction, the individual hermits formed small communities that devoted themselves to prayer and solitude. The Carmelites value prayer and community. They believe that prayer helps people form an intimate relationship with God, which flows into a life of service.

As their numbers grew, the Carmelites moved from Palestine to other parts of the world. In 1238, Simon Stock, an English Carmelite, led the community to become an order of friars. Similar to the Franciscans and Dominicans, the members of this order began working outside of their monasteries. They actively taught in universities. Around that time, an enclosed order of Carmelite nuns was also established.

In the fifteenth century the Carmelites experienced a major decline in members. However, in the sixteenth century, a reform of the Order was led by John of the Cross and Teresa of Jesus (Teresa of Ávila), and the Order was strengthened. Eventually, the reformed group became a separate Order known as the Discalced Carmelites. *Discalced* means "barefoot."

Two spiritual models who greatly inspire Carmelites are Mary and the Old Testament prophet Elijah. The earliest hermits were inspired by and devoted to Mary. They became known as the Brothers of Our Lady of Mount Carmel. Elijah is sometimes called the "fiery prophet" because Elijah was zealous for the Lord. Elijah is a special inspiration to the Carmelites because God spoke to him in a tiny whispering sound when he was in a cave on Mount Horeb. (See 1 Kings 19:12.) It was in hearing God's voice that Elijah was moved to speak out against injustice.

The Carmelites are formed of two separate Orders: the Discalced Carmelites and the Carmelites of the Ancient Observance. Within each, there are friars and nuns. Some men and women of the Carmelite family have ministries away from their communities. They teach, lead parishes, work in the missions, and develop other ministries around the needs of the people they serve. Other Carmelite friars and nuns stay in cloistered communities, where their only work is prayer.

Gifts for the Church

Sometimes we do not realize how much we have been blessed by God or how much we have to offer. Yet we are blessed with many gifts and talents, and God wants us to be generous. God himself is generous. God showers gifts on us all.

A *charism* is a specific gift or grace of the Holy Spirit which is given to benefit the Church by helping a person live out the Christian life or by building up the Church on Earth. In his letters, Paul speaks about the charisms of teaching, healing, and prophecy, among others. One of the Carmelite charisms is contemplation. Carmelites recognize and cherish this gift from God. They realize that he wants to build up the Church through them. By using their charism of contemplative prayer, Carmelites enrich the life of the whole Church. In contemplative prayer, the person praying is resting in God's presence, simply listening. From contemplative prayers have come many of God's gifts to the Church. Two famous Carmelites, Saint Teresa of Jesus (Teresa of Ávila) and Saint John of the Cross, left writings and directions for prayer that we still use today.

Activity

Think of the gifts God has given you. Which of these gifts help you live as a follower of Jesus and help build up the Church? What is challenging about using these gifts?

My gifts from God: _____

How I can use these gifts to make the Church stronger: _____

_____

My challenge in using these gifts: _____

_____

Holy Father, who, though urging all the faithful to perfect charity, never cease to prompt many to follow more closely in the footsteps of your Son, grant, we pray, that those you have chosen for this special calling may, by their way of life, show to the Church and the world a clear sign of your Kingdom. Amen.

Collect for Vocation to the Religious Life, Roman Missal

What Is Your Liturgical Year IQ?

How much do you know about the liturgical year? Take this fun quiz and find out!

1. The liturgical year begins on _____ .
   a. Easter Sunday
   b. New Year's Day
   c. the First Sunday of Advent
   d. Christmas Day

2. On January 1, we celebrate the Solemnity of _____ .
   a. the Epiphany of the Lord
   b. Pentecost Sunday
   c. Mary, the Holy Mother of God
   d. the Baptism of the Lord

3. _____ appears twice on the liturgical calendar.
   a. Advent
   b. Lent
   c. Easter
   d. Ordinary Time

4. _____ is the liturgical color for Lent.
   a. White
   b. Purple
   c. Green
   d. Pink

5. _____ is a holy day of obligation.
   a. The Transfiguration of the Lord
   b. The Assumption of the Blessed Virgin Mary
   c. The Annunciation of the Lord
   d. All Souls Day

6. At every celebration of Mass, we celebrate _____ .
   a. the Resurrection
   b. Advent
   c. Pentecost Sunday
   d. the Assumption of the Blessed Virgin Mary

7. Advent begins _____ Sundays before Christmas.
   a. one
   b. two
   c. three
   d. four

8. The Triduum begins on _____ and ends on Easter Sunday evening with Evening Prayer.
   a. Holy Thursday
   b. Holy Saturday
   c. Good Friday
   d. Palm Sunday

9. The Blessed Virgin Mary is honored on _____.
   a. the Ascension of the Lord
   b. the Assumption of the Blessed Virgin Mary
   c. the Epiphany of the Lord
   d. Pentecost Sunday

10. The liturgical seasons of _____ have the liturgical colors of white or gold?
   a. Ordinary Time and Lent
   b. Christmas and Easter
   c. Advent and Easter
   d. Advent and Lent

OUR CATHOLIC HERITAGE

What Catholics Believe

We share a common faith based on Sacred Scripture and on the Tradition of the Church founded on the teachings of the Apostles. Guided by the Holy Spirit, the Catholic Church teaches the authentic message of Jesus Christ.

How Catholics Worship

We celebrate our faith in worship when we give honor and praise to God. Worship is so vital for the Church that it is the first "work" of God's people. The official public worship of the Church is called the liturgy.

How Catholics Live

Living as Jesus taught is not easy, but God gives us lots of help. Our conscience and other special gifts help us learn God's will. When we turn away from sin and make good choices, we live as children of God.

How Catholics Pray

When we pray, we express our faith in God. We can pray alone. We can also pray with others when we gather for worship.

Doctrine Review

Sacred Scripture

God's Self-Revelation to humanity is
faithfully recorded in Sacred Scripture,
or the Bible. The Scriptures consist of
the forty-six books of the Old Testament
and the twenty-seven books of the New
Testament.

God is the true author of these sacred
writings because the Holy Spirit inspired
the people who wrote them. The Church
relies on the guidance of the Holy Spirit
to discern what God means to reveal to
us through the Scriptures. One of the chief duties of the pope and bishops is to
authentically explain the true meaning
of the Scriptures to the faithful.

The Old Testament

The forty-six books of the Old Testament include a variety of forms of writing,
such as stories, laws, history, poetry, and prayers. In the Old Testament, we
read the words of the prophets foretelling the coming of Jesus and his mission of Salvation. The coming of Jesus, our Savior, is also foretold through the
words and deeds of others, such as Moses and King David.

The first five books of the Old Testament, called the **Pentateuch**, are
important because they tell about the Creation and the Fall of Humanity, God's
Covenant with Abraham, the Passover, the Exodus, and the Covenant at Mount
Sinai. These books also teach that God ultimately rescues all humanity from
the slavery of sin through the Passover and Exodus of Jesus' Death and
Resurrection.

The New Testament

The twenty-seven books of the New Testament consist of the four accounts of
the Gospel; the Acts of the Apostles; twenty-one letters, or Epistles, written
by Saint Paul and other early Christians; and the Book of Revelation, which is
also known as the **Apocalypse**. Of these books, the most important are the four
Gospels, which tell about the teachings and actions of Jesus. The Gospels are
the basis for the Church's official teachings and practices, which we call the
Church's Tradition.

Because of the central importance of the Sacred Scriptures for our faith,
the Church uses them often in her liturgical prayer and worship. The Church
also encourages us to prayerfully read and reflect upon the Scriptures regularly in private and with others.

Activity

How well do you know the Bible? What are your favorite Scripture stories? Retell
one story from the Old Testament and one from the New Testament.

The Trinity

✝ "And I will ask the Father, and he will give you another Advocate to be with you always."

John 14:16

There is only one God. God reveals his name to Moses in Exodus 3:14, as **Yahweh**, which means "I am who I am." This Divine Name reveals that God is the source of Creation and the source of all truth and love. In Jesus God has also revealed himself to be One God in Three Divine Persons—Father, Son, and Holy Spirit—sharing equally the same one Divine Nature. That is why we refer to God as the Blessed, or Holy, Trinity. Grace is the help that God gives us to carry out his will. Grace introduces us into the fellowship of the Trinity.

Belief in the Trinity, One God in Three Divine Persons, is the central mystery of our faith. We know God as Three Divine Persons only because he has revealed himself to us in this way. We are not able to know the Trinity just by human intelligence alone. Since God alone is both the source of our existence and our Salvation, no creature should ever be regarded as being more important than God or as being a substitute for him.

In the Church's Tradition we speak about certain "works" for each of the Three Divine Persons. We speak of the Father as our Creator, the Son as our Savior, and the Holy Spirit as our Sanctifier. This is helpful to us in understanding God's nature, but we need to remember that all three Persons share equally in all the works of God.

We Honor God the Father as Our Creator

God created the universe **ex nihilo**, that is, from nothing. All that exists comes into existence solely through the power of God's will. Because the universe and all that is in it is created by God, it reflects and communicates God's glory and goodness. God intends for all his creatures, especially people, to reflect and share in his own truth, goodness, and beauty. Our own dignity, or "glory," comes from the fact that God has created us in his divine image and likeness. Throughout the Old Testament and through the teaching and example of Jesus in the New Testament, we learn that we are to approach our all-powerful Creator with confidence as our gentle, loving, compassionate, and merciful Father. We are called to do God's will as his loving children and to be thankful for his ever-faithful love and care for us.

Faith Words

Yahweh *Yahweh* is a Hebrew name for God meaning "I am who I am." In the Old Testament, this is God's sacred name, which he revealed to Moses.

ex nihilo *Ex nihilo* is a Latin phrase meaning "from nothing." It is used to describe how God created all that is, seen and unseen.

We Honor God the Son as Our Savior

The only Son of God, without losing his Divine Nature, became man, Jesus Christ. The Church calls this mystery the Incarnation. At the beginning of the Gospel of John, we find a beautiful summary of this mystery. John writes, "In

the beginning was the Word, / and the Word was with God. . . . / And the Word became flesh / and made his dwelling among us, / and we saw his glory, / the glory as of the Father's only Son, / full of grace and truth" (John 1:1, 14).

Jesus Christ makes it possible for us to share in the divine life, the very life of God. As true God and true man, Jesus Christ is the one and only true Mediator between God and people. The name *Jesus* means "God saves." *Christ*, which means "Anointed of God" in Greek and "God's Messiah" in Hebrew, is the title given to Jesus because he has been anointed by God to save his people.

While on Earth, Jesus, the Incarnate Word of God, proceeded by his words and actions to fully reveal God the Father's love for us. At the end of his life on Earth, Jesus, in obedience to his Father, died on the Cross to free us from sin and death. Jesus Christ has won for us Salvation through his Death and Resurrection. Before he ascended into Heaven, Jesus promised that his Father would send the Holy Spirit to the Church to be our advocate, or helper, until he returns at the end of time to bring about the perfection of God's kingdom.

We Honor God the Holy Spirit as Our Sanctifier

The Holy Spirit is the divine love that is shared by the Father and the Son. The Holy Spirit has been at work in creation from the beginning of time, guiding it to achieve the perfection planned by God. The Holy Spirit dwells in the People of God and helps us live as Jesus taught. The Holy Spirit strengthens us in holiness by giving us the seven Gifts of the Holy Spirit; which are wisdom, understanding, counsel, fortitude, knowledge, piety, and fear of the Lord. The Holy Spirit guides the Church in her efforts to understand the Scriptures and also protects the Church from falling into error when it teaches officially about faith and morals. The Holy Spirit is given to a person at Baptism, and his presence is strengthened in us at Confirmation.

Activity

Draw some symbols or images you feel might be used to represent the mystery of the Blessed Trinity. Be prepared to explain the meaning of your images.

Faith and Salvation

The message of the cross is foolishness to those who are perishing, but to us who are being saved it is the power of God.

1 Corinthians 1:18

Faith is both a gift from God and a human act by which the believer makes a personal commitment of the whole person to God, who invites the believer's response. In faith we entrust our mind, body, and spirit to God. This involves the assent of both our intellect and our will to the truth God has made known to us about himself. This Self-Revelation by God is found in Sacred Scripture and Sacred Tradition. Faith is one of the three Theological Virtues. Without faith we cannot hope to be saved—that is, achieve the communion with God for which he created us. We cannot acquire faith through our own effort. Faith is a gift from God, a grace that is given through the Holy Spirit.

Creation and the Fall

All of God's creatures have their own special good-ness. There is also a wonderful interdependence and order that exists among all the creatures of the universe. God created human beings to have both a physical body and a spiritual soul. Each person possesses a spiritual and immortal soul created directly by God. People have been chosen by God to be the stewards of his creation. God intends all creatures for the good of the entire human race.

Sacred Scripture tells us that our first parents, Adam and Eve, enjoyed a state of holiness and inti-macy with God and the happiness of living in Paradise. Unfortunately, they gave in to the temptation of the Evil One. They abused their freedom by rebelling against God and attempting to achieve their happiness apart from him. As a result of this Original Sin, our first parents lost for themselves and their descendants this state of original holiness. Because human nature has been weakened by Original Sin, we are subject to ignorance, suffering, and ultimately physical death.

Salvation Comes Through Christ

Salvation is the result of God's love for humanity and his desire that we enjoy everlasting happiness and eternal life with him. God the Father sent his only Son, Jesus, who freely offered himself to atone for our sins. Jesus' life, Passion, Death, Resurrection and Ascension make it possible for us to actually share in divine life. Jesus Christ is the one and only true Mediator between God and people.

Faith Words

fiat *Fiat* is a Latin word meaning "Let it happen" or "Let it be done."

Theotokos *Theotokos* is a Greek word mean-ing "God-bearer." The early Church used this word to express that Mary is truly the Mother of God.

The Church is catholic. We believe the Church is catholic, or universal, because it proclaims the totality of Christ's teaching and Salvation to the entire world through all time.

The Church is apostolic. We believe the Church is apostolic because it can trace its faith back to the teaching and practices of the Apostles. The Church is apostolic because the pope and bishops are the true successors of the Apostles. The pope, the Bishop of Rome and official head of the Church, is the successor of Saint Peter, who was appointed by Christ to be the head of his Church on Earth. The bishops are the visible source and foundation of the unity of their own diocesan churches. As successors of the Apostles, the bishops also provide their particular churches with a visible bond of unity with the pope and the universal Church.

Called to Witness

It is the mission of the Church to bear witness to the Good News of the saving deeds of God accomplished in Jesus. All members of the Church, not just clergy and religious, by virtue of their Baptism and Confirmation are responsible for carrying out this mission. All the baptized, who participate in the one priesthood of Christ, which is called the common priesthood of the faithful, by virtue of their Baptism, are called to holiness and to bear witness to Christ in their daily lives.

The Communion of Saints

All the members of the Church, both living and dead, are joined together in the Communion of Saints. This holy unity of people and things is brought about in a special way through the celebration of the Eucharist, the Sacrament of unity. Because of this unity, the Church on Earth remembers and prays for her members who have died and are in Purgatory, and also prays to the saints in Heaven for their help and assistance. The Church also looks to the angels, pure spiritual, personal, and immortal beings created by God with intelligence and free will, for protection and help. Angels are present with God in Heaven to give him glory ceaselessly. They are the messengers of his saving plan on behalf of the Church and all humankind.

Activity

List some opportunities a student your age might have to bear witness to Christ and the Gospel. Share your ideas with the others in your class.

Life Everlasting

When Christ your life appears, then you too will appear with him in glory.

Colossians 3:4

All people will continue in existence after their physical death. At the moment of death, each individual is personally judged by Christ in a *particular judgment* and is rewarded or condemned according to personal deeds. At the end of time all human beings will experience a resurrection of their bodies and all people will appear before the tribunal of Christ to give an account of their deeds in the *Last Judgment*.

The Raising of Lazarus
by Jacopo Tintoretto

Heaven and Hell

Each person determines whether they will spend eternity in Heaven or hell. God gives each human being both an intellect and a free will. All human beings are free to seek God and do his will as it is revealed to them in their conscience. Those who choose to seek God with a sincere heart and persevere in that choice until their death and die in a state of grace are welcomed by God into Heaven. No one knows what Heaven is actually like, but we do know that those who are welcomed into Heaven will enjoy the **Beatific Vision** in everlasting happiness with God.

If a person freely and deliberately sins gravely and rejects God's love and dies without first repenting and seeking his forgiveness, that person has chosen to spend eternity separated from God. Since we are created for union with God, Hell consists primarily of being eternally separated from God and his love.

God's Mercy

Through parables, such as the Lost Sheep and the Prodigal Son, Jesus taught that God is eager to welcome back any sinner, no matter how often or how grievously the person has sinned. God does not take any pleasure in the condemnation of the sinner, but rejoices when the sinner turns from sin and returns to him and his love. For this reason, Christ bestowed on the Church the power to forgive sin in his name, a power it exercises through the ministry of bishops and priests in the Sacrament of Penance and Reconciliation.

Faith Words

Beatific Vision The Beatific Vision is the contemplation of God, which brings everlasting happiness and peace.

All Souls Day All Souls Day is the day on which we pray for the souls undergoing purification in Purgatory. We celebrate All Souls Day on November 2.

Period of Purification

It is possible for a person to die in God's friendship and at the same time need more purification to achieve the holiness necessary before entering Heaven. Traditionally the Church has called this process of purification *Purgatory*, a final cleansing of remaining effects of one's sinfulness before entering the joy of Heaven. Rooted in this belief is the Church's practice of encouraging her members to offer prayers and sacrifices, especially the Holy Sacrifice of the Eucharist, for the souls in Purgatory. The Church believes the living can assist the dead in this way, just as the Church believes the saints in Heaven can assist us through their prayers. The Church has set aside November 2 as **All Souls Day**. On this day the Church offers prayers for all the faithful departed undergoing purification.

The Magnificat by Christopher Santer

The Assumption of the Blessed Virgin Mary

Because of Mary's unique role in God's plan of Salvation, she was preserved from the stain of Original Sin and all personal sin. After her death, Mary was taken up, body and soul, into the glory of Heaven. Mary shares in the glory of her Son's Resurrection in anticipation of the end of time when all the members of his Body will enjoy the resurrection of their own bodies. The Church remembers and celebrates Mary's Assumption into Heaven on August 15.

The End of Time

Only God knows when and how the world will end. But whenever it does happen, Christ will appear in glory, a universal resurrection will occur, all people will be judged, and the just will be forever united to Christ and live with him in the Kingdom of God. The material universe will undergo a transformation, and a "new creation" will be established. God will dwell in the midst of this new creation as the source of unending joy and happiness for all the just who will be able to see him face to face. All our longings as human beings for love, peace, justice, and unity will be completely and permanently satisfied.

Activity

In Heaven we will be perfectly happy. List some things that would make you happy right now. Then circle those you believe you will actually be able to experience in Heaven. Be prepared to explain your choices.

Sacraments of
✚ Christian Initiation

"You are my beloved Son; with you I am well pleased." *Mark 1:11*

The process of Christian initiation involves the celebration of three distinct but interrelated Sacraments: Baptism, Confirmation, and Eucharist. The Sacrament of Baptism marks the beginning of new life in Christ. The Sacrament of Confirmation marks the strengthening of this new life. The Sacrament of Eucharist nourishes us with Christ's Body and Blood to support Christ's life in us and continues our transformation in him.

Baptism

The water of the Sacrament of Baptism is a sacramental sign of our participation in Christ's Death and of our own death to sin. Baptism is also a sign of our participation in the Resurrection of Christ and our own rebirth to new life in Christ. Through Baptism, we are united to Christ and become members of the Church, the Body of Christ. The effects of this initiation into the life of Christ include the following: (a) Original Sin and any personal sins committed prior to Baptism are forgiven; (b) our new life in Christ establishes us as adopted children of the Father; (c) as members of Christ we become temples of the Holy Spirit; (d) we become sharers in the priesthood of Christ; and (e) we are freed from the slavery of sin and given access to true freedom in Christ.

Baptism of Christ by Paolo Veronese

At the celebration of the Sacrament of Baptism, the priest or deacon prays, "I baptize you in the name of the Father, / and of the Son, / and of the Holy Spirit" *(Rite of Baptism)*. The person being baptized is then immersed in the water, or water is poured over their head, three times. From ancient times it has been a custom in the Church for the faithful to bring their infants or young children to be baptized, since faith is a grace and gift of God that does not presuppose any human merit. In such cases the young children are baptized in the faith of their parents and of the Church.

Faith Words

age of reason The age of reason is the age at which children are able to distinguish between right and wrong, approximately age seven.

Confirmation

The Sacrament of Confirmation deepens and brings to maturity the grace of Baptism. Through the sacramental sign of anointing with Sacred Chrism, Christ pours out the Holy Spirit on those receiving the Sacrament. The Holy Spirit incorporates the newly confirmed more deeply into Christ and strengthens their bond with the Church. Finally, the Holy Spirit empowers the newly confirmed to enter fully into the Church's ministry and her mission, especially the mission to courageously bear witness to Christ in the world.

To be eligible for the Sacrament of Confirmation, a person must first be baptized. The candidate must also have attained the **age of reason**; must be willing to publicly profess faith in Jesus Christ and the Church; must be in a state of grace; must have the desire and intention of receiving the Sacrament; and must be willing to take on the duties of a disciple of Christ. In the rite of

Confirmation, the bishop (or priest acting in his behalf) lays hands on the the person being confirmed and anoints the person's forehead with Sacred Chrism as he prays, "(Name), be sealed with the Gift of the Holy Spirit." The Sacraments of Confirmation and Baptism place a permanent spiritual mark upon the soul. For this reason, Catholics receive these Sacraments only once.

Eucharist

The reception of the Sacrament of Eucharist for the first time marks the last step in the Catholic's initiation into the life of Christ and the Church. Catholics take their rightful place at the table of the Lord as full members of the Church. It is the beginning of the lifelong process of being nourished by Christ's Body and Blood in order to keep and increase life in Christ.

Sacramentals

Sacramentals are distinct from the Seven Sacraments. They are sacred signs (certain objects, actions, prayers, and blessings) instituted by the Church to help prepare us to receive the grace of the Sacraments.

Activity

The age for celebrating the Sacrament of Confirmation is not the same in every diocese. Some dioceses confirm at age seven; others at age ten; and the majority between the ages of fourteen and eighteen. What do you think is the best age to be confirmed? Be prepared to explain your choice.

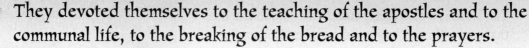

The Mass

✝ They devoted themselves to the teaching of the apostles and to the communal life, to the breaking of the bread and to the prayers.

Acts of the Apostles 2:42

The celebration of the Mass, which the Church also calls the Eucharist, is the greatest act of worship and praise the Church offers God through her liturgy. *Eucharist* is a Greek word that means "thanksgiving" or "to give thanks." The Mass is by its nature public and communal. It is the work of the whole Church and is not to be approached as a private devotion. Only a validly ordained priest can be the celebrant at the Mass and consecrate the bread and wine so that they become the Body and Blood of Christ. By virtue of our sharing in the one priesthood of Christ through Baptism, which is different than the ministerial priesthood of the ordained, we are to unite our prayers to those of the priest. The Church urges us to actively participate during Mass. At every Mass, it is Christ, our High Priest, who, acting through the ministry of the priest, offers himself in a sacrifice of worship to the Father.

Essential Elements of the Eucharistic Ritual

The Eucharistic celebration should always include the following elements: (1) the proclamation of the Word of God; (2) prayers in which the Body and Blood of Christ is offered in a sacrifice of thanksgiving to God the Father for his saving deeds and his many gifts to us, especially his Son, Jesus; (3) the consecration of the bread and wine into the Body and Blood of Christ; and (4) participation in the liturgical banquet in which the priest and the faithful receive the Body and Blood of Christ in an act of communion that unites them to Christ and one another. These four elements of the Mass make up a single act of worship. To these essential elements, the Church may add other elements in keeping with local customs and the nature of particular feast days. The liturgical celebration may at times include such elements as a formal procession, the singing of hymns, the sprinkling of the faithful with holy water, the use of incense, and so on. The whole Church—the Body of Christ, united with Christ as its Head, Christ and all the faithful members—celebrates the sacramental liturgy.

Faith Words

sacrificial meal The term *sacrificial meal* describes the Mass, which is both a holy sacrifice and a sacred meal.

A Memorial and a Sacrifice

The Mass is a **sacrificial meal**. The Church teaches that every Mass is both a memorial and a sacrifice. The Mass is a memorial because the Church celebrates the Eucharist in response to Jesus' command, "do this in memory of me." But the Church does more than just recall or remember Jesus and his work. The Eucharist makes Jesus and his work sacramentally present. The Mass is a sacrifice because through the sacramental signs of bread and wine and the words of consecration, Jesus' sacrifice on the Cross is made present again in our midst. It makes it possible for us to enter into and share in the one timeless offering of the one sacrifice of Jesus Christ. The Church offers the Eucharist as a holy sacrifice in reparation for the sins of the living and the dead and to petition God's blessings on the Church and the world.

The Mystery of Transubstantiation

At the heart of the Mass is the mystery of *transubstantiation.* That is the word the Church uses to describe the mystery of faith that through the words and actions of the priest and the power of the Holy Spirit, ordinary bread and wine become the Body and Blood of Christ without losing their normal appearances of bread and wine. Christ himself is truly and wholly present in his Body and Blood, Soul and Divinity, under the appearances of bread and wine. The Church uses the phrase "Real Presence" to express this truth of faith.

Holy Communion

Receiving our Lord in Holy Communion is an essential element of the Mass. The priest celebrant is obligated to receive Communion, and the Church urges Catholics to partake of this sacred banquet each time they participate in the Mass when they are in the state of grace and rightly disposed. Every Catholic has the obligation to receive Communion at least once during each year between the First Sunday of Lent and Pentecost Sunday. When we receive Holy Communion, Christ unites us to himself and to one another, nourishing us with his own strength and holiness.

Essential Signs

The essential signs used by the Church to effect the Sacrament of the Eucharist include the use of unleavened wheat bread and grape wine, which recall the kind of bread and wine Jesus used at the Last Supper. They also include the words of consecration Jesus himself used at the Last Supper. (See Luke 22:18–19.)

Activity

Make a list of all the actions and responses the faithful are called upon to do or say when participating at Mass. Compare your list with those of others in your class.

Sacraments of Healing

✝ "But now we must celebrate and rejoice, because your brother was dead and has come to life again; he was lost and has been found."

Luke 15:32

◆ ◇ ◆

While he was on Earth, Jesus healed people both spiritually and physically. He forgave sinners and cured various infirmities of body and mind. Jesus then empowered and commissioned the Church to continue healing in his name after he ascended to Heaven. It is through the two Sacraments of Healing that the Church continues the healing ministry of Jesus. The Sacraments of Healing are Penance and Reconciliation (also known as the Sacrament of Conversion and Confession) and Anointing of the Sick.

Penance and Reconciliation

Through the Sacrament of Penance and Reconciliation, we receive spiritual healing by obtaining forgiveness for any sins we commit after Baptism. Three actions are required of the penitent in this Sacrament. First, the penitent must make an expression of sincere sorrow or contrition for having sinned. Authentic contrition involves **conversion**—turning away from sin and resolving to avoid sin in the future. Second, the penitent is required to confess their serious sins to the priest. It is important to remember that the Church teaches that to obtain forgiveness it is necessary to confess all serious sins. The Church also teaches the importance of making a careful and thorough examination of conscience before receiving the Sacrament. Though we are not required to confess venial sins, the Church strongly recommends it. Third, the penitent must have the intention to do the penance assigned by the priest and make reparation for the harm their sins have caused and to do any works of reparation the priest may assign.

The priest, in the name of Christ and the Church, then pronounces the words of absolution through which the penitent's sins are completely forgiven. Only validly ordained priests may pronounce the words of absolution. They receive this authority, or *faculty,* from the Church. The bishop normally gives this faculty to all the priests ministering in his diocese. The Church teaches that receiving this Sacrament is the Catholic's ordinary means of reconciliation with God and the Church.

Faith Words

conversion From a Latin word meaning "to turn around," *conversion* means "a turning away from sin."

Spiritual Effects of the Sacrament of Penance and Reconciliation

Celebrating the Sacrament of Penance and Reconciliation provides the penitent with spiritual healing. The penitent is reconciled with God and restored to the state of God's grace. The penitent is also reconciled to the Church and, if the confession of mortal sin was necessary, can once again receive Holy Communion. The eternal punishment merited through serious sin is removed, and at least part of the temporal punishment we receive because of our sins is also removed. It should be noted that the temporal punishment due to sin can be further pardoned through indulgences. The penitent experiences a sense of peace and spiritual consolation. Serenity of conscience is restored. Finally, the penitent receives an increase of spiritual strength for pursuing good and resisting the temptation to sin in the future.

Anointing of the Sick

The Sacrament of Anointing of the Sick brings special graces to those experiencing the difficulties that accompany serious illness or old age. However, it is the custom of the Church to administer this Sacrament at other times as well, such as when a person is about to undergo a serious and possibly life-threatening surgery. The Church also encourages communal celebrations of Anointing of the Sick at which many elderly and those suffering from physical or emotional illness are anointed. In all cases the Church requires a bishop or priest to administer this Sacrament.

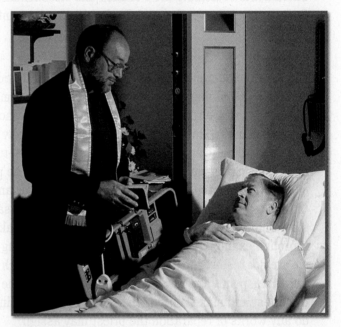

The Sacrament of Anointing of the Sick is intended to help people deal with their illnesses and unite them to the sufferings of Christ. Those being anointed can also obtain forgiveness of sins if they are unable to do so through the Sacrament of Penance and Reconciliation. On occasion, the Sacrament of Anointing of the Sick has been reported to effect physical healing when this has been helpful to the sick person's Salvation.

The Rite of Anointing

In this Sacrament, the priest, acting in the name of Christ and the Church, anoints the forehead and hands of the sick or elderly person. Other parts of the body may also be anointed in keeping with circumstances and local custom. The priest also prays certain liturgical prayers asking that God's strength, healing grace, and forgiveness be bestowed upon the person. The oil used in the anointing in the celebration of this Sacrament is called the Oil of the Sick. It is specially blessed for this purpose by the bishop.

Activity

Have you ever known someone who has received the Sacrament of Anointing of the Sick? Discuss with a classmate what takes place in this Sacrament.

Sacraments at the Service of Communion

✝ For this we toil and struggle, because we have set our hope on the living God, who is the savior of all, especially of those who believe.

1 Timothy 4:10

◇ ◇ ◇

The Sacraments at the Service of Communion are Holy Orders and Matrimony. Through these Sacraments, Jesus continues to minister to the Church, fostering its growth in faith, service, and unity.

Holy Orders

Through the Sacrament of Holy Orders, the Church ordains bishops, priests (or presbyters), and deacons. The word *ordain* means "to set aside" or "to empower a person to carry on the work of the Apostles." Bishops, as the rightful successors of the Apostles, possess the fullness of the ministerial priesthood. Priests are united to the bishops and carry out their priestly duties as the bishops' co-workers. Deacons are helpers of the bishops and priests and are ordained for specific tasks of ministerial service on behalf of the Church. These duties include proclaiming the Word of God, witnessing sacramental marriages, administering Baptism, and works of **pastoral** care and charity. Deacons are not empowered to lead the celebration of Mass, hear confessions, or anoint the sick. Deacons carry out their ministry under the pastoral authority of the bishop. Unlike bishops and priests, deacons, unless they intend to become priests, may be married before they become deacons. Only men are called to the ordained priesthood and to the diaconate and only official **episcopal** authority has the right and responsibility to call to ordination those whom it judges suitable to carry out the tasks entailed by ordained ministry.

Faith Words

pastoral *Pastor* is the Latin word for "shepherd." *Pastoral* describes the work of bishops and priests in "shepherding," or guiding and caring for, people in the Church.

episcopal The word *episcopal* is used to describe bishops or the objects, actions, and events in their ministry.

Rite of Ordination

Only bishops can ordain other bishops, priests and deacons. In the ordination of priests to the office of bishop, three ordained bishops must participate. In an ordination of a priest, the bishop places his hands on the head of the baptized man being ordained. The bishop prays the Solemn Prayer of Consecration asking God to bestow upon this man the grace of the Holy Spirit to empower him to carry out his ministerial duties. Those ordained to be a priest or bishop are also anointed with Sacred Chrism. In the ordination of a deacon, the bishop lays his hands on the candidate's head in silence. Then he kneels before the bishop, who prays over him. Like the Sacraments of Baptism and Confirmation, the Sacrament of Holy Orders places a permanent spiritual mark on the soul of the man being ordained.

Matrimony

The Sacrament of Matrimony, or Marriage, consists of a baptized man and a baptized woman freely and mutually making promises through which they agree to give themselves entirely to each other in a lifelong covenant of faithful and fruitful love that is open to the gift of children. Marriage is a public state that affects the life of both the Church and society. Because of this, it is fitting that this Sacrament be celebrated publicly in the presence of the faith community. At a minimum, the Church requires that the marriage promises be exchanged in the presence of a priest or deacon, who represents the Church, and two additional witnesses. The Church encourages the couple to celebrate the Sacrament within the celebration of Mass. The baptized couple are actually the ministers of this Sacrament because their mutual promise of love and fidelity effects the Sacrament.

Effects of Matrimony

Through the Sacrament of Matrimony, God gives the couple special graces to sustain them, to help them grow in love for each other and to fulfill their marriage obligations. Their mutual love and their life together are signs of Christ's love for the Church. Through their physical love for each other, which is the complete giving of themselves to each other and the sharing of God's creative power, the married man and woman become one. This is why the Church teaches that sexual love is reserved for married couples only. Catholic parents also accept the responsibility of sharing their faith with their children. The love and care parents give their children is a reflection of God's love. In turn, children owe their parents gratitude and assistance. This obligation is necessary for harmony within the family. The Church considers the Catholic family to be a *domestic Church* because family members are called to nurture one another in faith and to witness to the Gospel through their hospitality, charity, and compassion.

Activity

Make a list of some of the qualities you feel are important for an ordained priest to have.

Conscience

✝ For the whole law is fulfilled in one statement, namely, "You shall love your neighbor as yourself."

Galatians 5:14

God created us in his own image, with a spiritual soul having both an intellect and a free will. We are by nature destined to find everlasting happiness in God. To achieve that destiny, however, we are obliged to "do good and avoid evil," which is the fundamental moral law. The role of our conscience is to help us recognize good and evil and choose good over evil. However, this is not always that easy. Because human nature has been wounded by Original Sin, we are subject to errors of judgment and are inclined to seek evil when exercising our freedom. On the positive side, the Holy Spirit guides us toward moral maturity, a maturity that finally reaches its fulfillment in Heaven.

Making Moral Decisions

There are three elements involved in determining the morality of human acts: the object, the intention, and the circumstances. The object refers to the nature of the act we are considering. Some acts, such as helping a poor person or forgiving an enemy, are naturally good. Some acts, such as stealing from the poor or seeking vengeance against an enemy, are by their nature evil. For an act to be judged morally good, the object of that act must be good. The intention refers to our reason for doing the act. An act can be morally wrong if we have an evil intention for doing it. For example, a person might give to the poor solely to gain the praise of others without any real concern for the poor. The circumstances also affect the morality of an act. For example, in the Gospels we read the story of the poor widow who gave a few cents to the Temple. The goodness of her moral act was greater than that of the rich people who gave large amounts of money. Due to her financial circumstances, hers was a much larger act of generosity. For an act to be judged morally good, the object, the intention, and the circumstances must all be good. We are not allowed to seek a good moral goal by using immoral or evil means for achieving it.

Faith Words

virtue A virtue is an ability to make morally good decisions that lead to the habit of doing good. Christian virtues are considered gifts from God that we can develop into habits of Christian living.

Morality and Freedom

We are morally responsible for our acts because we have free will. The acts we freely and knowingly choose to do belong to us, and so do the consequences that come from those acts. But in some cases, circumstances can diminish our ability to choose freely and knowingly, and therefore diminish our moral responsibility. Such circumstances include ignorance that we are not responsible for, being forced to act by others, fear, and other psychological and social factors. Lack of information, however, does not automatically excuse us. We have the obligation to form our conscience in keeping with the moral law and to make an effort to become informed of the true moral nature of actions before we choose them. Reading and reflecting on the Word of God is a sure source for forming our conscience. The moral teachings of the Church and the advice and good example of the faith community also help us form a right conscience.

Virtue and the Moral Life

Virtue is the spiritual power or habit and firm disposition to do good. Like all good habits, virtues can be acquired by repeatedly choosing to do particular morally good acts and choosing to avoid particular morally evil acts. Such repeated good moral choices help us develop a reliable intellect and a strong will, enabling us to behave in ways that reflect faith and good reasoning.

There are four virtues called Moral Virtues. They are prudence, justice, fortitude, and temperance. These virtues are also known as the Cardinal Virtues. Prudence is the virtue that helps us sort out the potential good or evil of a situation and to make good moral judgments. Justice is the habit of treating others fairly in all our dealings with them. Fortitude is the habit of being willing to choose the right moral course even in difficult circumstances and when faced with opposition. Temperance is the habit of living in moderation and maintaining control over our natural desires.

The Theological Virtues

The three virtues of faith, hope, and charity are called Theological Virtues for two reasons. First, they are gifts from God. We do not acquire them by our own effort, though we are obligated to exercise them through the use of our free will. Second, God is their object. These virtues help us to believe in, hope in, and love God above all else.

Activity

Whom do you consider your best source for advice on moral matters? Be prepared to explain your choice.

Sin and Mercy

"I am the good shepherd. A good shepherd lays down his life for the sheep."

John 10:11

The reality of sin and God's ever-present mercy and willingness to forgive us are two themes that run throughout both the Old Testament and the New Testament. In one sense, Scripture is the story of God's efforts to save us from our sinfulness and to reunite us to himself.

The Nature of Sin

Sin is an act contrary to human reason because it leads us away from the goal for which we are destined—to be together with God. Sin is any free choice that we knowingly make that goes against God's Law and his plan for creation. We can sin by freely doing what we know is against God's Law (sins of commission) or by freely choosing not to do what we know is right (sins of omission). When we sin, we live contrary to the way Jesus teaches us to live.

The Church distinguishes between mortal sin and venial sin. Mortal sin is a serious violation of God's Law. It is called "mortal" (meaning "deadly") because it sets itself against and turns our hearts away from God's life-giving love, or sanctifying grace. If we die without seeking forgiveness, mortal sin results in eternal separation from God, or eternal death. Three conditions must be present for an act to be judged a mortal sin: (1) the action must be gravely wrong; (2) we must fully know and understand that the act is gravely wrong; (3) we must make a free choice to commit the sin.

Venial sin is an offense against God's Law that is not gravely wrong. Venial sin does not separate us from God's love but weakens our relationship with him and the Church community. While forgiveness of mortal sin requires us to receive the Sacrament of Penance and Reconciliation, venial sin can be forgiven through expressing our sorrow and performing good works. However, the Church encourages the practice of confessing venial sins in the Sacrament of Penance and Reconciliation.

Mortal sins and venial sins committed by individuals are called personal sins. We also have a personal responsibility for the sins committed by others when we cooperate with them. Scandal, the act of knowingly causing another to sin by our words or example, is a very serious offense and is strongly condemned by Jesus.

Faith Words

grace Grace, a gift that God freely gives us, is God's life within us, which fills us with his love and enables us to do his will and to respond to our vocation to become his adopted children.

sanctifying grace Sanctifying grace is the grace of God sharing his divine life with us and that heals us of sin and makes us Christlike.

God's Mercy

God's mercy is revealed throughout the Old Testament. It is fully revealed in the Person of Jesus, who, in obedience to the Father, died on the Cross to free us from the slavery of sin. The effect of God's mercy is to bestow on us Salvation from sin. We are moved by the **grace** of God's mercy to reject our sinfulness and to seek and accept God's forgiveness. Through the action of the Holy Spirit, our sinfulness is replaced by the righteousness of Christ. In the Sacrament of Baptism, we receive God's **sanctifying grace** and the gift of new life in Christ and the gift of justification. This sanctifying grace unites us intimately with God and enables us to participate in the very life of God. It makes us the adopted children of God the Father and heirs to his kingdom.

God continually helps us in our daily lives to live our new life in Christ. This help, called actual grace by the Church, never interferes with our personal freedom. But it does call forth in us free choices that correspond to God's will for us, because it touches our deepest longing to be together with him.

Conversion and the Christian Life

Conversion means "to turn around." Applied to the Christian life, it refers to turning from sin and seeking to follow God's will. A central element of Jesus' message was to call sinners to conversion. We have many examples of conversion in both the Old Testament and the New Testament. One of the most well known is the conversion of Paul from being an enemy of the early Church to becoming one of the greatest Apostles.

There is another kind of conversion that is also very important for Christians. It takes the form of turning from "being good" to "being better." For example, we may feel we are already being generous enough to the poor. But upon hearing a missionary preach, we may decide to be much more generous. This is a kind of conversion also. Maturing in Christ entails a lifetime of such conversions to ever-greater love for God and neighbor. Just as it is always God's grace that prompts conversion from a life of sin, conversion to growing more Christlike also depends on the presence and action of God's grace.

Activity

What kinds of conversion are needed in today's world? If you were planning to speak to your class about conversion, what would your message be?

The Beatitudes

Rejoice and leap for joy on that day! Behold, your reward will be great in heaven.

Luke 6:23

God has created in us the desire for true happiness—true happiness that can be experienced only through union with God. In the Old Testament God revealed to the Israelites that the path to union with him and to fullness of life and true happiness lies in following the Mosaic Law, or Law of Moses. This Law, summarized in the Ten Commandments, provides us with a plan for living in union with God, in loving communion with one another, and in harmony with all creation.

The Beatitudes as Revolutionary Ideas

Jesus proclaimed the Beatitudes as the path to happiness. *Beatitude* is another word for "blessedness" or "happiness." We find the most complete expression of the Beatitudes in Matthew's Gospel at the beginning of the Sermon on the Mount in Matthew 5:3–12. As "rules" for achieving happiness, the Beatitudes completely went against what the people of Jesus' time had come to believe would give them happiness. In fact, the very things that Jesus seemed to be saying would bring happiness (being poor, being hungry and thirsty, being meek, being persecuted, and so on) were the things the people felt were the causes for unhappiness. The same can be said for virtually all that Jesus taught in the Sermon on the Mount.

The Beatitudes and the Kingdom of God

To understand the Beatitudes it is essential that we examine them in the context of Jesus' overall teaching about the Kingdom of God. The Beatitudes clearly do not make sense as guides to living successfully in any earthly kingdom. To survive and "be happy" in any earthly kingdom people strive to acquire as much wealth and power as possible. People stand up for their rights and often defend them with violence.

All this makes sense if God has no part in our lives and we are expected to "take care of ourselves." But Jesus came to announce and inaugurate the Kingdom of God. Jesus calls us to rely on God's love and mercy. This does not mean we are to sit idly by allowing God to do everything for us. It does mean that we embrace the Beatitudes through the gift and inspiration of the Holy Spirit. We cooperate with God, who is establishing a society whose members live together in mutual love, justice, and peace.

Faith Words

Beatitude *Beatitude* is another word for "blessedness" or "happiness." A Beatitude is also any one of the eight guidelines about how to live and find real happiness in God's kingdom that Jesus taught in the Sermon on the Mount.

Beatitudes: A Summary

Beatitude	Our Challenge
Blessed are the poor in spirit, for theirs is the kingdom of heaven.	Learn to put all our trust in God rather than in material possessions.
Blessed are they who mourn, for they will be comforted.	Learn not to expect perfect happiness on Earth. Grow in hope and confidence that God can and will provide us with perfect happiness in his kingdom.
Blessed are the meek, for they will inherit the land.	Learn that happiness does not come from self-promotion and gaining control over others. It comes from treating one another with gentleness and patience.
Blessed are they who hunger and thirst for righteousness, for they will be satisfied.	Learn that being upset with the injustice and evil we see around us is a result of God's grace and an invitation to strive to promote a just society.
Blessed are the merciful, for they will be shown mercy.	Learn that the very foundation of God's kingdom rests on our being willing to forgive those who wrong us. Refusing to forgive and seeking vengeance only continue the cycle of hatred and violence.
Blessed are the clean of heart, for they will see God.	Learn that growing in friendship with God is our single most important task on Earth.
Blessed are the peacemakers, for they will be called children of God.	Learn that as children of God, we have a basic responsibility to help others forgive each other and live in peace together.
Blessed are they who are persecuted for the sake of righteousness, for theirs is the kingdom of heaven. *Matthew 5:3–10*	Learn that we may be made fun of or insulted whenever we are truly working to do what is right and to promote God's kingdom. We should be reassured that we are on the right track.

Activity

First, decide which of the Beatitudes you personally consider the most difficult to follow. Next, choose the one you feel is the easiest for you to follow. Be prepared to discuss the reasons for your choices.

The Ten Commandments:
Love of God

✝ "I, the LORD, am your God, who brought you out of the land of Egypt, that place of slavery."

Exodus 20:2

The Ten Commandments are a set of standards and norms that God has revealed to us to guide us to true happiness. They help us avoid harming ourselves and others. They reflect the natural law that God established from the beginning of time to order creation. It is this same natural law, available to us through our reason, that provides the foundation for all moral rules and civil laws.

The first three of the Ten Commandments focus on our relationship with God. The remaining seven focus on our relationship with one another and with all creation. Each of the Commandments imposes a grave moral obligation on us.

The Ten Commandments prepare the way for the New Law of Christ, which fulfills and perfects what God has revealed in the Ten Commandments. Finally, it is important to recall that God in his mercy and love always provides the grace we need to do what he has commanded of us.

I am the Lord, your God.
You shall not have other gods beside me.

The First Commandment provides the foundation for the others. It commands us never to regard any person or thing to be more important than God. It calls us to believe in, hope in, and love God above all else. To raise any creature above God in any way is a form of idolatry. The First Commandment also forbids us to make "gods" of money, power, and fame by looking to them rather than to God to give us happiness and fulfillment.

Many people do not realize that the First Commandment also warns against superstition. Superstition is a form of idolatry, as is belief in divination (fortunetelling, horoscopes, palm reading, and astrology) and magic (such as satanism and witchcraft).

The Church allows and encourages the use of sacred images (statues, crucifixes, pictures of saints, and so on) in its prayer and worship. These are not the same as the "gods" the First Commandment forbids. They are not objects of worship, nor are they considered to have any magical powers. Sacred images are intended to help us better focus our hearts and minds on God.

Faith Words

blasphemy Blasphemy is the act of showing contempt for God or for sacred things through one's words or actions.

perjury Perjury is the act of lying after having made an oath to tell the truth, with God as one's witness.

You shall not take the name of the LORD, your God, in vain.

The Second Commandment obliges us to show proper reverence and respect to God in keeping with his holiness and his nature as our Creator. Actions, such as **blasphemy**, or showing disrespect and irreverence for God and things of the Church, are forbidden by this Commandment. The Second Commandment also forbids us from using God's holy name disrespectfully and from committing **perjury**, or making false oaths. When we call upon God to witness to a lie, we commit perjury.

The Second Commandment forbids us to treat disrespectfully any person or object that has been consecrated to God. Being disrespectful of priests and religious brothers and sisters, making fun of sacred objects and rituals, and being disruptive during Mass are all examples of ways people might—often unknowingly—violate the Second Commandment. If a person consciously intends to show irreverence and disrespect to God when doing such things, they commit a very serious offense against the Second Commandment.

Remember to keep holy the LORD's Day.

The Third Commandment tells us we must set aside one day each week to focus in a special way on giving honor to God and on nurturing our relationship with him. In the Jewish tradition the last day of the week, the Sabbath, is set aside for that purpose. In the Christian tradition, Sunday, the first day of the week and the Lord's Day, is set aside in memory of Jesus Christ's Resurrection.

The Church teaches that all Catholics must "keep holy the LORD's Day" by participating in the Mass each Sunday and on holy days of obligation. The Mass is the highest form of honor and worship we can offer to God.

In obedience to the Third Commandment, the Church also teaches that in addition to participating in Mass, Catholics are to refrain from all unnecessary work or business activities that would prevent them from giving proper worship to God. Sunday is intended in God's plan for humanity as a day of rest for the body as well as a day for the nourishment of the soul. Likewise, Christians are not supposed to make demands of others that might prevent them from offering worship to God on the Lord's Day.

Activity

List some objects and activities in our society today that you think some people tend to turn into "idols" by regarding them as more important for their happiness than God.

The Ten Commandments:
Love of Neighbor

"Do to others as you would have them do to you."

Luke 6:31

The Fourth through Tenth Commandments show us how we should respect and relate to others in the human family. The moral principles they present are well known. They are revealed to us by our loving God. We can also know these principles through the use of reason and by reflecting on the natural law.

Honor your father and mother.

The Fourth Commandment deals with how we are to relate to those in authority over us. It is God's will that children honor, respect, and obey their parents. All those who exercise legitimate authority over us derive their authority from God. So we should honor and obey them as God's representatives.

You shall not kill.

The Church teaches that the Fifth Commandment includes other serious obligations beside the obvious one, that we are forbidden to kill others. Every human life is sacred from the moment of conception until natural death, because each human being has been personally called into existence by God and bears his image and likeness. The Church forbids direct abortion and imposes the canonical penalty of excommunication for this crime against human life. The Church also forbids euthanasia, or "mercy killing" of the elderly or physically or mentally ill or disabled. The Fifth Commandment forbids suicide and any other deliberate acts that unnecessarily threaten the life or health of ourselves or others. The Church also teaches that medical research on unborn children is forbidden.

You shall not commit adultery.
You shall not covet your neighbor's wife.

The Sixth and Ninth Commandments command us to respect our bodies and the gift of sexuality with which God has blessed us. We are to nurture the virtues of chastity and temperance. The Church teaches that, besides adultery, other acts to be considered serious sins against the Sixth Commandment include masturbation, sexual intimacy outside of marriage, pornography, homosexual practices, incest, and rape. Since the gift of human sexuality includes our capacity to procreate, and since one of the purposes of marriage is to bring forth children, the Church considers it wrong for a couple to use artificial means to prevent a pregnancy, no matter how legitimate their intentions might be.

Faith Words

plagiarism Plagiarism is the use of someone's ideas or works as if they were one's own.

covet To covet means to have an excessive desire for pleasure or possessions.

You shall not steal.

Stealing in any form is an offense against the Seventh Commandment. Stealing can take many forms. Not paying a worker a just wage is a form of stealing. Charging a customer an unfair price and not giving an employer a fair day's work for one's wages are forms of stealing. **Plagiarism**, or claiming another's creative work as one's own, is a form of theft. Wasting the earth's resources also violates the Seventh Commandment, since it is stealing from others and from future generations. Stealing from or defrauding the poor and needy of their goods or services is an especially grave offense.

You shall not bear false witness against your neighbor.

When we tell a lie, we say what is false in a way that we try to deceive one's neighbor. The Eighth Commandment forbids all lying regardless of how we communicate the lie: orally, in writing, or through means of objects, gestures, or actions. The more a person or group needs and has the right to a particular truth, the more grave is the sinfulness of the lie that prevents the person or group from obtaining it. For example, intentionally lying to a jury regarding the innocence of a person suspected of a crime is a grave sin.

You shall not covet your neighbor's goods.

The Tenth Commandment forbids us from coveting our neighbors' possessions. To **covet** means "to have an excessive desire for what rightfully belongs to someone else." The Tenth Commandment also forbids envy. Envy is the state of feeling angry or saddened that other people have something we do not have and creates an immoderate desire in us to acquire it for ourselves. Envy is one of the seven capital sins.

Precepts of the Church

There are certain specific duties Catholics have in addition to obeying the Ten Commandments. They are called the precepts of the Church and include the following:

1. Participate in Mass on all Sundays and holy days of obligation.
2. Confess serious sins once a year.
3. Receive the Eucharist at least once during the Easter Season.
4. Fast and abstain on days appointed by the Church.
5. Contribute to the Church's support.

Activity

On a separate sheet of paper, try to rewrite the Fifth through Tenth Commandments using "You shall" statements rather than "You shall not" statements.

Social Justice

Children, let us love not in word or speech but in deed and truth.

1 John 3:18

The unity that exists between the Three Divine Persons of the Trinity is a model of how people should live and share with one another in community. *Social justice* is the term used to describe the Church's mission to continue Jesus' service to the poor and the oppressed. Jesus came to bring glad tidings to the poor, liberty to captives, and recovery of sight to the blind. (See Luke 4:18–19.) The Church continues this ministry by reaching out to care for and support the poor and the oppressed in society today.

Seven Key Themes

There are seven themes that summarize the heart of the Church's teaching on social justice and our obligation to promote it.

Life and Dignity of the Human Person—The sacredness and dignity of the human person is the basis upon which a moral society is built. We live in a world where that dignity has often become secondary to our materialism. Abortion, assisted suicide, and the death penalty all promote disrespect for human life. We must strive to restore respect for all human life.

Call to Family, Community, and Participation—We are created to live in community. Extreme individualism has caused a change in the structure of our society and a shift in our values. The family is the central social institution and we must support and strengthen family life. We are called to become involved in society and help it foster peace, justice, and love through its political and economic institutions and practices.

Rights and Responsibilities—Human dignity can only be protected and a healthy community established if human rights are protected and responsibilities met. Just as we want others to respect our rights and dignity, so we have the responsibility to respect the rights and dignity of all others as if each were "another self." Basic human rights all people possess include, among others, the right to life; political and religious freedom; freedom of conscience; adequate food, clothing, and shelter; education; and adequate medical treatment.

Faith Words

solidarity Solidarity is the unity we share with all our brothers and sisters, who are made in the image of God. It is an eminently Christian virtue that practices the sharing of spiritual goods even more than material ones.

stewardship Stewardship is responsibility of managing what belongs to another person. We are stewards of God's creation.

Option for the Poor and Vulnerable—To measure the morality of any society, we need only look to see how the most vulnerable and dependent of its members are faring: children, the sick, the disabled, the elderly, and the poor. These are the people to whom Jesus ministered above all others. Catholics have a special obligation to reach out to defend the rights of the poor and vulnerable and to call all of society to do the same.

Dignity of Work and the Rights of Workers—The economy is intended to be at the service of the people. Too often people are mistreated and taken for granted in the name of financial and economic growth. Work has a natural dignity because it is by nature a continuing participation in God's creation. People have the right to engage in productive work and to be paid a fair wage for their labor. People also have the right to organize and join labor unions, own private property, and exercise economic initiative.

Solidarity—As children of the same loving Father, we belong to one human family here on Earth. We are called to foster this **solidarity** at the local, national, and international levels. This means the Church is called to oppose all forms of division and prejudice: racial, ethnic, religious, or economic. We are called to help others value the differences each culture contributes to human society and to work together toward peace, justice, and harmony among all people throughout the world.

Care for God's Creation—God appointed us as stewards of the earth. Our faith requires us to protect our environment, all God's creatures, and one another. We are called to oppose the exploitation of the earth's limited resources for the sole purpose of gaining wealth or benefiting the few. We are also to protect the earth from needless pollution.

Social Concerns

Given the Catholic's fundamental duty to promote social justice, most parishes have established social concerns, or **stewardship**, committees. Their purpose is to help parishioners identify and pursue activities intended to bring about a more just and peaceful community. Typical activities include supporting the Pro-Life Movement, sponsoring food pantries and homeless shelters, and helping the elderly.

Activity

Make a list of those groups of people in need of help in your local community. How many of these groups is your school presently seeking to help in some way? What can you personally do?

Prayer

"And I tell you, ask and you will receive; seek and you will find; knock and the door will be opened to you."

Luke 11:9

Prayer and the Catholic life are inseparable. Prayer is deeply rooted in the Church's living Tradition and has always been an integral part of the Church's life. Aided by the Holy Spirit, the Church teaches each new generation of Catholics to pray. The Catholic family, through the guidance and example of parents, is the first place children come in contact with this Tradition and receive instruction in prayer. The Word of God, the liturgy of the Church, and the Theological Virtues of faith, hope, and charity are sources God gives us to inspire and shape Catholic prayer.

Some Principles of Prayer

Prayer is basically talking to and listening to God. This "conversation" revolves around five basic topics: blessing and adoration, praise, thanksgiving, petition, and intercession. In prayer we praise the goodness and love of God and thank him for his many gifts and ongoing care for us. We tell God of our needs and those of others, asking his help in meeting them. We ask God for forgiveness for our own sins and the sins of others.

In keeping with the Church's tradition of prayer, we are encouraged to appeal to the saints who have gone before us, asking them to join us in offering our prayers to God. Throughout the history of the Church Mary, the Mother of Jesus, has always been given an important place in the prayer life of Catholics. The Church teaches that God always hears our prayers and always answers them, always providing what is best for us.

It is not unusual, however, to experience difficulties when we pray. We can become distracted by the events around us or by various tasks we need to do. We may experience periods of "dryness" during which God seems to be absent from us. In reality, God is always present with us in prayer no matter what feeling we may be experiencing.

Faith Words

novena A novena is a Catholic devotion in which specific prayers are said on nine consecutive days.

pilgrimage A pilgrimage is a journey to a holy place or sacred site for spiritual or devotional reasons.

Quiet Prayer

We do not need to use words to pray. When we are quiet and simply focus our attention on God, we are praying. During those times when we are silent the Holy Spirit speaks to our hearts. Just reflecting on a Scripture passage or a story from the Gospels can be a form of prayer. When the beauty of nature helps us become aware of the beauty and wisdom and power of God, we are praying even if we do not say a word.

Vocal Prayer

The Church has a rich source of formal prayers that it has developed over the centuries. These include prayers, such as the Sign of the Cross; the Hail Mary; the Rosary; Acts of Faith, Hope, Love, and Contrition; prayers to the Holy Spirit; and so on. When we pray by using one of these traditional prayers, it is called "vocal prayer," even though we may not be praying the words aloud.

Liturgical Prayer

Liturgical prayer is the official, public prayer of the Church. In liturgical prayer we pray through the power of the Holy Spirit with and in Christ who presents our prayers to the Father. For that reason liturgical prayer is the highest and most perfect form of prayer we can offer to God. Besides the Mass, the chief forms of liturgical prayer include the celebration of the other Sacraments and the Liturgy of the Hours.

The **Liturgy of the Hours** involves reciting certain psalms, Scripture passages, hymns, and prayers at set times throughout the day. Many religious, especially those living in monasteries, gather for Morning, Daytime, Evening, and Night Prayer.

Popular Devotions

Besides participation in the liturgy, the Church encourages the faithful to participate in devotions. Devotions are not a substitute for liturgical prayer, but flow from the liturgy and deepen our participation in it. Some of the more common devotions include praying the Rosary, the Stations of the Cross, or a **novena** to a saint; adoration of the Blessed Sacrament; and making a **pilgrimage** to a holy place or shrine.

Activity

List all the times you can think of when you prayed this past week. Now on a scale of one to ten, how strong do you think your prayer life is? If you feel you need improvement in your prayer life, what are some things you might do?

The Lord's Prayer

✝ *"Your Father knows what you need before you ask him."*

Matthew 6:8

◆ ◇ ◆

The Lord's Prayer holds a central place in the Church's life of prayer for several reasons. First, it is the prayer Jesus personally taught his disciples—and through them the whole Church. Second, the Lord's Prayer is a summary of all that Jesus reveals to us about how we should relate to God and treat each other. The Lord's Prayer has often been referred to by the Church as "the little Gospel." Besides the opening words in which we address the Father, there are seven distinct petitions in the Lord's Prayer.

Our Father, Who Art in Heaven

By teaching us to address God as *our* Father, Jesus is teaching us that we are not to view our relationship with God as a private matter. No one has a special, private claim on God. God is the Father of all people. In approaching God, we are to remember that we are members of a family. All people are our brothers and sisters. Perhaps the most important lesson Jesus teaches us through these opening words is that we should approach God as a loving, caring Father. We are to approach our loving Father, fully confident that he loves us and is eager to receive us. Through the words, "who art in heaven," Jesus reminds us that we are to balance this sense of intimacy with deep respect and reverence for the Father, who is Lord of Heaven and Earth.

Hallowed Be Thy Name

By making this the first petition of the prayer and using the word **hallowed**, Jesus is teaching us that above all else we should desire and seek the Father's glory and praise. With all our hearts, we pray that people in every age may come to know, honor, and praise our loving God.

Thy Kingdom Come

By his words and deeds, Jesus Christ showed us that the Father promised to one day establish his kingdom of perfect justice, peace, unity, and happiness. Likewise, in words and deeds, Jesus gave us certain "previews" of what this kingdom is like. In this second petition of the Lord's Prayer, Jesus teaches us that we have a special duty to pray continually, asking the Father to hasten the arrival of the kingdom.

Faith Words

hallowed Used in the opening words of the Our Father, this word means "holy," "sacred," or "revered."

trespass *Trespass* means "to commit a sin."

Thy Will Be Done on Earth as It Is in Heaven

Jesus taught by word and example that our happiness is the result of obedience to God's will. Disobedience to God's will is the source of human misery and evil. Jesus Christ teaches us that we are to pray that the human family learns to obey God the Father's will perfectly, just as it is obeyed in Heaven. Such obedience has the effect of hastening the day when God's kingdom will arrive.

Give Us This Day Our Daily Bread

In this petition, Jesus teaches us to turn to God our loving Father each day in trust and confidence, knowing that he knows and will provide the appropriate goods we need both spiritually and materially. This petition reminds us that we are to share our blessings with others. The earth's goods are intended to be shared with all people. There is more than enough for everyone if we share.

Forgive Us Our Trespasses as We Forgive Those Who Trespass Against Us

In this petition Jesus teaches us to ask the Father's forgiveness for our sins, which seems normal enough. However, Jesus has included a condition in our request. Jesus tells us we are to ask the Father to forgive us *only if and to the same degree that we forgive those who **trespass** against us.* We are to be willing to forgive one another if we expect the Father to forgive us. The forgiveness of our sins depends not only on God's willingness to forgive us but also on *our willingness* to forgive one another.

Lead Us Not into Temptation, but Deliver Us from Evil

In these final petitions, Jesus teaches us to ask the Father's continuing help and protection from falling prey to evil and from becoming victims of the effects of the evil of others.

When we pray the Lord's Prayer, we are reminded of all the central truths of the Gospel. At the same time we ask the Father for all that is really essential for human happiness.

Activity

Print the Lord's Prayer on an index card, or a sheet of paper, using your best printing. When you go home, tape it to your bathroom or bedroom mirror as a reminder to say it each day.

Doctrine Review

What Catholics Believe

Word Power

Circle the letter before the word or phrase that best completes each sentence.

1. Revelation is   **a.** secret information.   **b.** what God has let us know about himself.
   c. what science has learned about God.   **d.** only made known to the pope.

2. The Bible contains   **a.** everything God wants to reveal.   **b.** the writings of the pope
   and bishops   **c.** writing, inspired by the Holy Spirit, about our relationship with
   God.   **d.** the history of the world.

3. Epistles are   **a.** letters.   **b.** weapons.   **c.** missionaries.   **d.** laws.

4. We call God the Blessed Trinity because   **a.** there are three gods.
   b. there are three names for God.   **c.** there is One God in Three Divine Persons.
   d. there are three Divine Natures in Jesus.

5. The Incarnation means that   **a.** Jesus earned the right to be called God.
   b. God's own Son became a man without giving up being God.   **c.** God's Son
   appeared like a man on Earth.   **d.** Jesus sends the Holy Spirit to be with us.

6. Mary is called *full of grace* because   **a.** God chose her to have a unique role in
   Salvation.   **b.** she was a very good mother to Jesus.   **c.** she answers our
   prayers.   **d.** she was always a virgin.

7. Jesus Christ brought about Salvation from sin through his   **a.** miracles.
   b. preaching and kindness.   **c.** prayers to his Father.   **d.** Death on the Cross.

8. People who belong to a non-Catholic religion   **a.** can never go to Heaven.   **b.** must
   be married to be saved.   **c.** can be saved if they seek God with a sincere heart and
   follow their conscience.   **d.** must go to Purgatory before they can get into Heaven.

9. The four Marks of the Church include   **a.** one and holy.   **b.** one and infallible.
   c. holy and love.   **d.** apostolic and infallible.

10. Mary's Assumption refers to her   **a.** holiness.   **b.** being Jesus' mother.
    c. always being a virgin.   **d.** being taken up into Heaven body and soul.

What Do You Think?

Turn to page 96 and read the Nicene Creed. Which parts of the Creed are the easiest for
you to understand? Which parts do you feel that you need to know more about? Explain
your answers.

Doctrine Review

How Catholics Worship

Word Power

Circle the letter before the word or phrase that best completes each sentence.

1. In the Sacrament of Baptism we do *not* become   **a.** freed from Original Sin.
   b. adopted children of the Father.   **c.** ordained priests.   **d.** temples of the Holy Spirit.

2. The Sacrament of Confirmation   **a.** marks the end of our religious education.
   b. deepens our Baptism.   **c.** takes the place of our Baptism.   **d.** takes away
   Original Sin.

3. The Church considers the age of reason to be about   **a.** age seven.   **b.** age three.
   c. age ten.   **d.** age fourteen.

4. The word *Eucharist* means   **a.** "celebration."   **b.** "thanksgiving."   **c.** "praise."
   d. "holiness."

5. The word *transubstantiation* describes how the bread and wine   **a.** remind us of the
   Last Supper.   **b.** remind us of Jesus.   **c.** become the Body and Blood of Jesus Christ.
   d. must be made from certain ingredients.

6. In the Sacrament of Penance and Reconciliation, we are   **a.** forgiven Original Sin.
   b. forgiven sins committed after Baptism.   **c.** required to confess all sins.
   d. required to confess at least one serious sin.

7. The Sacrament of Anointing of the Sick should be received   **a.** by anyone who is
   suffering in old age or is seriously ill.   **b.** once each year.   **c.** only in danger of death.
   d. instead of confession.

8. Baptized men who receive the Sacrament of Holy Orders become   **a.** priests or lectors.
   b. bishops or monsignors.   **c.** deacons, priests, or bishops.   **d.** brothers or sisters.

9. Deacons who are not planning to become priests can   **a.** be married before they are
   ordained.   **b.** become bishops.   **c.** preside at the Eucharist.   **d.** hear confessions.

10. The Catholic Church has called the Christian family   **a.** the real Church.   **b.** the
    domestic Church.   **c.** a parish church.   **d.** a diocese.

What Do You Think?

Imagine that you are planning a program to prepare students your age for Confirmation.
What would you require the candidates to do? What kind of instruction would you plan?

Doctrine Review

How Catholics Live

Word Power

Circle the letter before the word or phrase that best completes each sentence.

1. Conscience is our ability to **a.** decide what is holy. **b.** tell good from evil. **c.** stay away from sin. **d.** always be good.

2. Virtues are **a.** good moral habits. **b.** sacred signs. **c.** laws of the Church. **d.** rules to live by.

3. A mortal sin is **a.** less serious than a venial sin. **b.** serious offense against God's Law. **c.** not freely chosen. **d.** never forgiven.

4. Venial sins **a.** must always be confessed. **b.** separate us from God. **c.** are less serious than mortal sins. **d.** are more serious than mortal sins.

5. The Beatitudes **a.** take the place of the Ten Commandments. **b.** refer only to the Kingdom of God. **c.** are rules for achieving true happiness. **d.** only apply to priests.

6. The Ten Commandments reflect **a.** the natural law. **b.** the Beatitudes. **c.** the teaching of the Apostles. **d.** the laws of the Catholic Church.

7. Catholics are required to participate in Mass **a.** once each year. **b.** only at Eastertime. **c.** on certain holy days. **d.** on all Sundays and holy days of obligation.

8. The Commandment that obliges us to honor our parents is the **a.** Second Commandment. **b.** Fourth Commandment. **c.** Sixth Commandment. **d.** Eighth Commandment.

9. The Church teaches that all human life is sacred **a.** from the moment of birth. **b.** from the moment of Baptism. **c.** from the moment of conception. **d.** from the moment a baby can breathe on their own.

10. The Commandment against adultery is the **a.** First Commandment. **b.** Second Commandment. **c.** Fifth Commandment. **d.** Sixth Commandment.

What Do You Think?

What is the most difficult moral problem for students today? How would you advise your classmates to deal with it? To whom would you go for help?

Doctrine Review

How Catholics Pray

Word Power

Match the words in Column A with the phrases in Column B.

A

_____ 1. prayer

_____ 2. vocal prayer

_____ 3. quiet prayer

_____ 4. Liturgy of the Hours

_____ 5. liturgical prayer

_____ 6. hallowed

_____ 7. trespass

_____ 8. novena

_____ 9. pilgrimage

_____ 10. the Lord's Prayer

B

a. the Church's official public prayer

b. a visit to a sacred place

c. talking and listening to God

d. holy, sacred, or revered

e. praying by using the Church's traditional prayers, such as the Hail Mary

f. sometimes referred to as "the little Gospel"

g. meditating on Scripture

h. to commit a sin

i. prayed throughout the day

j. prayed for nine days

What Do You Think?

Imagine that you are getting ready to publish a prayer book for students. Which prayers would you include? What intentions would you pray for? At what times during the day would you suggest students pray?

FAVORITE LESSONS AND CELEBRATIONS

The school year is just about over. You have learned many things in your religion classes. Think about what you have studied and celebrated this year, and answer the following questions.

Which Bible story in this book did you enjoy the most?

_____

What did you learn from this story?

_____

_____

Which person from the Bible stories in this book is your favorite? Why?

_____

_____

_____

_____

_____

_____

_____

_____

Name three things you learned about the Catholic faith that you did not know before this year.

_____

_____

_____

Which saint did you most enjoy learning about? Why?

_____

_____

_____

_____

Which holy person did you most enjoy learning about? Why?

_____

_____

_____

_____

Which prayer celebration did you like most this year? Why?

_____

_____

_____

_____

_____

END-OF-YEAR PRAYER

A Prayer of Thanksgiving

All: In the name of the Father, and of the Son, and of the Holy Spirit. Amen.

Leader: God Father of all, as we have studied the story of your Church this year, you have given us many blessings. We have learned about the Marks of the Church, the growth of the Church throughout the ages, Church and culture, and the renewal of the Church. We have heard your call to be disciples and to make the values of your kingdom known to all. We ask your continued blessing in the name of Jesus Christ, your Son and our Lord and Savior, through the Holy Spirit.

All: Amen.

Reader 1: A reading from the Acts of the Apostles.
(Read aloud Acts 3:42–47 from the Bible.)

Leader: What do we have in common with the early Church?
(Pause for silent reflection.)
Let us pray a litany of thanksgiving.

Reader 2: We are grateful for the Marks of the Church: one, holy, catholic, and apostolic. They remind us of our uniqueness as Catholics.

All: We thank you, Lord.

Reader 3: We are grateful for the Church's ability to resolve conflicts by calling leaders together to meet and be guided by the Holy Spirit.

All: We thank you, Lord.

Reader 4: We are grateful for the artists and architects throughout the ages whose works have brought us into a deeper awareness of God's presence among us.

All: We thank you, Lord.

Reader 5: We are grateful for the Church's ability to acknowledge mistakes and set a clear course for the future.

All: We thank you, Lord.

Reader 6: We are grateful for the liturgy and prayer traditions of the Church, which the Church has renewed to better reflect Christ's saving presence in our lives.

All: We thank you, Lord.

Reader 7: We are grateful for our Church as she reaches out to all people in the world in the name of justice and charity.

All: We thank you, Lord.

Reader 8: We are grateful for the Church's quest for the unity of all Christians.

All: We thank you, Lord.

Reader 9: We are grateful for Ecumenical Councils, which help the Church respond to the needs of her members and clarify the Church's understanding of her role in the world.

All: We thank you, Lord.

Reader 10: We are grateful for the leadership of the pope and bishops, who direct the Church under the guidance of the Holy Spirit.

All: We thank you, Lord.

Reader 11: We are grateful for our call to continue Christ's mission as we anticipate the coming of the Kingdom of God.

All: We thank you, Lord.

Leader: All-loving Father, we are most thankful that you sent your Son to be our Savior and Brother. We are grateful that you sent the Holy Spirit to be with us. We appreciate one another as we nurture each other in our faith. We express our gratitude for all these things in the name of Jesus Christ our Lord.

All: Amen.

Glossary

age of reason The age of reason is the age at which children are able to distinguish between right and wrong, approximately age seven. *(page 407)*

All Souls Day All Souls Day is the day on which we pray for the souls undergoing purification in Purgatory. We celebrate All Souls Day on November 2. *(page 405)*

alms Alms are donations of time, money, or goods to people in need. *(page 301)*

Apocalypse The Apocalypse, or Book of Revelation, is the last book of the Bible. It describes the end of the world in symbolic language. *(page 397)*

apostolic The Catholic Church is apostolic because Jesus Christ founded the Church on the Apostles, and the Church is faithful to the teachings of Jesus Christ passed on to her by the Apostles. *(page 33)*

Beatific Vision The Beatific Vision is the contemplation of God, which brings everlasting happiness and peace. *(page 405)*

Beatitude *Beatitude* is another word for "blessedness" or "happiness." A Beatitude is also any one of the eight guidelines about how to live and find real happiness in God's Kingdom that Jesus taught in the Sermon on the Mount. *(page 419)*

blasphemy Blasphemy is the act of showing contempt for God or for sacred things through one's words or actions. *(page 421)*

canon law Canon law is the collection of the laws of the Catholic Church. *(page 115)*

catechesis Catechesis is a process of faith formation that includes education and participation in the life of the Catholic community. *(page 277)*

catholic The word *catholic* means "universal." With a capital C, it describes the Church founded by Jesus Christ on the Apostles. *(page 57)*

Christendom Christendom is the name given to the growth of the Church in territory and in both temporal, or political, and spiritual authority resulting in the pope's authority exceeding that of the emperor and eventually kings. *(page 115)*

Church The Church is the living Body of Christ, the People of God. The Catholic Church is one, holy, catholic, and apostolic. The word Church means "convocation," or gathering together. *(page 69)*

Church Fathers The early Christian leaders of the first eight centuries of the Church whose teachings helped develop Christian doctrine are known as Church Fathers. *(page 91)*

conversion From a Latin word meaning "to turn around," *conversion* means "a turning away from sin." *(pages 338 and 411)*

Counter-Reformation The Counter-Reformation was the sixteenth-century movement of reform instituted by the Catholic Church to counter the increasing strength of Protestantism and bring about true reform of the Church. *(page 218)*

covet To covet means to have an excessive and disordered desire for pleasure or possessions. *(page 423)*

Crusades The Crusades were military attempts by Christians to free the Holy Land from Muslim control. *(page 173)*

denomination A denomination is an individual, organized religious body that is a form of a particular faith. *(page 243)*

devotion A devotion is a special way of praying to God the Father, Jesus, and the Holy Spirit, or of expressing love for Mary and the saints. *(page 185)*

Doctor of the Church "Doctor of the Church" is the title that the Church gives to saints whose writings have greatly helped others understand matters of faith or doctrine. *(page 48)*

doctrine Doctrine refers to an official teaching or a body of official teachings of the Church. *(page 127)*

ecumenical council An ecumenical council is a worldwide gathering of all the bishops called by the pope and convened by him. Ecumenical councils clarify the teachings of the Church. *(page 91)*

ecumenism Ecumenism is the movement to establish unity among all Christians to which the Church is called by the Holy Spirit. *(page 265)*

encyclical An encyclical is a pastoral letter from the pope to the whole Church and even the world in which the pope clarifies or reinforces Catholic teachings. *(page 289)*

episcopal The word *episcopal* is used to describe bishops or the objects, actions, and events in their ministry. *(page 413)*

Eucharist The Eucharist is the central Sacrament of the Church. It is the source and summit of the Christian life. In the Sacrament of the Eucharist, bread and wine become the Body and Blood of Jesus Christ through the power of the Holy Spirit and the words and actions of the priest. *(pages 45 and 369)*

excommunication Excommunication is a penalty incurred by the committing of a grave offense against the Catholic religion. It excludes a member of the Church from the Eucharist and other Sacraments and from exercising any office or ministry in the Church. *(page 231)*

ex nihilo *Ex nihilo* is a Latin phrase meaning "from nothing." It is used to describe how God created all that is, seen and unseen. *(page 399)*

faith Faith is the assurance of things hoped for, the conviction of things not seen (based on Hebrews 11:1). Faith is one of the three Theological Virtues. It is the gift of God's invitation to believe in him and the grace-filled response to that invitation. *(page 149)*

fiat *Fiat* is a Latin word meaning "Let it happen" or "Let it be done." *(page 401)*

free will Free will is the freedom to choose to do what is right or what is wrong. *(page 231)*

grace Grace, a gift that God freely gives us, is God's life within us, which fills us with his love and enables us to do his will and respond to our vocation of being his adopted children. *(page 417)*

hallowed Used in the opening words of the Our Father, *hallowed* means holy, sacred, or revered. *(page 429)*

Heaven Heaven is eternal life and everlasting happiness with God, and with all people who love God and others, after death. *(page 173)*

Hell Hell is everlasting suffering and separation from God. *(page 173)*

heresy A heresy is a teaching that is contrary to Church doctrine. *(page 91)*

icon An icon is a holy image of Jesus, the Virgin Mary, or the saints, often made out of gold leaf and other special materials. *(page 127)*

indulgence An indulgence is the removal of all or some of the temporal punishments for sins that we must suffer in Purgatory for the effects of our sins on Earth that have already been forgiven. *(page 173)*

Latin Latin was the common language spoken in the Roman Empire. It is the basis for many European languages. *(page 127)*

liturgy The liturgy of the Church is the official, public worship of God. It includes the celebration of Mass and the other Sacraments. Christ is always present and leads the Church in the celebration of the liturgy. *(page 103)*

Liturgy of the Hours The Liturgy of the Hours is the Church's official prayer for certain times of the day and night. It is also called the Divine Office. It consists of psalms, readings, hymns, and prayers. *(pages 243 and 332)*

Magisterium The teaching office of the Church, guided by the Holy Spirit, to authentically and accurately interpret the Word of God—Scripture and Tradition. *(page 33)*

Marks of the Church One, holy, catholic, and apostolic. The Marks of the Church are the four attributes and essential characteristics of the Church and her mission. *(page 403)*

Mass The Mass is another name for the celebration of the Sacrament of the Eucharist. It is taken from the Latin word *missa,* meaning "sent," a word once used to send the faithful forth at the end of the celebration. *(page 161)*

mendicant order A mendicant order is a religious community of men or women who dedicate themselves to living the Gospel ideal of poverty and belong to a way of living and preaching the Gospel approved by the Church. *(page 185)*

Messiah The Hebrew word Messiah means "Anointed One of God"; the Anointed One God promised to send his people. Jesus is the Messiah promised by God. *(page 332)*

monastery A monastery is a lifelong residence for monks or nuns. *(page 149)*

monasticism Monasticism is a way of living the Gospel in which men (monks) and women (nuns) live in community and devote themselves to prayer, work, and learning. *(page 149)*

Mosaic Law The Mosaic Law, or Law of Moses, sets forth rules and practices that the Jewish people have followed since the time of Moses. The Ten Commandments, the basis of Mosaic Law, are found in the Bible, in Exodus 20 and Deuteronomy 5:6–21. The Book of Leviticus contains further details of the Law. *(page 57)*

natural law The natural law is the foundation of the moral law for everyone. It is part of human nature and allows people to know the difference between good and evil. *(page 115)*

novena A novena is a Catholic devotion in which specific prayers are said on nine consecutive days. *(page 306 and 427)*

papal infallibility Papal infallibility is the doctrine that when the pope speaks officially for the Church on a matter of faith or morals, he is guided by the Holy Spirit and what he says is free from error. *(page 265)*

Paschal Mystery The Paschal Mystery is the saving event of the Passion, Death, Resurrection, and Ascension of Jesus Christ. The Paschal Mystery is the center of God's plan of Salvation. *(page 103)*

pastoral *Pastor* is the Latin word for "shepherd." Pastoral describes the work of priests and bishops in "shepherding," or guiding and caring for, people in the Church. *(page 413)*

pastoral letter A pastoral letter is a message from a bishop or bishops giving guidance to the members of the Church or society. *(page 289)*

Penance and Reconciliation The Sacrament of Penance and Reconciliation is a Sacrament of Healing in which the penitent is forgiven the sins they commit after Baptism by a priest and are reconciled with God and the Church. *(page 219)*

Pentateuch The Pentateuch is the first five books of the Old Testament. *(page 397)*

perjury Perjury is the act of lying after having made an oath to tell the truth, with God as one's witness. *(page 421)*

piety Piety is one of the seven Gifts of the Holy Spirit which leads to devotion to God. *(page 185)*

pilgrimage A pilgrimage is a journey to a holy place or sacred site for spiritual or devotional reasons. *(page 427)*

plagiarism Plagiarism is the use of someone's ideas or works as if they were one's own. *(page 423)*

predestination Predestination is the teaching that states that God determines whether someone is saved or damned before they are born. *(page 231)*

presbyters Presbyters were the appointed religious leaders, or elders, of the early Church. In the Church today, the term *presbyter* means "priest." *(page 57)*

presider A presider is a priest who leads a sacramental or liturgical celebration as well as consecrates the bread and wine during Mass. *(page 409)*

Protestant Reformation The Protestant Reformation was the early sixteenth-century religious movement begun in Europe by Martin Luther that set out to reform some of the doctrines and practices of the Catholic Church. The efforts of Luther and other reformers resulted in the development of Protestantism. *(page 207)*

Purgatory Purgatory is a final state of purification from sin after death. *(page 207)*

ritual The combination of words and actions used in the celebration of the liturgy. *(page 338)*

Sacrament A Sacrament is a sacred sign and cause of grace instituted by Christ, entrusted to the Church. The Seven Sacraments are the main liturgical actions of the Church. They make us sharers in Divine life, and continue God's saving action among us. *(page 45)*

sacramental life The sacramental life of the Church is the way in which the Church celebrates the liturgy and the Seven Sacraments. Through the Church's sacramental life, we are united with Christ. *(page 45)*

sacrificial meal The term *sacrificial meal* describes the Mass, which is both a holy sacrifice and a sacred meal. *(page 409)*

sanctifying grace Sanctifying grace is the grace of God sharing his divine life with us and that heals us of sin and makes us Christlike. *(page 417)*

schism Schism is the refusal of submission to the pope (the Roman Pontiff) or of communion with the members of the Church subject to him. *(page 126)*

social justice Social justice is respect for human dignity demonstrated through actions that promote human rights. *(page 289)*

social teachings The social teaching of the Catholic Church is based on the respect for human dignity, human solidarity, and the principles of justice and peace. *(page 288)*

solidarity Solidarity is the unity we share with all our brothers and sisters, who are made in the image of God. It is an eminently Christian virtue that practices the sharing of spiritual goods even more than material ones. *(page 425)*

stewardship Stewardship is the managing and caring for the property of another person. We are called to be stewards of God's creation. *(page 425)*

Theotokos *Theotokos* is a Greek word meaning "God-bearer." The early Church used this word to express that Mary is truly the Mother of God. *(pages 265 and 401)*

transubstantiation Transubstantiation is the term used to name the sacred mystery in which bread and wine are changed into the Body and Blood of Christ through the power of the Holy Spirit and the words and actions of the priest, through which the whole Person of Christ in his humanity and divinity becomes truly and substantially present under the appearances of bread and wine. *(pages 161 and 410)*

trespass *Trespass* means "to commit a sin." *(page 429)*

Trinitarian Trinitarian means "reflecting the unity of the Blessed Trinity." The Church is Trinitarian because it reflects the unity of the Trinity by being the People of God, the Body of Christ, and the Temple of the Holy Spirit. *(page 33)*

vernacular The vernacular is the language that is native to the people of a region or a country. *(page 243)*

virtue A virtue is an ability to make morally good decisions that lead to the habit of doing good. Christian virtues are considered gifts from God that we can develop into habits of Christian living. *(page 415)*

Yahweh *Yahweh* is a Hebrew name for God meaning "I am who I am." In the Old Testament, this is God's sacred name, which he revealed to Moses. *(page 399)*

Index

Credits

COVER: Gene Plaisted, O.S.C., The Crosiers

SCRIPTURE ART: Tim Ladwig

Photo and art locators denoted as follows: Top (T), Center (C), Bottom (B), Left (L), Right (R), Background (Bkgd).

PHOTOGRAPHS: Every effort has been made to secure permission and provide appropriate credit for photographic material. The publisher deeply regrets any omission and pledges to correct errors called to its attention in subsequent editions. Unless otherwise acknowledged, all photographs are the property of RCL Benziger.

ix Dennis Marsico/Corbis; ix Gérard Degeorge/Corbis; 22 Dennis Marisco/Corbis; 22 Gérard Degeorge; 23 Bill Wittman; 23 Gene Plaisted, OSC/The Crosiers; 27 (Bkgd) Scala/Art Resource, NY; 34 Gérard Degeorge/Corbis; 36 Fernando Bizerra Jr/EPA/Newscom; 38 (Bkgd) Peter Van Rhijn/SuperStock; 41 Ron Chapple/FPG Internat'l, LLC; 48 The Granger Collection, New York; 50 Gene Plaisted, OSC/The Crosiers; 53, 60 Bettmann/Corbis; 60 Sean Sexton Collection; 62 Reuters News Media, Inc./Corbis; Darren Modricker/Corbis; 67 Bob Daemmrich/Stock Boston; 67 Michael Newman/PhotoEdit; 70 Gene Plaisted, OSC/The Crosiers; 70 The Granger Collection, New York; 72 Scala/Art Resource, NY; 74 Andrew Ward/Life File/PhotoDisc; 85 Martha Cooper; 92 Pinacoteca Civica Castello Sforzesco, Milan, Italy/Mauro Magliani, SuperStock; 94 Time Life Pictures/Getty Images; 96 Rhodri Jones/Panos Pictures; 104 Oleg Nikishin/Getty Images; 105 Otto Lang/Corbis; 105 Robert Estall/Corbis; 106 Macduff Everton/Corbis; 107 Courtesy of Reginia McAloney; 113 Nathan Benn/Corbis; 116 Giraudon/Art Resource, NY; 118 Scala/Art Resource, NY; 120 Jules Frazier/PhotoDisc; 125 2001 Artists' Right Society (ARS), New York/ADAGP, Paris/SuperStock; 125 Simeone Huber/Stone; 125 Zefa Visual Media, Germany/Index Stock Imagery; 126 (BL) Ancient Art & Architecture Collection/Ronald Sheridan Photo Library; 126 (BR) Staatliche Museen zu Berlin—Prubisher Kulturbesitzm Gemaldegalerie/Jorge P. Anders; 128 Bettman/Corbis; 130 Rev. Andrey Davydov; 131 University of Aberdeen Library; 132 Joel W. Rogers/Corbis; 143 Gianni Dagli Orti/Corbis; 143 Adam Woolfitt/Corbis; 145 Charles O'Rear/Corbis; 147 Courtesy of Saint Benedict's Prep School; 150 The Bridgeman Art Library/Getty Images; 150 The Cummer Museum of Art and Gardens, Jacksonville, FL/SuperStock; 152 Scala/Art Resource, NY; 153 Valley of Our Lady Monastery; 154 Galen Rowell/Corbis; 159 Gail Mooney/Corbis; 160 The J. Paul Getty Museum; 164 Ruggero Vanni/Corbis; 165 Angelo Hornak/Corbis; 165 Dagli Orti/The Art Archives; 165 Dan Heller/Dan Heller Photography; 166 Steve Vidler/SuperStock; 171 Abed Khateeb/AP/Wide World; 171 InterNetwork Media/PhotoDisc; 174 Steve Vidler/SuperStock; 176 Archivo Icongrafico, S.A./Corbis; 177 Gustavo Tomsich/Corbis; 178 (Bkgd) The Huntington Library, Art Collections and Cotanical Gardens, San Marino, CA/SuperStock; 185 Nik Wheeler/Corbis; 185 Roger Wood/Corbis; 186 Erich Lessing/Art Resource, NY; 188 Carmelnet.org; 189 Sami Sarkis/Alamy Lmited/Alamy.com; 190 Universal/Robert Stigwood/Kobal Collection; 201 Hulton/Archive/Getty Images; 203 Arthur Tilley/FPG International, LLC; 205 David Madison Sports Images; 208 The Walters Art Museum, Baltimore; 210 Jean Dominique Dallet/SuperStock; 212 SuperStock; 215 Getty Images; 217 G & M David deLossy/Getty Images; 221 Dorling Kinersley/Dorling Kindersley Media Library; 229 AP/Wide World; 232 Courtesy of the National Portrait Gallery, London; 234 Arte & Immagini srl; Instituto e Museo di Storia della Scienza, Firenze/Corbis; 242 Bettmann/Corbis; 244 H. Rogers/Art Directors and TRIP Photo Library; 246 Missouri Historical Society Photograph and Print Collection/Archdiocese of Saint Louis; 248 Stephen Sudd/Getty Images/Stone; 259 Eddie Adams/AP/Wide World; 259 Harold Chapman/The Image Works, Inc.; 261 Lori Adamski/Peek/Stone; 264 David Lees/Corbis; 268 Brothers of the Christian Schools, Rome; 269 Myrleen Ferguson Cate/PhotoEdit; 270 InterNetwork Media/PhotoDisc; 273 Gene Plaisted, OSC/The Crosiers; 276 Tamas Kovacs/AP/Wide World; 278 Mark Gibson/Index Stock Imagery, Inc.; 282 Eliol Ciol/Corbis; 285 Joel Andrews/The Lufkin Daily News/AP/Wide World; 287 Sam Panthaky/AFP/Getty Images; 289 David Young-Wolff/PhotoEdit; 290 Mary Kate Denny/PhotoEdit; 292 COTERA/AP/Wide World; 294 Joseph Sohmo/ChromoSohm, Inc./Corbis; 297 Mark Romanelli/Getty Images; 299 Ryan McVay/PhotoDisc; 302 Museo di San Marco dell'Angelico, Florence, Italy/Bridgeman Art Library; 302 Tony Gutierrez/AP/Wide World; 304 Jeffrey Jones/The Independent Gallup/AP/Wide World; 305 Jim Whitmer; 305 Rob Crandall/Rainbow; 306 Michael Denora/Stone; 322 James L. Shaffer; 324 Galen Rowell/Corbis; 325 Richard T. Nowitz/Corbis; 326 University of Dayton; 328 James Frank/Stock Connection, Inc., Alamy Limited; 330 San Miniato al Monte, Florence, Italy/Briodgeman Art Library; 331 EyeWire Collection/Getty Images; 333 All rights reserved. Vie de Jésus MAFA 24 Rue du Maréchal Joffre, F7800 Versailles; 334 Elio Simonetti/The Fontanini/Roman, Inc.; 334 Taxi/Getty Images; 336 Myrleen Ferguson Cate/PhotoEdit; 338 Bill Wittman; 338 Skjold Photographs; 339 David Young-Wolff/PhotoEdit; 340 Laura James/Private Collection/Bridgeman Art Library; 341 AP/Wide World; 341 Roger Lemoyne/Getty Images; 344 EyeWire Collection/Getty Images; 349 Jonathan Nourok/PhotoEdit; 350 George and Monserrate Schwartz/Alamy Limited; 353 SuperStock; 356 Scala/Art Resource, NY; 358 Brad Mitchell/Alamy Limited; 360 Francis G. Mayer/Corbis; 362 Jack S. Blanton Museum of Art, The University of Texas at Austin; 363 The Image Bank/Getty Images; 364 Anatoly Sapronenkov/Tretyakov Gallery, Moscow/ SuperStock; 366 Art Institute of Chicago; 367 Ariel Skelley/Corbis; 368 Hermitage, St. Petersburg, Russia/Bridgeman Library; 369 Ami Vitale/Alamy Limited; 370 Richard Cummins/Folio, Inc.; 371 Lennart Nilsson/Albert Bonniers Forlag AB; 373 Galleria dell' Accademia, Venice, Italy/Bridgeman Art Library; 374 P.Chichikov/Ponkawonka.com; 376 Erich Lessing/Scala/Art Resource, NY; 378 Philadelphia Archdiocesan Historical Research Center; 378 Saint John Neumann Shrine; 379 Society of Saint Vincent de Paul, Los Angeles; 380 Arte & Immagini srl/Corbis; 382 Bettmann/Corbis; 384 Private Collection/Archives Charmet/Bridgeman Art Library; 385 J. Stock/StockShot/Alamy Limited; 386 Brian Jackson/AP/Wide World; 387 Skjold Photographs; 389 Ralf-Finn Restoft/Corbis; 390 Hulton Archive Photos/Getty Images; 391 Jim Whitmer/Jim Whitmer Photography; 393 Jose Luis Pelaez, Inc./Corbis; 398 Reunion des Musees Nationaux/Art Resource, NY; 399 Gene Plaisted, OSC/The Crosiers; 400 Scala/Art Resource, NY; 401 Gene Plaisted, OSC/The Crosiers; 402 Chris Bland/Eye Ubiquitous/Corbis; 403 Chris Sheridan/Catholic New York; 405 Cameraphoto/Art Resource, NY; 406 Christopher Santer/www.pacemstudio.com; 407 Scala/Art Resource, NY; 408 Gene Plaisted, OSC/The Crosiers; 413 Gene Plaisted, OSC/The Crosiers; 414 Mark E. Gibson/Rainbow; 415 Corbis; 417 Gene Plaisted, OSC/The Crosiers; 418 Gene Plaisted, OSC/The Crosiers; 419 Bachmann/PhotoEdit; 423 Tim Brown/Stone; 424 David Woodfall/Stone; 425 AFP/Corbis; 426 Jean-Marc Bouju/AP/Wide World; 428 Gene Plaisted, OSC/The Crosiers; 429 Milt & Joan Mann/Cameramann International, Ltd.; 430 Gene Plaisted, OSC/The Crosiers; 445 Gene Plaisted, OSC/The Crosiers; 445 Scala/Art Resource, NY; 445 Bill Wittman; 446 Steve Allen/Brand Pictures

ART: ix Elizabeth Wolf; 19, 20 Elizabeth Wolf; 20 Michael DiGiorgio; 21, 24 Elizabeth Wolf; 31 John Hovell Kirchoff Wohlberg, Inc.; 32, 35 Tim Ladwig; 37 Arvis Stewart; 44, 46 Tim Ladwig; 46 Roman Dunets; 55 Dave Jonason, Clare Jett & Associates; 56, 58 Tim Ladwig; 61 Michael DiGiorgio; 68 Tim Ladwig; 85 Philippe Fix; 90, 92, 102 Tim Ladwig; 102 Roman Dunets; 114 Tim Ladwig; 119 T.L. Ary, Mendola Artists; 147 Linda Wingerter; 148 (TL) Roman Dunets; 148 Tim Ladwig; 153 Arvis Stewart; 172, 174 Tim Ladwig 177 Arvis Stewart; 183 Tom Leonard; 184 Roman Dunets; 184 Tim Ladwig; 201 Elizabeth Wolf; 206 Roman Dunets; 211 Arvis Stewart; 217 Jean and Mou-Sien Tseng; 218, 220 Tim Ladwig; 230, 231 Roman Dunets; 235 Kirchoff/Wohlberg; 242, 244 Roman Dunets; 245 Renee Daily; 247 Kirchoff/Wohlberg; 264 Roman Dunets; 264, 266 Tim Ladwig; 288 Roman Dunets; 300, 342, 354 Tim Ladwig; 364 Linda Wingerter; 369, 372 Robin DeWitt; 387 Jean and Mou-Sien Tseng; 388 Renee Daily; 396 Michael DiGiorgio; 444 Roman Dunets; 444 Tim Ladwig; 444 Arvis Stewart; 444 Tom Barrett; 445 Tim Ladwig; 445 Elizabeth Wolf.

Acknowledgements

Thomas C. Fox, "Scholars hail Elizondo's vision." *National Catholic Reporter,* July 14, 2000, www.natcath.com/NCR_Online/archives/071400/071400g.htm; "Jean Donovan: 'Except for the Children.'" Religious Task Force on Central America and Mexico, www.rtfcam.org/martyrs/women/jean_donovan.htm; Fr. George W. Kosicki, C.S.B., "The Mercy Saint's secret: Trade in your misery for Jesus' mercy." *Marian Helper,* Summer 2001, p. 15; Stephen Stelle, Obituary of "Father Daniel Egan." *Catholic New York,* February 17, 2000, p. 24; From "O TPI™A°IO™ YMNO™" ("Thrice Holy") from *Holy Cross Liturgical Hymnal,* pp. 30–31. Copyright © 1988 by Holy Cross Orthodox Press. Reprinted by permission of Holy Cross Orthodox Press; Stanzas 1, 3, 9, and 11 from "Song of the soul that rejoices in knowing God through faith" from The *Collected Works of St. John of The Cross,* translated by Kieran Kavanaugh and Otilio Rodriguez. Copyright © 1979, 1991 by Washington Province of Discalced Carmelites, ICS Publications, 2131 Lincoln Road, NE, Washington, D.C. 20002–1199, U.S.A., www.icspublications.org; Abridgment of "Most Beloved Lord Father" by S. M. Celeste from Chapters XXII, "In the chambers of the Holy Office of the Inquisition" from *Galileo's Daughter* by Dava Sobel, pp. 243–244. Copyright © Dava Sobel. Reprinted by permission of Walker and Company, Inc.; David Cho and Kelly Heyboer, "Honor and Memories for Seton Hall Hero." *The Star-Ledger,* August 28, 2000, front page; Joseph Cardinal Bernardin, *The Gift of Peace: Personal Reflections.* Chicago, IL: Loyola Press, 1997, pp. 128–129; U.S. Catholic Bishops, "Economic Justice for All." Office for Social Justice, Archdiocese of St. Paul and Minneapolis, www.osjspm.org.cst.eja.htm; Matthew Bunson et al., *John Paul II's Book of Saints.* Huntington, IN: Our Sunday Visitor, Inc., 1999, p. 79; "Hunger Basics: Frequently Asked Questions." Bread for the World, www.bread.org/hungerbasics/faq.html; John Paul II, "Address of John Paul II To His Beatitude Christodoulos, Archbishop of Athens and Primate of Greece." The Vatican, www.vatican.va/holy_father/john_paul_ii/speeches/2001/documents/hf_jp-ii_spe_20010504_archbishop-athens_en.htm; Kennis Wessel, Ph.D., "Paganism and Christianity—Side-by-Side in 999." The Ponca City News, www.poncacitynews.com/millennium/Pages/page6.html; Helen Prejean, C.S.J., Speech from Albany, New York, January 24, 1995. Father Terrance Halloran, http://members.aol.com/twhalloran/pageC.html; John Paul II, *Evangelium Vitae* (Encyclical Letter). The Vatican, www.vatican.va/holy_father/john_paul_ii/encyclicals/documents/hf_jp-ii_enc_25031995_evangelium-vitae_en.html; Viktor E. Frankl, *Man's Search for Meaning.* Washington Square Press, www.rjgeib.com/thoughts/frankl/frankl.html; Austin Flannery, O.P., *Vatican Council II: The Conciliar and Post-Conciliar Documents, New Revised Edition.* Boston, MA: St. Paul Books and Media, 1992, p. 975; Margaret Plevak, "Jazz great's encounter with Mass led him to Catholicism." Catholic Herald, November 2, www.archmil.org/news/ newslet2.asp?recid=379; "Calling Forth and Inspiring New Models." The Leaven Center, www.leavencenter.com/WhoWeAre.html; Sydney J. Harris, "Strictly Personal." Quoteland.com, Inc., www.quoteland.com/search.asp?query=Regret+for+the+things; Jonas Salk, "Dreams." www.quoteproject.com/subject.asp?subject=3; Joseph Cardinal Suenens, "Leon-Joseph Cardinal Suenens Information." John Carroll University, www.suenens.org/cardinal_suenens_information.htm; Erwin Panofsky, *De Administratione ad Scriptum Consecrationis.* Princeton, NJ: Princeton University Press, 1946; John Paul II, "Homily at The Abbassyin Stadium of Damascus." The Vatican, www.vatican.va/holy_father/john_paul_ii/homilies/2001/ documents/hf_jp-ii_hom_20010506_damascus_en.html; Walter M. Abbott, S.J., *The Documents of Vatican II.* The America Press, 1966, pp. 718–719; *Catechism of the Catholic Church, Second Edition.* Washington, D.C., United States Catholic Conference, Inc., 1994, pp. 218 and 559; Jack Weatherford, *Savages and Civilization: Who Will Survive?* New York, NY: Crown Publishers, Inc., 1994, p. 46; "St. Thomas Aquinas." Kevin Knight, www.newadvent.org/cathen/14663b.htm; "Who Were the Knights Templar?" and "The Warrior Monks: The Templar Beauséant." Stephen Dafoe and Alan Butler, www.templarhistory.com/who and www.templarhistory.com/beausant; Sister Thea Bowman, "Naming Of Our New Buildings." The Catholic Community Forum, www.catholicforum.com/stfrancis/Parish%20News/Bulletins/sfa_bulletin051400.html; David Waters, "Bishop Patterson's History," and "World's Greatest Preacher Article." Bountiful Blessings, Inc., www.bbless.org/bishopgepatterson.html, www.bbless.org/worldgreatestpreacher1.html; Misty Bernall et al., *She Said Yes: The Unlikely Martyrdom of Cassie Bernall.* Farmington, PA: Plough Publishing House, 1999; Eileen Egan and Kathleen Egan, O.S.B., *Prayertimes with Mother Teresa.* New York, NY: Bantam Doubleday Dell Publishing Group, Inc., 1989, pp. 42 and 43; "Jesse Manibusan." St. John Vianney Parish, www.stjohnvianneybettendorf.org/Guests/jmanibusan.html; Mike Rimmer, "Scarecrow and Tinmen." Premier, www.premieronline.co.uk/pages/ feature/feature_scarecrow.htm; Elimu logo and text from www.elimu.org. Reprinted by permission of ActionAid; "Prayer for Christian Unity 2001." The Vatican, www.vatican.va/roman_curia/pontifical_councils/chrstuni/documents/ rc_pc_chrstuni_doc_20001215_prayer-2001_en.html; Rev. Peter Klein, *The Catholic Source Book, Third Edition.* Orlando, FL: Harcourt Brace and Company, 2000, pp. 125, 126, 286, 300, 311, 362, and 434; Paul Evans, "Benedictine Monks of Santo Domingo de Silos Chant." Rolling Stone LLC, www.rollingstone.com/recordings/review.asp?aid=17796; Rev. Canon James T. Irvine, "Benedictine Prayer 2." St. Luke's, www.user.fundy.net/msgr/WEBPrayerHANDBOOK_3_benedictine_prayer_suggestion_2.htm; Jim Forest, *Praying with Icons.* Maryknoll, NY: Orbis Books, 1997, p. 23; Tony Castle, *The Light of Christ: Meditations for Every Day of the Year.* New York: Crossroad Publishing Company, 1987, p. 248; Brother Angelo Devananda, *Mother Teresa: Contemplative in the Heart of the World.* Ann Arbor, MI: Servant Books, 1985; Jim Forest, "A Biography of Dorothy Day." The Catholic Worker Movement, www.catholicworker.org/dorothyday/ddbiographytext.cfm?Number+72; Peter Ackroyd, *The Life of Thomas More.* New York, NY: Bantam Doubleday Dell Publishing Group, Inc., 1998. Republished with permission of The Crossroad Publishing Company, from *Hildegard of Bingen: Mystical Writings* edited and introduced by Fiona Bowie and Oliver Davies, Copyright (c) 1990 by Crossroad Publishing Company. Permission conveyed through Copyright Clearance Center, Inc. From *Perpetua's Passion: The Death and Memory of a Young Roman Woman* by Joyce E. Salisbury. Published 1997 by Routledge, New York. Reprinted with permission. From *Ad Caeli Reginum* (Encyclical of Pope Pius XII on Proclaiming the Queenship of Mary), promulgated on October 11, 1954. Full text appears at http://www.vatican.va/holy_father/pius_xii/encyclicals/documents/hf_p-xii_enc_11101954_ad-caeli-reginam_en.html. Reprinted with permission.

In appreciation: Our Lady of Mount Carmel Church, Nutley, NJ; St. Ann Church, Parsippany, NJ; St. Ann Melkite Catholic Church, West Paterson, NJ; St. Anselm Church, Wayside, NJ; St. Margaret Church, Morristown, NJ; St. Patrick Church, Yorktown Heights, NY; St. Peter the Apostle Church, Parsippany, NJ; Craig Baker, www.schooluniforms.com